DATE DUE			
DEC 2			
OCT 2 1			

Sources and Resources

Sources and Resources

The Literary Traditions of Christian Humanism

by Barry Ulanov

NP

The Newman Press · 1960 · Westminster, Maryland

Nihil obstat: Edward A. Cerny, S.S., S.T.D.
Censor Librorum

Imprimatur: Francis P. Keough, D.D.
Archbishop of Baltimore

September 22, 1959

The *nihil obstat* and *imprimatur* are official declarations that a book or pamphlet is free of doctrinal and moral error. No implication is contained therein that those who have granted the *nihil obstat* and *imprimatur* agree with the opinions expressed.

Library of Congress Catalog Card Number: 59–14807
Printed in the United States of America

For Nicholas

whose middle name is Augustine

Preface

WE OWE MUCH TO THE HUMANISTS OF THE SEVERAL renaissances—Italian, French and English, Spanish and Portuguese. Their systematic revival of the classical past gave to history some of its most notable physical properties: mass, extension, density. Their confidence in human nature and the energies they devoted to human affairs gave to man a deeper sense of self-reliance and an increased respect for the disciplines of learning in which the humanists expressed their trust and to which they consecrated their time. Ever since, we have called these branches of knowledge "humanistic," a tribute first of all to the men who developed them while they developed themselves in the fourteenth, fifteenth, and sixteenth centuries, and then to the studies themselves. The tribute is deserved. It has, in the word itself and in the ideas that inform it, overtones of both the humanitarian and the humanizing.

The true humanist has always been, as his name suggests, a man propagating a faith, a faith in letters, a faith in learning, a faith in the power of the humanities to eliminate some of the most degrading of all forms of pain and suffering, those that follow from ignorance. If he is a doctrinaire adherent of any of a dozen or more naturalistic schools, he will seek his nostrums at least as eagerly and as often in the sciences as in the humanities. If he is a Christian humanist, he will not turn to any one discipline for salvation, but will probably rely more on studies in theology and philosophy, in history and the arts than in the sciences, to discover or rediscover sources of human wisdom and resources of human performance.

The principal literary resource of the Christian humanist for nearly two thousand years has been rhetoric. In it the art of persuasion is linked to that of figure to make concept and precept understandable and thus more useful, no matter how massive, how extensive, or how dense. In it, obscure and ambiguous ideas are made intelligible by the devices of analogy and allegory, contradiction and resemblance, personification and exaggeration, enlargements of identity or diminishings, deliberate harshness of sound or sweetness—every sort of trick of music and logic and grammar. It was never the purpose of the master rhetoricians merely to illustrate, to enforce or reinforce moral truths; certainly from Augustine to Newman, thinkers of consequence never employed the vast apparatus of rhetoric only to demonstrate their ease in its artificialities. Rarely is an art so debased as rhetoric is when by definition or explication it is reduced to a question that contains its own answer or to a mere show of eloquence.

When one traces, however incompletely and inadequately, the development of Christian sources into Christian humanist resources, one discovers many things about the nature of language, of literature, of history, and of man. One learns at last, I think, that the rhetoric used with such great virtuosity, by Augustine and Boethius, Gregory and Bernard, Dante and Thomas and Shakespeare and Pascal and all the others, conceals an even greater unction. At the center of their works, even those swathed in contradiction, exaggeration, and irony, is some encounter between man and God. To bring to other men the substance of that meeting, or to indicate how it may be elicited or already has been effected in a man or in his world, is the aim of the Christian humanist writer. He has the greatest trust of all in human nature; to human affairs he devotes all his energies. For wherever he sees the creature, he understands the creative essence; whenever he comes upon the known, always changing, he reflects upon the unknown behind it, endlessly immutable. His subject is, to borrow a figure from the rhetoric of Kierkegaard, the depths of the possible. I have chosen in this volume to confine myself to a diverse group of writers who are generally united by ideas and devices, by a whole vocabulary and way of thinking that is associated more particularly with the work of St. Augustine than with that of any other man. This is not to suggest that there is no other language for Christian humanism or that there are no other habits of thinking possible for Christian humanists, but simply to indicate that almost always in the West, after the fourth century, when the paths of God and man met the rhetoric in which the meeting was reported was Augustinian. This has been true regardless of the immediate training of the writer, whether he has read Augustine at length or only cursorily or not at all: so much has this tradition been in the air, on our tongues, and in our minds in the words of the Bishop of Hippo.

It will be clear, I think, that the men gathered together here represent in their divergences some of the breadth of Christian humanism, some of the ways the Augustinian approach has been reshaped and reformed to fit different temperaments, different issues, different societies, different eras. I hope it will be equally clear that all are united by well-founded intuitions of hope.

BARRY ULANOV

Acknowledgments

THE AUTHOR AND THE NEWMAN PRESS EXPRESS THEIR gratitude to the following publishers who have granted permission to reproduce copyrighted material:

Appleton-Century-Crofts, Inc., New York, for *Concerning the Teacher*, by St. Augustine, translated by George G. Leckie, copyright 1938 by D. Appleton-Century Company, Inc.

Benziger Brothers, Inc., New York, for *St. Thomas Aquinas*, by Gerald Vann, O.P.

George Braziller, Inc., New York, for *The Diary of a Writer*, by F. M. Dostoevsky.

The Bruce Publishing Company, Milwaukee, for *The Interior Life of St. Thomas Aquinas*, by Martin Grabmann, translated by Nicholas Aschenbrener, O.P.

Columbia University Press, New York, for *The Philosophy of Marsiglio Ficino*, by Paul O. Kristeller, copyright 1943 by Columbia University Press.

E. P. Dutton & Company, Inc., New York, for *Western Mysticism*, by Edward Cuthbert Butler, O.S.B.

Fathers of the Church, Inc., for *The City of God*, by St. Augustine, translated by D. B. Zema, S.J., G. G. Walsh, S.J., *et al.*; for *Christian Instruction*, by St. Augustine, translated by John J. Gavigan, O.S.A.; for *Divine Providence*, by St. Augustine, translated by Robert P. Russell, O.S.A.; for *Letters*, by St. Augustine, translated by Sister Wilfred Parsons, S.N.D.; for *On Music*, by St. Augustine, translated by Robert Catesby Taliaferro; for *Soliloquies*, by St. Augustine, translated by Thomas F. Gilligan, O.S.A.; and for *Funeral Ora-*

tions, by St. Gregory Nazianzen, translated by Leo P. McCauley, S.J.

Harvard University Press, Cambridge, Massachusetts, for *De Consolatione Philosophiae*, by Boethius (The Loeb Classical Library), translated by Rev. H. F. Stewart, D.D., and E. K. Rand; and for *The Steps of Humility*, by St. Bernard of Clairvaux, translated by George Bosworth Burch.

B. Herder Book Company, St. Louis, for *The Christian Latin Literature of the First Six Centuries*, by Abbé Bardy, translated by Mother Mary Reginald, O.P.; and for *The Trinity*, by St. Thomas Aquinas, translated by Sister Rose Emmanuella Brennan, S.H.N.

The Liberal Arts Press, Inc., New York, for *The Mind's Road to God*, by St. Bonaventure, translated by George Boas.

The Marquette University Press, Milwaukee, for *Humanism and Theology* (1943 Aquinas Lecture), by Werner Jaeger.

Mediaeval Academy of America, Cambridge, Massachusetts, for *On the Sacraments of the Christian Faith*, by Hugh of St. Victor, translated by R. J. Deferrari.

Methuen and Company, Ltd., London, for *Thought and Letters in Western Europe*, by M. L. W. Laistner.

Morehouse-Gorham Company, Inc., New York, for *On the Song of Songs*, by St. Bernard of Clairvaux, translated by a Religious of C.S.M.V.

The Oxford University Press, New York, for *Documents of the Christian Church*, edited by Henry Bettenson; for *Poems*, by Gerard Manley Hopkins; and for *The Divine Comedy*, by Dante Alighieri, translated by John D. Sinclair.

Pantheon Books, Inc., New York, for *Pensées*, by Blaise Pascal, translated by H. F. Stewart.

Henry Regnery Company, Chicago, for *The Letters of St. Bernard of Clairvaux*, translated by Bruno Scott James.

Sheed and Ward, Inc., New York, for *The Church of the*

Word Incarnate, by Charles Journet, translated by A. H. C. Downes; for *Faith and Prejudice and Other Unpublished Sermons*, by John Henry Cardinal Newman, copyright 1956 by Sheed and Ward, Inc., New York, and for *Autobiographical Writings*, by John Henry Cardinal Newman, copyright 1957 by Sheed and Ward, Inc., New York.

University of California Press, Berkeley, California, for *Platonism Ancient and Modern*, by Paul Shorey.

University of Chicago Press, Chicago, for *The Renaissance Philosophy of Man*, by Elizabeth Forbes.

Joseph F. Wagner, Inc., New York, for *The Catechetical Instruction*, by St. Thomas Aquinas, translated by J. B. Collins, S.S.

Yale University Press, New Haven, Connecticut, for *Aristotle's De Anima with the Commentary of St. Thomas Aquinas*, translated by Kenelm Foster, O.P., and S. Humphries, O.P.

Thanks are also due to Professor Émile Cailliet for permission to quote from *The Great Short Works of Pascal*, translated by himself and Dr. John C. Blankenagel.

Contents

Sources and Resources

CHAPTER 1

Lions and Gardens

IN ONE OF THE MOST ELOQUENT DEFENSES OF AN ART THE world has ever known, Giovanni Boccaccio said, "It is now sufficiently clear to reverent men, that poetry is a practical art, springing from God's bosom and deriving its name from its effect, and that it has to do with many high and noble matters that constantly occupy even those who deny its existence." But that was six hundred years ago, when Boccaccio wrote his *Genealogy of the Gentile Gods,* when it was clear indeed to reverent and to irreverent men that poetry was a practical art and that it, like all else, sprang from God's bosom. Poetry was a practical art to Boccaccio and his contemporaries and the saints and scholars from whom they drew their inspiration, because poetry was an art of revelation and poets revealers of God's will as He had made it known to His creatures and shown it forth in His creation. As best they could, they looked into the enigmas of creation and the mysteries of men and reported what they had seen, joyful when it was good, sorrowful when it was evil, and delighted always, either at the magnificence of those who sought sanctity and found it, or at the uproarious spectacle of the others—so many more in number—who fought clumsily, gracelessly, with bestial ineptness to elude their beatitude. And what they saw, they saw whole, as part of a plan, and their part in it purposeful. Never, under any circumstances, would they have defended their craft as "self-expression" or explained their profession in terms of the inanities of aesthetics. They were pleased to look at people and places and events *sub specie aeternitatis,* but with eyes and ears, with senses generally made alert by the things of this world.

Have we lost this keenness of view and soundness of hearing and fineness of taste and touch and smell? Certainly, on the surface at least, the arts in our time, as for many generations before it, do not seem to be created under the aspect of eternity. The prevailing mode in the arts for at least a century has been what is called realism or naturalism, a mode for which an elaborate apologetics has been constructed, apparently scientific in tone and rich in the justification of sense experience. We too look and listen and report what we see and hear, report more accurately, we often say, because our tools are more accurate, because we have test tubes and calipers and slide rules with which to measure the integers and entanglements of human relations and the ample discoveries of science with which to check our findings. We pride ourselves on the candor of our reports, on the shamelessness of our unveilings, on the surgical precision of our probings. How is it, then, that so small an area of human life is covered in our novels, that poetry has become so largely the solipsistic outpouring of tortured souls, that ambiguity has become a positive value, that the Virgin Mary and Jesus Christ have disappeared from our literature, and that goodness is little more in the so-called creative works of our time than an embarrassing smirk which rightfully earns our contempt?

Somewhere in the passing of the four or five hundred years that we like to call centuries of progress there disappeared the breadth of view and fullness of understanding that make the mere reading of Dante or Chaucer or Boccaccio or Augustine or Shakespeare a creative adventure for the Christian spirit. Somewhere along the perilous line of literary history a narrow literalness replaced the seeing in depth which distinguishes the work of the Christian humanists, and the senses of the soul were traded in for factory-made telescopic lenses which, for all their power, never seem to be able to reveal more than dirt under the carpet and cesspools beneath the cerebellum. And as long as we continue to fool ourselves with the notion that the writer is a scientist, necessarily weighed down with laboratory equipment and trained only to observe ephemera and to document the transient, the product is likely to remain the same: infinite emptiness in a little room.

Those of us, whether readers or writers, who are heirs to the Christian humanist tradition have another course open to us and much larger resources to fall back upon. We can reach back into our own past and revel in it and take heart. Over a period of a millennium and a half or more, from St. John the Evangelist to St. John of the Cross, at the very least, we can find nourishment and encouragement in the root and the flower of a literature thoroughly and beautifully and movingly Christian. We can find in others who came after—Shakespeare and Donne and Herbert and Crashaw, Pope and Swift and Fielding and Sterne, Wordsworth and Hopkins and Newman, to speak of only one country's literature—the same lights, a little dimmed perhaps, but shining within with the same wisdom and put together with a related power and looking forward to the same glory. We can recognize in the saints of every era the literary skills which God's graces confer, no matter what the guises, and not be ashamed to be stirred by the tidings of comfort and joy expressed in the simple French of Sainte Thérèse or by the consecration of the trivial exclaimed in impassioned Spanish by Sister Josefa Menendez.

There are traps in this course too. It is easy to be deluded into thinking that the Christian truths contained in the writings of avowed Christian poets and canonized saints are exuded with the bludgeoning directness of a pious ejaculation. They are not. As revealers of God's word and God's will, such writers are aware always that, however sharp their insights and however immediate their experiences, they see only as in a mirror, darkly, and that by the time the insights and the experiences have been communicated on paper there is a further refraction between the reader and the writer to be overcome. The best of them, accordingly, take early account of this fact and the very particular mystery which is life itself and start by drawing a veil over their creations, finding sanction for this procedure in the parables of Christ. This is, in fact, as Boccaccio explains, what fiction is, "a form of discourse, which, under guise of invention, illustrates or proves an idea; and, as its superficial aspect is removed, the meaning of the author is clear." "If, then," he continues, "sense is revealed from under the veil of fiction, the composition of fiction is not idle nonsense."

Thus do the great Christian writers arrive at the procedure which informs almost all their matter: the allegorical method. A very clear explanation of the method is Dante's in his letter to Can Grande della Scala, in which he dedicates the third canticle of the *Commedia*, the *Paradiso*, to that lord of Verona and explains his use of allegory:

> . . . there is one meaning that is derived from the letter, and another that is derived from the things indicated by the letter. The first is called *literal*, but the second *allegorical* or *mystical*. That this method of expounding may be more clearly set forth, we can consider it in these lines: "When Israel went out of Egypt, the house of Jacob from a people of strange language; Judah was his sanctuary and Israel his dominion." For if we consider the *letter* alone, the departure of the children of Israel from Egypt in the time of Moses is signified; if the *allegory*, our redemption accomplished in Christ is signified; if the *moral meaning*, the conversion of the soul from the sorrow and misery of sin to a state of grace is signified; if the *anagogical*, the departure of the sanctified soul from the slavery of this corruption to the liberty of everlasting glory is signified. And although these mystical meanings are called by various names, they can in general all be said to be allegorical, since they differ from the literal or historic . . .

Ultimately, this working method owes its rational order and logical structure to St. Augustine, whose most lucid and cogent presentation of these ideas is to be found in his *De Doctrina Christiana*. The philosophy of allegory, as a central procedure for all thinking writers whose sights are not trained exclusively upon this world, antedates St. Augustine by some centuries, however; it is to be found, at least implicitly, in the works of Cicero and Virgil in the figures with which they veil the doctrine of *pietas*, for example, and in the miraculous transformations of people into trees and streams in the *Metamorphoses* of Ovid, to whom ideas were most plausible when personified.

A whole phalanx of the *personae* of allegory can be drawn from the great Christian writers in illustration of the method. St. Gregory the Great shows how "the nature of every thing is compounded of different elements," by citing "Holy Writ" where "different things are allowably represented by any one thing." Take lions as an example:

> . . . the lion has magnanimity, it has also ferocity: by its magnanimity then it represents the Lord, by its ferocity the devil. Hence it is declared of the Lord, *Behold, the Lion of the tribe of Judah, the Root of David hath prevailed*. Hence it is written of the devil, *Your adversary, the devil, like a roaring lion, walketh about seeking whom he may devour*. But by the title of a "lioness" sometimes Holy Church, sometimes Babylon is represented to us. For on this account, that she is bold to encounter all that withstand, the Church is called a "lioness," as is proved by the words of the blessed Job, who in pointing out Judea forsaken by the Church, says, *The sons of the traders have not trodden, nor the lioness passed by it*. And sometimes under the lioness is set forth the city of this world, which is Babylon, which ravins against the life of the innocent with terribleness of ferocity, which being wedded to our old enemy like the fiercest lion, conceives the seers of his forward counsel, and produces from her own body reprobate sons, as cruel whelps, after his likeness.[1]

We are all familiar with the various figurative meanings attached to gardens, whether or not we have always penetrated to the third and fourth levels of communication intended by Christian writers. For medieval man, the significance of a garden—ordered or disarranged, effulgent with the plenty of a Paradise suitable to the splendor of preternatural man or frosty with the sterility of Adam fallen and banished—was palpable, convincing, something he understood by direct and by literary experience. He lived close to the soil and his writers, his singers, his bards spoke to him in images he could understand, in narratives at once redolent of eternity and rough with the smell and touch of the earth he knew so well. Thus the many gardens of medieval literature, of Chaucer's tales and Boccaccio's, of *Beowulf* and the *Roman de la Rose;* thus Dante's dark wood, the enchanted gardens of the fairy tales, and the many elaborate symbolic botanies of encyclopedists and philosophers to whom horticulture was nothing less than a reasoned index of the sins and virtues, the successes and failures, the charity and cupidity of man on pilgrimage from this world to the next.

A return to allegorical methods and materials in this twentieth century requires something more than an elementary knowledge of zoology and botany. Even a thorough acquaintance with the fanciful bestiaries and herbals of the Middle Ages will not be enough. For even as the commandments and counsels of the Church were translated effectively into the terms of the daily lives of medieval and Renaissance men, so must they be rendered again, in a language we speak, in a world we understand, in colors and textures and sounds and tastes and odors we recognize.

The first level, the literal, of modern allegory will be quite different, must be, from the letter of medieval and Renaissance writing. But the second and third and fourth planes—those that go to make up the spirit of any allegorical communication

—should obviously be the same for Christian writers and readers in this not-so-clearly-Christian era as it was in that time so unmistakably concerned to emulate the ministry and passion and death and resurrection of Christ, and to understand those who loved Him and those who did not, and to make sense of those who followed after Him and those who did not.

Can we lose by such an effort? Will we be deprived of some of our precious scientific objectivity if we spend somewhat less time on a drop-by-drop analysis of the secretion of the glands and somewhat more on the description of human dignity? Will our picture be incomplete if we find, now and then, some joy in the maternity of Mary the Mother of God to go along with the sorrow we discover so frequently in the neurotic Mom of motion pictures, clinical case histories, and slick magazine screeds? The questions, of course, are rhetorical; the answer to all of them is a resounding "no!"—or at least it will be if we realize the size of the Incarnation and its meaning for everything and everybody, even for writers seeking subject-matter and techniques with which to explore it, if we see with St. Irenaeus that Christ "came to save all through Himself" and that therefore

> He passed through every stage of life . . . was made an infant for infants, sanctifying infancy; a child among children, sanctifying those of this age, an example also to them of filial affection, righteousness and obedience; a young man among young men, an example to them, and sanctifying them to the Lord. So also amongst the older men; that He might be a perfect master for all, not solely in regard to the revelation of the truth, but also in respect of each stage of life.[2]

This, then, is not a less complete but a fuller picture; not a less scientific observation of the facts of life but a more broadly encompassing documentation of the world God created, adding to the partial measure of human reason some of the voluminous riches of revelation. The resources of this tradition are endless, its possibilities now as before as large as the gifts of man. Its methods, as Boccaccio said of poetry, are practical, for it rests securely upon the most realistic of all literary foundations, upon the certainty that not only has a man a body but a soul as well.

CHAPTER II

The Patristic Assimilation

THE FIGURE OF SAINT AUGUSTINE, WORKING AWAY ASSIDUously at *The City of God* with the barbarian hammering at the gates of man, is familiar enough and captivating enough. It has the stature of a saint. It suggests the heroic virtue by which we know a saint. It also possesses some of the color and craft of the myth-making imagination: it is to the imagination that the figure makes its appeal. And yet, actually, the story does not go far enough; its colors are too pale, its craft is insufficient; it is all too much like pagan myth in its emptiness at the heart and smallness of the spirit. This is the Saint Augustine of fancy, not the Father of the Church of fact.

No, entirely too much is missing in that familiar narrative. It reduces the battle to the size of time and space, assaying Augustine's achievement entirely in terms of concentration, of staying-power and physical courage. However long he should be able to work away at his *magnum opus;* whatever wisdom he should be able to pack into it; whomever he could get to read it, with the enemy pressing, pressing, pressing from outside—that should be his accomplishment. In this version of the tale, it is the enemy's failure that counts rather than the saint's persistence: as long as the enemy delays, so long is Augustine enabled to go on with his work. In fact, however, there is far more to the tale, a more genuine heroism, a more formidable achievement, for the barbarian was already within the gates when this saint—and all the others whom we honor by that special dignity that goes with Fatherhood—worked so diligently at their salvation and ours.

How far Augustine and all the Fathers had to reach to get

at the enemy! He was all over; he was in everything. The language the Fathers spoke, the garments they wore, the political institutions under which they lived, the very most treasured of human intimacies—all had been shaped and turned by pagans far removed in spirit, if not in time, from the truths revealed now, in time, by God made man. The arguments of the pagans dominated philosophy. The arguments had considerable cogency and masterful extension. Could any human reach far enough to take them in, to take them *on* in spiritual combat and intellectual joust?

Augustine's answer to the pagan argument is forthright: "We worship God," he says to the barbarian: it is not heaven and earth, a world-spirit or any other spirits in any ordinary sort of living being that we worship. "We adore God who made heaven and earth and all that they contain, God who made every kind of soul, from the lowest that lives without sensation and intellection through the sentient up to the soul that can think." This is no god of lust, this One God of the Fathers, no soothsayer, no mere magician, no personification, no Jupiter or Apollo or Mercury:

> the God we worship [Augustine continues] . . . constituted, for each of the natures He created, an origin and purpose of its being and powers of action. He holds in His hands the causes of things, knowing them all and connecting them all. It is He who is the source of all energy in seeds, and He who put rational souls, or spirits, into the living beings He selected, and He who gave us the gifts of speech and language.
>
> The God we worship chose certain spirits and gave them the power of foresight, and through them He makes prophecies. To others he gave the gift of healing . . .
>
> His sovereignty and power reach to the lowest things. All things that grow and sustain animal life, both liquids and solids, He produced and made appropriate for different natures. He gave us the earth, the fertility of soil, and foods for men and

beasts. All causes, primary and secondary, come within His knowledge and control . . .[1]

Thus is the battle joined, with much fervor and with much strength.

There were many besides Augustine, of course, who fought. Leo the Great, just a few years after the writing of *The City of God*, turned back Attila the Hun, apparently with nothing more than the power of his presence and the eloquence of his words. But is this Leo's most spectacular achievement of this kind or is it the excoriation of the Eutychian heretics? Or is it his excommunication of the zealot Hilary of Arles who would not bow to papal authority? One can criticize a pope so determined to prove that Peter was, far more than merely one among equals with the apostles, the mediator between them and Christ; so determined indeed that he would excommunicate an obviously holy man. But one can also understand—if one reads him carefully enough, and moves with enough concern and caution into his time—a devotion to the truth that would accept no compromise, overlook no breach, conciliate no failure, not even the minor lapse of a saintly French bishop. "Is there anything more unreasonable than to be unwilling to submit to the authority of the most wise and learned?" he asks. "But this is what one does," he continues, "when, in contempt of the oracles of the prophets, of the apostles, and of the gospel, he listens only to himself, [and] becomes a teacher of error because he has not been willing to be only a disciple of the truth."

The counsel of truth is the counsel of reason. It is also the counsel of humility. Leo never tires of stressing the size and stability and incalculable majesty of the "humiliation by which the Master and Creator of immortals was willing to become a man, subject to death . . ." It is this humiliation by which the Church recognizes the titles to nobility of its Lord. This self-abasement of the Maker of man is the foundation stone upon which the great structure of Christian humanism is to be erected. For "He became as truly man as he remains immutably God." And "since the Son begotten before all time has received in time a new birth, there exists a new order of things. He who in his own nature is invisible has made himself visible to ours; the incomprehensible has put himself within reach of our conception; the source of all beings has begun to be . . ."[2]

This is, again and again, the answer to the barbarian. It was the answer not only to the pagan outside, in a society partly converted to Christianity, but also to the pagan within each of the Christians. "Have we no worth, we poor men, of all creation?" the suffering Boethius exclaims, speaking for himself and for many others, in the first book of his *Consolation of Philosophy*. And the answer comes, from Leo, from Augustine, from Boethius, from all the Fathers, the answer of the Incarnation, the answer of freedom: "All beings endowed with reason also possess the power to choose or to refuse." That is Philosophy's answer to all the problems posed in the *Consolation*, in the last book of that subtle masterpiece, couched in terms so general that all, pagan or Christian or anyone, anywhere on the road in-between, can find at least the outline of salvation in its pages.

The worth of us "poor men" is obvious enough to those who believe: God so loved the world that He gave His only Son. To those to whom the signs are still hazy and the things signified even more clouded, the problem of freedom is the pointer. It is the line of speculation which must, inevitably, bring those who follow it to the Incarnation. It is Philosophy's role in the *Consolation* to lead Boethius, and through him all men, to confront the Incarnate God. That is also the central task of the Fathers. All saw, at one time or another, the persuasive strength of Freedom as the angelic messenger of the Incarnation. Again and again they saw and named and explicated the forerunning place of Freedom: It brings men closer to the truth, and prepares them for the moment when truth comes closer to men, when "the source of all beings has begun to be."

There is no better place to begin the study of Christian humanism today than in the past, that past which is the beginning of our present. For all for whom the Incarnation occupies the major position in history, the Fathers must seem tutelary geniuses guiding civilization from the chaos of an incomplete nature to the peace and balance and order of a world whose destiny is begun here but completed elsewhere. The past which is the age of the Fathers must, then, necessarily seem the beginning of our present. Certainly, it is there and then that the study, the speculation, the research, the discipline, and the dedication of the modern Christian humanist must begin. For it was in that world, sorely divided among careering barbarians, careening pagan states, and Christians, that the terms were defined, the weapons forged, the battle-lines engaged. It was then that Christianity and secularism were first clearly pitted against each other. And it was in those alternately terrifying and thrilling centuries that Christians were given the insights, the intuitions, the methods, the wisdom, and the strength with which to win their battles.

Once Apostolic times were over, the Christian was obviously, even to unconvinced pagans, more than an agonizing eccentric. To many he had become an inspiring leader. But now that the mission of the Church on earth had taken firm hold, order had to be established, procedure outlined, practice defined. These were the functions of the Fathers, of Athanasius writing on the Trinity and the Incarnation, of Ambrose on the sacraments, of Augustine on grace and free will, of Jerome in the production of a version of the Scriptures for the use of the Latin churches, of Clement and Origen and Basil and John Chrysostom in their homilies and letters and exhortations on the letter and spirit of Holy Writ. These were the functions of all the inspired Gregorys: of Gregory the Great, whose commentaries on the *Book of Job* offer the modern scholar an encyclopedic guide to the Scriptural and poetic vocabulary of the Fathers; of Gregory Nazianzen, orator and poet, letter-writer and eulogist, as a writer facile and certainly not without worldly temptations, but committed—life and soul and worldly inclinations as well—to the Church which could assure his leaving this world in a state of grace; of Gregory of Nyssa, the brother of Basil, who was in his love of Christ and making of everything Christian in His image the founder, perhaps, of systematic mystical theology.

It is not altogether remarkable that the problems each of these men faced were so much alike, that everywhere it was a matter of pagan challenge and barbarian attack, overt or covert. Each had to decide for himself just how commendable he found the inheritance of Greece and Rome—pagan Greece and Rome—and just how commendable he could make Christianity by his acceptance or rejection of the pagan inheritance. It is something more than the natural concatenation of events that makes the answers of each of these men so much like those of the others. They, each of them, decided to make patient use of their pagan legacy, that they might be able to pass on to us, considerably fatter in the flesh and more discerning in the spirit, their Christian patrimony.

To what sort of use did they put their classical inheritance? The kind Augustine advises in the *De Doctrina Christiana*, a parallel in taking to St. Paul's attitude in giving: as the Apostle was, in order to make the good tidings better known, "all things to all men," the Father suggests that Christians take all things from all men in order to make the good tidings more adaptable both in pagan and Christian communities:

all the teachings of the pagans have counterfeit and superstitious notions and oppressive burdens of useless labor, which anyone of us, leaving the association of pagans with Christ as our leader, ought to abominate and shun. However, they also contain liberal instruction more adapted to the service of truth and also very useful principles about morals; even some truths about the service of the one God Himself are discovered among them. These are, in a sense, their gold and silver. They themselves did not create them, but excavated them, as it were, from some mines of divine Providence which is everywhere present, but they wickedly and unjustly misuse this treasure for the service of demons. When the Christian severs himself in spirit from the wretched association of these men, he ought to take these from them for the lawful service of preaching the Gospel. It is also right for us to receive and possess, in order to convert it to a Christian use, their clothing, that is, those human institutions suited to intercourse with men which we cannot do without in this life.[3]

The candor of Augustine's statement is matched, in spirit in any case, by others to the same effect. St. Gregory Nazianzen's funeral oration on his brother, St. Caesarius, makes a similar point: in all learning, the core is God.

From geometry and astronomy, that branch of learning so dangerous for others, he selected what was useful, that is from the harmony and order of heavenly bodies he learnt admiration for the Creator. Yet, what was harmful he avoided. He did not attribute all being and becoming to the motion of the stars, as do those who set up their fellow servant, creation, in opposition to their Creator. But he referred, as is reasonable, their motion, as all other things, to God.[4]

It is vital to our point to read the Fathers themselves on their use of pagan antiquity. Otherwise, it is all too easy, even for such a scholar as Werner Jaeger, to make a statement like this one:

today it no longer needs to be proved that there has been a permanent tendency of revival throughout the last millennia of Western civilization—not to speak of the East which is a problem in itself. That tendency has culminated in certain historical periods. In this sense we now speak without hesitation of the Roman civilization of Cicero's own time and of the Augustan age as a renaissance of Greek cultural ideals. Another example of which we speak too little is that of the fourth century, A.D., when a complete revival of classical Greek literature and thought took place in the Greek Christian East, and a revival of Roman literature in the Latin speaking West culminating in St. Augustine. There are still people who do not realize that what we have in both hemispheres of the late Roman empire at that time was one of the most creative civilizations which history has ever seen. The synthesis of Christian religion and classical Greek and Roman culture which it effected became classical in its turn for the following centuries of the Middle Ages, and for countless millions of people it still is.[5]

One cannot quarrel with the tribute to the age of the Church Fathers as "one of the most creative civilizations which history has ever seen." One must take exception, however, to what Professor Jaeger seems to find creative in this civilization; for if he is accurate in the terms of his description, what was accomplished by rhetoricians such as Gregory of Nyssa and Augustine, by ecclesiastical authorities such as Ambrose and Gregory the Great, by polemicists such as Leo and Athanasius, by Scripture scholars such as Jerome and Basil and Chrysostom, was nothing more than a glorified compromise in which the place of Christianity was as high as, but no higher than, that of "classical Greek and Roman culture." One must do more than take exception, one must—if "one" is among those cited earlier, those for whom the Incarnation occupies the center of human history—one must altogether reject this notion of a synthesis of pagan culture and Christian religion which has so long dominated the teaching of these materials in our schools, Christian as well as secular, and insist rather on the facts as the Fathers faced them and named them, fought for them and remade them. It is one thing, after all, to take from the pagans "liberal instruction . . . adapted to the service of truth and . . . useful principles about morals . . . their gold and silver." It is quite another to take their "counterfeit and superstitious notions and oppressive burdens of useless labor," the sort of thing which would be inevitable in any mere synthesis of Christian and pagan cultures.

The zeal with which Leo, a man humble in his faith and directed by conviction more than most to the humility of the Founder of his faith, prosecuted any variation on the truth which should mark any sort of departure from it is worth remembering. The irony with which Augustine rejected the crude personifications of the pagan Pantheon is worth recalling. The tender solicitude with which pontiff and council, theologian and rhetorician, teacher and student, bishop and priest and monk defined and defended the smallest even as the largest Christian truth—literally, in the case of Athanasius, not yielding an iota—is worth keeping in mind. Holding all this firmly before one, how can one accept, for a moment, this curious concept of a compromising corps of Church Fathers whose proudest boast is of having molded a synthesis? If this were true, rather than founders they should be followers; rather than originators, imitators; rather than fathers, sons—and we should all be considerably the poorer for their synthetic achievement.

No, the Patristic assimilation did not consist of being assimilated; the Fathers were the appropriators, not the appropriated; the conquerors, not the vanquished. It is true that Christians, in general, fought the barbarians very differently from the way the barbarians fought against them; that, old or new, Greek or Roman, Goth or Vandal, what the barbarian offered in war, the Christian took in peace, and sooner or later made his own if it contained any part of a truth that could be used for the greater glory of God. The Fathers, a very special breed of Christians, were very selective in their culling of the pagans. As a result they did achieve one kind of synthesis, the unification of all that belonged together, men or ideas, nations or philosophies, for that is the function, perhaps beyond all the others, of the Church of Christ, *unam sanctam apostolicam.* This is the synthesis Augustine proclaims in the *De Moribus Ecclesiae Catholicae.* Addressing the Church, he says,

> Thou bringest into the bond of mutual charity every relationship of kindred, and every alliance of affinity. Thou teachest servants to cleave to their masters from delight in their task rather than from the necessity of their position. Thou renderest masters forbearing to their servants from a regard to God their common Master, and more disposed to advise than to compel. Thou unitest citizen to citizen, nation to nation, yea, man to man, from the recollection of their first parents, not only in society but in fraternity. Thou teachest kings to seek the good of their peoples; thou counsellest peoples to be subject to their kings. Thou teachest carefully to whom honor is due, to whom regard, to whom reverence, to whom fear, to whom consolation, to whom admonition, to whom encouragement, to whom discipline, to whom rebuke, to whom punishment; showing how all are not due to all, and how to all love is due, and how injury is due to none.[6]

That is the assimilation the Fathers sought to accomplish, and much of the time, at least, did. It is that example, that synthesis, that assimilation which is classical for all time.

CHAPTER III

St. Augustine: "And So It Shall Be Opened"

THE OPENING SENTENCE OF THE *Confessions* OF ST. Augustine is well enough known and widely enough celebrated: "Great art thou, O Lord, and greatly to be praised, great is thy power and thy wisdom infinite." It sums up all that the *Confessions* is about as a book, and all that Augustine's life as a Christian was dedicated to say, to sing, to shout. The concluding sentence of the great work is not well enough known; it is hardly known at all, for it brings to a conclusion the thirteenth book of the *Confessions*, and most editions stop at the ninth or tenth. When they do go on through the additional books, most readers do not; for the story of Augustine stops at the beginning of the tenth.

Does one miss much, missing the last three books? Not much of Augustine the philosopher, very little of Augustine the theologian, and almost none of Augustine the autobiographer; but of Augustine the poet, of Augustine the Christian, of Augustine the humanist, of Augustine the man, one misses very much, too much. Especially does one miss, one realizes after making up the loss, the rolling amens of Book XIII, that astonishing avalanche of rhetoric which pours down upon the reader in the form of thirty-eight short chapters, thirty-eight boulders, to come to a stop with its blunt proclamation: *sic aperietur*—and so it shall be opened.

What shall be opened? Many things, Augustine says: our rest in God and God's rest in us, the "grand sanctification" that God shall offer to our repose, our salvation. In cruder terms, we might say it is the gates of heaven that will be opened. But the opening starts here on earth, starts with us, starts with our bumbling attempts to make sense of Scripture.

It ends with our invocation of God: "I call upon thee, O my God, my mercy," Augustine begins the thirteenth and last book of the *Confessions;* "I invite thee into my soul," he says, "thee that createdst me, and who hast not forgotten me, that had forgotten thee." He calls upon God for rest, for eternal rest, and an understanding of some sort of the nature of God, an understanding that can be communicated. That, finally, is what shall be opened: the knowledge of God, the difference between God and man, Who He is and who we are. "And what man is he that can teach another man to understand this? Or what angel, another angel? Or what angel, man? Let it be begged of thee, be sought in thee, knocked for at thee; so, so shall it be received, so shall it be found, and so shall it be opened."

This is the Augustine who stands above all others who put their words to God's use. This is the Augustine who binds together classical past and Christian present in a bond of mutual charity, that charity which, he reminds us in the *De Doctrina Christiana*, is the only commandment of Scripture. This is the Augustine one finds if one goes beyond the slogans and homilies, the textbook formulas and illuminated holy cards to which so much of his work has been reduced. If one wants another sort of man, a weaker sort of commandment, a more accommodating and worldly teaching, one should go elsewhere; Augustine is not the man one seeks, nor is what was opened for him and what he opens for us what one wants opened.

Inevitably Augustine became a figure of legend. He is the very model of a modern legend. "The Story of a Sinner Who Became a Saint," one pamphlet about him is subtitled. Grouped around him are other appealing figures of the kind legend-makers and mythologizers quickly appropriate: his mother, so prolific of tears; his blustery father, postponing baptism like the slickly crafted curmudgeon of the play *Life with Father;* his mistress, mother of his son Adeodatus, left in a lurch large enough for a ten-twent-thirt melodrama. His conversion in the garden is equally theatrical; only St. Paul's vision on the Damascus road can rival the incantatory repetition of *tolle lege, tolle lege*—"Take up and read; Take up and read"—and the ardent response and the text from St. Paul seen through tears: "Not in rioting and drunkenness, not in chambering and wantonness, not in strife and envying: but put ye on the Lord Jesus Christ, and make not provision for the flesh." Even the theft of pears from an orchard next to his family's vineyard becomes an event and a *sermo*, a word for significant instruction.

Inevitably, with such a gift for signifying tales, Augustine became a central interpreter of Christian doctrine. To him, Protestants appealed in time of revolt. From him, Catholics protested against the appeals in time of counter-reformation. For a millennium he was the touchstone of understanding and the provider of light. His works formed a great bridge suspended across civilization to join Orient and Occident, Romans and Greeks and Christians, Cicero and Plato and Ambrose. We do not have to see the world spun around him, as Adolf Harnack does, "the miserable existence of the Roman Empire in the West . . . prolonged . . . only to permit Augustine's influence to be exercised on universal history," to recognize in him the intellectual and spiritual leader of the Christian West.

If, however, we accept the figure of legend and the interpreter of doctrine at face—or historians'—value, we lose the Augustine of the thirteenth book of the *Confessions*, we abandon the method he himself struggled to make commendable to all, and we miss almost entirely the most substantial of his contributions, the one that really signified. What we lose is Augustine the exegete. What we abandon is the allegorical method. What we miss almost entirely is that fruitful reading of Scripture which made possible the extension of his influence, as even his most dogged detractors agree, over almost all human activities, social and political and cultural, as well as religious.

Every vast view of Augustine is an exegetical one. Each comes from Scripture: the two cities; the psalms as a figure of the Church; the curative strength of charity, that most positive "motion of the soul whose purpose is to enjoy God for His own sake and one's self and one's neighbor for the sake of God"; and the debilitating power of concupiscence, that most weakening of all the motions of the soul, "bent upon enjoying one's self, one's neighbor, and any creature without reference to God."

We are today so far withdrawn from the Bible that this consuming interest of Augustine must to many seem merely quaint, a curious habit of the only incompletely learned of the Dark Age, bent in their monkish way over a book too far removed from pocket size to be really absorbing and too remote from the age of scientific discovery to be really useful. But science is not Augustine's discipline or desire; wisdom is. The source of wisdom is Scripture. Thus to Scripture he goes —relentlessly. To say of his works that they are full of Scripture is to offer what would have been to him the highest of compliments. Scripture is his food, his fullness, his faith. To say Scripture is to say Wisdom, whose book the Bible is. To say Wisdom is to name her whose votary Augustine is.

In a letter written to a foolish young pagan, happily or unhappily named Licentius, whom Augustine tutored at Cassiciacum, he describes the demeanor of Wisdom:

> wisdom first fetters her votaries and then tames them with training exercises; afterwards she sets them free and gives herself to be enjoyed by them. Those whom she has made expert by temporary obligations she will afterwards hold in an eternal embrace—and

there is nothing more delightful than this or more enduring. I admit that these beginnings are somewhat hard, but I would not call achievement hard because it is so sweet, nor would I call it soft because it is so lasting.

Will Licentius refuse to become one of Wisdom's supporters? Will he rebuke his teacher, and answer him contemptuously, like the slave in Terence's play, *Adelphœ*, "So you're pouring out your maxims here, Old Wisdom?" Augustine has an answer for the answer:

Better catch [the maxims], then, because I am pouring out, not outpouring. If I sing and you dance to another tune, it will not bother me, for my song has its own charm, even if it does not stir feet to the dance, because it is sung in the full key of charity.

Augustine goes on to examine the faults in a vaporous but not untouching yard of verse Licentius had dedicated to him, "The Poem of Licentius to His Master Augustine." He becomes taken up, as he often was, with literary, with rhetorical, matters. Even these, however, become something more. The art of verse-making is turned deftly into a metaphor; rhetoric and poetic are put to the moral purpose which every faculty has for Augustine:

If your verse were defective by reason of unregulated rhythm, if it did not abide by its own laws, if it offended the ear of the listener by uneven quantities, you would certainly be ashamed, and you would neither delay nor leave off your study and practice of the metrical art, counting no effort or toil too much so long as you could regulate, correct, straighten out and smooth off your lines. But, when you yourself are disordered and undisciplined, when you do not abide by the laws of your God, when you are not in accord with the honorable wishes of your friends, or even with your own reputation as a scholar, do you think all that is to be disregarded and forgotten? Your self-esteem is lowered by the sound of your own language, but you think it is a smaller thing to offend the ears of God by your disorderly behavior than to arouse the criticism of the grammarians by your disordered lines.[1]

Many of Augustine's works translate the language of the arts in the same way and assign them the same labor, the *opus Dei.* Such books are the *De Doctrina Christiana*, the *De Magistro*, the *De Musica*, the *De Ordine*, the works on the Sermon on the Mount, on the first three chapters of *Genesis*, on the spirit and the letter, and related biblical commentaries. Like the last books of the *Confessions*, these works are no longer much read, except by scholars. And they serve even scholars chiefly as a guide to Augustinian diction and a key to medieval Scriptural method. These are not recondite works, however. They do not require special training to read, to understand, or put to use. The *De Doctrina Christiana*, for example, is a remarkably compact treatise on the nature of Christian doctrine and the way it is communicated in Scripture. After a brief but not at all superficial summary of those things which are of signal importance to Christians—the nature of God, the Incarnation, the Resurrection, the Church—Augustine proceeds to the distinction around which his exegetical method revolves, between *things* and *signs*, which represent things. Some things, he explains, are to be *enjoyed*, to make us happy; such things are those which, "by a certain association with us are accountable to God, such as a man or an angel, or which, related to us, require the grace of God through us, such as our body." Other things, of a more transitory nature, are to be used only to attain our end in God; they are not to be enjoyed in themselves; they are means, not ends.

The bulk of the *De Doctrina* is filled with Augustine's prescriptions and proscriptions for the interpretation of signs. He distinguishes among different kinds of rhetorical figures, probes the obscurities of signs, and advances the cardinal rule for discerning figure in Scripture:

> we are not to attempt to interpret a literal expression as if it were figurative. Therefore, I must first point out the method of making sure whether a passage is literal or figurative. In general, that method is to understand as figurative anything in Holy Scripture which cannot in a literal sense be attributed either to an upright character or to a pure faith. Uprightness of character pertains to the love of God and of our neighbor; purity of faith, to the knowledge of God and our neighbor.[2]

Having discovered that a passage is literal or figurative, "it is easy, by employing the rules concerning things . . . to reflect upon it under all its aspects until we reach the idea of truth, particularly when practice, invigorated by the observance of piety, is added to it."

He recognizes the need for the study of grammar and rhetoric, for an understanding in depth of trope and metaphor, irony, antiphrasis, and other figures. He recommends, if adopted with prudence, the application of the rules of the Donatist heretic Tyconius for penetrating obscure passages in Scripture. Finally, he outlines the methods and manners suitable to the profession of the preacher. With an astonishing compendiousness, he reduces to the size of a very short treatise the substance of Ciceronian rhetoric, discourses eloquently, if briefly, on style, and draws in radiant lines an aureole around his own career as a rhetorician, perhaps the most handsomely endowed and comprehensively educated of them all.

The purpose of the *De Magistro* is essentially the same as that of the *De Doctrina*, the exposition of signs. All words are signs that prod the memory, Augustine explains to his son Adeodatus. In this marvelously readable dialogue, Augustine, the teacher, the *Magister*, outlines his functions and those of language. He does so with captivating swiftness. For all the speed, however, he never becomes glib. He recognizes the knottiness of the problem: "For discussing words with words is as entangled as interlocking and rubbing the fingers with the fingers, in which case it may scarcely be distinguished—except by the one himself who does it—which fingers itch and which give relief to the itching."

Augustine takes his son through the rough science of signs, scratching away methodically at each itch until he has exposed the truth beneath the surface, the thing covered by the sign. He is eager that Adeodatus understand that some things can be discovered without signs, such things as those of nature, the sun, the moon and the stars, the land and sea—all "are shown through themselves by God and nature to those who perceive them." Other things we learn through recognition and association: it is not the name "head-covering" or "hat" that identifies a hat, but the sight of it, with which we then associate its denominating term. We accept, as a series of conventions, sounds, the parts of speech, the rules of grammar, and the head-coverings given all of these by the habits of spelling. But it is the cognitive process that follows the convention that matters. It is not, for example, the sound of *coenum*, filth, that bothers us, but what it stands for. A change of one letter can raise filth to heaven—*coenum* to *coelum*. Therefore, it is the final lesson of this discipline, and the central concern of the teacher as well, to explain that we do not learn through outward show, but only through "the guardian truth within the mind itself." Words remind us to "consult" that truth within.

This is the nub of Augustine's analysis of language. The guardian truth is the true teacher, God Himself: "for He who is said to reside in the interior man is Christ." Once again, the insight rests on a Scriptural reference; once again, it is Paul who leads Augustine: "Strengthened by his Spirit in the inner man, that Christ may dwell in your hearts through faith" (Eph 3:16, 17). He alone is the Master, the teacher. To his teachings alone should we give heed. This we do as best we can, according to our moral and intellectual limitations, when we consult the voice of wisdom living in each of us. Signs lead us to things; we check the accuracy of signs and the meaning of things by consultation with that interior truth which is the ultimate measure of all experience, a truth we know because of the presence of God within all of us.

There is, Augustine is saying, a reality to which signs and things must conform. It is, God be praised, a measurable reality. It is not, God once again be praised, merely the teacher's truth: "For who is so stupidly curious," Augustine asks, "as to send his son to school in order that he may learn what the teacher thinks?" If you have learned anything, he says to his son, you understand from whom—or you do not understand at all:

For if you know that what I have said is true, then had you been questioned about each statement you would have said that you did know it. You see, therefore, from whom you have learned these matters. Surely, not from me to whom you would have given the correct answer if questioned. However, if you do not know that they are true, neither the inner man nor I have taught you; not I, because I can never teach; not the inner man, because you have it not yet in you to learn.[3]

The great effort the disciple of Augustine must make is to drag up from the lowest depths within him all that is buried there. He must continually expose to the searching light of analysis whatever has been pushed into the dark corners of his memory. Memory is all; everything that one is and has been is stored within it. It records experiences pitilessly. Through the understanding and the will, one discriminates between the solid materials and the waste packed away in the memory. The relation of these perceptions of Augustine to the layers of consciousness—to the subconscious, the unconscious, and the preconscious—discovered by modern psychologists should be self-evident.

Like the cure of the psychoanalyst, Augustinian therapy is very much concerned with an emerging and expanding consciousness. We get to know ourselves as we get to know the world: by constant exploration. The Christian combat begins with honest and fearless self-examination. It is this sort of analysis which unites all of Augustine's writings and imposes upon them an organizing structure. The tone of the *Confessions* is the prevailing one here. But that tone is like a verbal sign; it is where it leads that matters, not what it is in itself. Where it leads, of course, is to the awareness of the presence of God, the all-present God.

Founder of the form of self-analysis called *Soliloquium*—soliloquy—Augustine examines himself, the nature of his body and his soul, and the nature of truth, in a series of exchanges in which his reason is personified to permit the tension of dialogue. Once again, he demonstrates the purpose of the liberal arts. Those well trained in them

> bring to light in the process of learning knowledge that undoubtedly is buried in oblivion within them, and, in a way, they disinter it. Moreover, they are not content and they cannot contain themselves until they behold in all its breadth and fullness the whole countenance of Truth, whose splendor already glows in a certain measure in these arts.[4]

The splendor has to be glimpsed through the darkness, the truth amidst falsehood. The comforting fact is that they can be discovered here below. How? By a nearly mathematical pursuit of order. On the level of the individual, the attempt is, through the analytical researches of the soliloquy, by the submission of language to minute scrutiny, by the incessant probing of signs, to make all one does comprehensible to oneself and accountable to God. On the highest and broadest plane, it is a search for purpose and plan in the universe, for the design that puts evil in its place and good where it belongs, that makes much, if not all, comprehensible to man and, as always, accountable to God. On both levels, it is the overwhelming desire for understanding which makes possible the enormous body of Augustine's writings, fitted together, perception by perception, subject by subject, discipline by discipline, until nearly the full range of human speculation has been encompassed.

What the treatises on language, the *Confessions*, and the soliloquies are to the inquiry into the nature of the individual, the *De Ordine* is to the investigation of the design of the universe. Like the other works I have been discussing here, it is a small one. Like them too, its queries are nonetheless on the grand scale, its view vast. The promontory from which Augustine looks out over creation is sketched in the opening paragraph:

> To perceive and to grasp the order of reality proper to each thing, and then to see or to explain the order of the entire universe by which this world is truly held together and governed—that, Zenobius, is a very difficult and rare achievement for men. Moreover, even if one had this power, he is not thereby enabled to find an audience fitted for such divine and hidden things, either by personal worth or by an acquired habit of learning. And yet there is nothing that the most gifted minds search out more eagerly . . . nothing that these are more desirous of hearing and learning than how it is that God has a care for human affairs . . .

All the writing of the *De Ordine* is of the same literary quality, of a related rhetorical order. Through analogy and conjunction, contrast and disjunction, Augustine sets before Zenobius, a government worker whose identity is now long lost in the annals of declining and falling Rome, the manifold operations of order. He finds the parts of a flea "marvelously fitted and framed, while human life is surrounded and made restless by the inconsistency of countless disorders." But only "uninstructed men . . . on account of their feeble mentality, are unable to grasp and to study the integral fittingness of things. They think that the whole universe is disarranged if something is displeasing to them . . ." The root of their mistaken judgment is their failure to examine themselves, to acquire self-knowledge through meditation. Only by tracing "in solitude the impressions of opinion which the course of daily life has made" or correcting them through the application of the liberal arts can one get to know oneself. Only by the soul thus returning to itself can it understand the beauty of the universe—namely, its unity, its harmony, the exquisitely hoed and harrowed interrelationships of the "divine planting."

Through argument and discussion with friends, he reports to Zenobius, Augustine has been led through the night, past the dawn, to go to the baths, "for that place was comfortable and suitable for our disputation . . ." Suddenly they all notice "a bitter" cockfight beginning to take shape before them. They decide to stay and watch—with reason, for in the fight they find, if not resolved, at least clarified, the points at dispute in their discussion of order:

For what do the eyes of lovers [of truth and beauty] not encompass; where do they not search through to see beauteous reason signaling something thence?—reason which rules and governs all things, the knowing and the unknowing things, and which attracts her eager followers in every way and wherever she commands that she be sought. Whence indeed and where can she not give a signal?—as was to be seen in those fowls: the lowered heads stretched forward, neck plumage distended, the lusty thrusts, and such wary parryings, and, in every motion of the irrational animals, nothing unseemly—precisely because another Reason from on high rules over all things. Finally, the very law of the victor: the proud crowing, the almost perfectly orbed arrangement of the members, as if in haughtiness of supremacy. But the sign of the vanquished: hackles plucked from the neck, in carriage and cry all bedraggled—and for that very reason, somehow or other, beautiful and in harmony with nature's laws.

Watching the cockfight leads to reflections on the behavior of the rooster, on their own pleasure in the display of beauty, and on the truths that lie beyond the senses. It is a novella of the kind in which Renaissance romance writers delighted, a brief excursion to supplement and implement the main points of the larger narrative. It has in its conclusion the mark of *suavitas*, that most agreeable sweetness which identifies the true Augustinian tale. This is the pursuit of wisdom as Plato and Socrates understood it, through all the moments of one's life, not excepting a cockfight at dawn before the public baths:

> We were saying to ourselves: Where does law not reign? Where is the right of commanding not due to a superior being? Where is there not the shadow of consistency? Where is there not imitation of that beauty most true? Where is there no limit? And, thus admonished that there should be a limit to our watching the chickens, we went whither we had proposed to go, and there, as best we could, we garnered into this part of the notebook all the points of our nocturnal discussion—carefully indeed, for the points were recent; and at any rate, how could such striking things escape the memory of three diligent inquirers?

Providence is the goal of the inquiry of the *De Ordine*. It was written early in Augustine's life as a Christian, at the end of the year of his conversion, 386. In it, he searches out for himself the relation of reason and revelation, the extent to which the directing hand of God may be discovered in creation, and, once found, the orders of knowledge that follow upon its discovery. The definitions offered do not by any means exhaust the subject. All of Augustine's works which touch on Divine Providence and order in the universe—and most do—do not exhaust the subject, nor does he pretend that they do. But incomplete as they are, these definitions are necessary starting points for the Christian humanist. To them, directly or indirectly, Augustine returns over and over in his works.

The morning after the cockfight Augustine offers to Licentius one approach to order. It might be called the definition according to the life of the spirit: "Order is that which will lead us to God, if we hold to it during life; and unless we do hold to it during life, we shall not come to God." With this principle established in the first of the two books of his treatise, he turns in the second to a description of the life of moderation and of the wisdom and tranquillity which are its fruit. "A grand view of life, a succinct but complete view," Alypius admits, but how can it be achieved by mere mortals? This leads Augustine to a definition and discussion of reason—"a mental operation capable of distinguishing and connecting the things that are learned."

The ensuing chapters on reason in art offer the interested reader a grand and succinct and definitive introduction to medieval art theory. For those in the years from the fifth century to the fifteenth who did not get their view of art from Augustine directly could not help being influenced by Augustinian thinking. It dominated almost all schooling and practice in the visual arts, and in music, poetry, and oratory for a thousand years. In brief, Augustine teaches that "what pertains to reason" in the pleasure of the senses "is that in which there is a certain rhythmic measure." He points to an unreasonable design or, rather, that which is without design at all:

considering carefully the parts of this very building, we cannot but be displeased because we see one doorway toward the side and another situated almost, but not exactly, in the middle. In things constructed, a proportion of parts that is faulty, without any compelling necessity, unquestionably seems to inflict, as it were, a kind of injury upon one's gaze. But, the fact that three windows inside, one in the middle and two at the sides, pour light at equal intervals on the bathing place—how much that delights and enraptures us as we gaze attentively is a thing already manifest, and need not be shown to you in many words. In their own terminology, architects themselves call this *design*, and they say that parts unsymmetrically placed are without design.

This is a general rule in the arts and in all of man's creative activities. Rhythm accounts for the sweetness in songs and obviously is paramount in dancing. It is to be found in the numbering and measuring of man's resources accomplished by the art of dialectics. It is even more a part of rhetoric, the delicately balanced, numerically ordered art of persuasion, "its lap heaped high with charms which it [scatters] to the crowd so that the crowd might deign to be influenced for its own good." Wherever things are numerically proportioned, there is reason, there is power, truth, wisdom, and beauty. From "the science of right reasoning and the power of numbers" come the insights which lead to the all-essential, all-purposeful ideas of order, which in turn lead to some grasp of the sacred mysteries and account in some satisfactory fashion for the activities and privations we call evil in a universe in which God is omnipotent.

It is not sufficient to make excellently measured things. Birds do as much. But they build their carefully constructed nests without understanding what they are doing. Man, on the other hand, understands what he does. Not only can he use numbers, he can grasp their nature. "Nothing else," Augustine concludes, "ranks me above the brute animal except the fact that I am a rational animal." Once again, he makes all of man's activities parallel and unites to a perception of design in the universe the ordering of one's own soul through conscious, rational effort:

Indeed, it is not by faith alone, but by trustworthy reason, that the soul leads itself little by little to most virtuous habits and the perfect life. For, to the soul that diligently considers the nature and the power of numbers, it will appear manifestly unfitting and most deplorable that it should write a rhythmic line and play the harp by virtue of this knowledge, and that its life and very self—which is the soul—should nevertheless follow a crooked path and, under the domination of lust, be out of tune by the clangor of shameful vices.

The result of such an effort is man's beatitude. It brings together all the orders of knowledge into a cohesive, massive unity and up to a majestic vision of eternity. What does one see? What does one know? What questions are answered? Augustine asks, in effect: What can there be left to see? What does one not know or need to know? What questions can there be for one who has achieved harmony of soul?

What should we say? Everyday expressions present themselves, but they have been rendered sordid by things of least worth. I shall say no more, except that to us is promised a vision of beauty—the beauty through whose imitation all other things are beautiful, and by comparison with which all other things are unsightly. Whosoever will have glimpsed this beauty—and he will see it who lives well, prays well, studies well—when will it ever trouble him why one man, desiring to have children, has them not, while another man casts out his own offspring as being unduly numerous; why one man hates children before they are born, and another man loves them after birth; or how is it not absurd that nothing will come to pass which is not with God—and, therefore, it is inevitable that all things come into being in accordance with order—and nevertheless God is not petitioned in vain?[5]

Augustine went on from the degree of consciousness

achieved in the *De Ordine* and the treatises on language and signification to the far-flung perceptions of the *De Trinitate* and the *De Civitate Dei.* He moved from inquiry to assertion and from the comparative confinement of small-scale dialogues to the expansiveness of large-scale philosophical treatises. But the sovereign truth remains the same in all of them: there is in creation a discoverable design. At whatever level we perceive it, through whatever means, it leads to that reality to which all that is is conformable, to that being in whom all is rooted, to God Himself. One can approach that truth through the zealous arraignment of pagan failures and the noble vision of ultimate Christian triumph of *The City of God,* or one can come directly to it in the fifteen books *On the Trinity,* especially in the twenty-fifth chapter of the twelfth book, in which Augustine substitutes for the Platonic doctrine of reminiscences the Christian doctrine of illumination. In both imposing works, it is elaboration one finds rather than anything new, elaboration of a sufficient complexity to make enormously useful the earlier, simpler, more straightforward statements of the same material.

It is hard to accommodate the fullness of vision of *The City of God* without the preparation offered for it by the comparatively dim foreshadowings of the *De Ordine.* Even after the stunning experience of the splendor of the *De Civitate Dei* one turns gratefully to the pages of the early little work, happy to turn for a little while from the monumental to the miniature. In the same way, after the charged language of Book XII of the *De Trinitate,* the *De Magistro* is a relief, not only because of the diminution in size, but because there the doctrine of illumination is to be found in words of much greater simplicity and directness. In the involuted language of the work on the Trinity, we are told "that the intellectual mind is so formed in its nature as to see those things, which by the disposition of the Creator are subjoined to things intelligible in a natural order, by a sort of incorporeal light of an unique kind; as the eye of the flesh sees things adjacent to itself in this bodily light, of which light it is made to be receptive, and adapted to it." In the simpler words of the *De Magistro,* we are told to examine and confirm the truths we know by means of "the guardian truth within the mind itself," that is to say, through consultation with Christ Himself, who dwells in each of us as the interior teacher.

Whether one seeks general illumination from Augustine or the particular doctrine of illumination, looks for an understanding of the general structure of his career or of one of his particular philosophical or theological positions, the best and the most gratifying approach is the chronological one. Through it, doctrines are unveiled and lasting things signified —those things which are to be enjoyed and not merely to be used. By means of such a passage through the books of Augustine, the magnitude of his achievement is revealed—not the space on the library shelves the volumes occupy, but the career of meditation and contemplation which they reflect and offer to others. Here it is, intact, numerically precise, and with that sweet proportion which to the Augustinian indicates reason, beauty, and wisdom.

It is all a matter of degree—of seven degrees, as Augustine himself points out in his treatise on the magnitude of the soul. Degree by degree, we mount in contemplation until we come to the Highest Cause, the Supreme Author, the First Principle of all things:

> When it has been achieved, we shall truly see the vanity of all things under the sun, and we shall discern how far distant are mundane things from those that really are. Then shall we know how true are the Articles of Faith (credenda) that have been enjoined, and how well and wholesomely we have been nourished by Mother Church. We shall see into the nature of our bodies so as to consider the Resurrection of the Flesh to be as certain as

the rising of the sun. We shall have such understanding of the Mystery of the Incarnation and the Virgin Birth, as to brush aside impatiently all cavilling. And such pleasure is there in the contemplation of Truth, such purity, such sincerity, such undoubting faith, that one now feels one had never really known what previously we had seemed to know; and death is no longer feared, but desired as the greatest gain, that the soul may be free to cleave wholly to the whole Truth.[6]

Thus we come to the last thing. To it all other things and signs have pointed. If we have followed Augustine in an orderly, rhythmically measured progression of signs and things, we have inevitably been brought to the desire "to be free to cleave wholly to the whole Truth."

CHAPTER IV

Boethius: Wisdom's Consolation

In Pavia, just outside Milan, Italy, in what looks like an alley, there is a church in retreat from the world, but not the sun: San Pietro in Cielo d'Oro, St. Peter in a Golden Sky—the Pavians' fanciful way of describing the dome of their church. Upstairs, in the main altar, repose what are proclaimed to be the bones of St. Augustine. Downstairs, in the crypt, into which too some of the golden sun creeps, rest the bones of that figure we know simply by the name of Boethius, whose full name, in full patrician splendor, was Anicius Manlius Torquatus Severinus Boethius, who is known, as a result of the local cult at Pavia, as St. Severinus Boethius.

In the cant phrases of the popular historians of medieval thought, who dispose of Boethius in a few pages or even fewer paragraphs, he is "the last Roman philosopher," "the first of the schoolmen," "the interpreter of the ancient world and its wisdom," and, most notably, author of the best read book of the Middle Ages, the *Consolation of Philosophy*. Indeed the *Consolation* was without rival for perhaps thirty generations of readers, from Boethius's own time to Shakespeare's, from the sixth to the sixteenth century. Its author, then, cannot be dismissed in a few conventional phrases, even phrases so often repeated as to seem stipulated in a contract with the licensers of the Middle Ages.

The *Consolation* still commands our attention, still demands to be read and understood. While it is no longer quite the controversial work it was for so many commentators for so many years, for some there are still serious misgivings about the solidity of the faith attested to in it; and where there are not misgivings, there are misapprehensions about the method and meaning of the work. For too many, even of the learned, the *Consolation* is still a work of philosophy quite removed from theology and not even ancillary to it. For too many, only the obscure facts of Boethius's life, made darker by dozens of conflicting glosses, and the easy susceptibilities of the notoriously susceptible Middle Ages can account for the cult at Pavia. All that is missing in such an accounting is the particular genius of Boethius, which is as much that of a saint as of an artist, and which surely best explains, at least in the timeless terms of Divine Providence, the wisdom of interring his bones directly beneath those of St. Augustine.

The facts of Boethius's life are not unimposing, however little they may really explain his appearance in the Roman calendar. He was born into a prominent Roman senatorial family about the year 475. When he was seven, his father was consul. At an early age he was orphaned and his education undertaken by a pious nobleman, whose daughter he later married. In his early thirties, he himself became consul. A learned and trustworthy man, he was dispatched on important missions by the Emperor Theodoric, and his two sons were also raised to the rank of consul about two years before their father's disgrace. When Boethius's fall came, then, it was from the greatest heights.

The accusations are not clear, but in the fuzzy records the atmosphere of disloyalty to the Ostrogoth emperor prevails. Boethius was a popular man, of noble birth, and with a wide reputation for wisdom and learning. He had participated in the defense of a prominent senator, also of consular rank, who had been accused of plotting with the Byzantine government against Theodoric. He may too have been the victim of the animosity of an Arian ruler directed against the leading member of an orthodox Christian senate. In any case, he was condemned to death, and after spending the months in prison described in the *Consolation*, was executed.

It is senseless to attempt to decide whether or not Boethius was a martyr. Considering the kind of evidence upon which such a decision would have to be made, it is not only senseless, but impossible. It is enough to look at his achievement, one so large that not all the fuzziness of poor documents can efface it. I am not speaking of his attainments as a scholar, as a name dear to specialists; I am not hailing the sort of achievement usually memorialized in footnotes and nowhere else. Nor do I say that we must be impressed because his name is so significant in the Middle Ages in so many manuscripts—not even because his *Consolation* appeared in so many editions, was pirated by so many, translated by so many, and so many of stature, into Anglo-Saxon by Alfred the Great, into Old German by Notker, into Middle English by Chaucer, into the English forever associated with her name by Queen Elizabeth. No, important as each of these facts is, it is no one of them that should, at first, anyway, halt us in the contemplation of Boethius. It is rather his astonishing range, his perseverance, his assiduous pursuit of the highest level of accomplishment.

Boethius's duties were certainly responsible ones, sufficiently consuming of time and energy to occupy all of his life away from his family. But Boethius—who more than fulfilled Augustine's prescription for the good life of a balance of right reasoning and the science of numbers—was a master of the Quadrivium who was determined to communicate his own mastery of mathematical disciplines to others. He wrote a *De Musica* and *De Arithmetica*, which are still preserved, and a *De Geometria* which is lost. A master of Greek, he planned to translate not less than all of Aristotle and Plato into Latin. He actually managed to do the *Categories* and *De Interpretatione*, which have survived, and the other logical treatises of Aristotle, which have not. He also translated the

Isagoge of the Neoplatonist Porphyry, and on it, as upon the Aristotelian *Organon* and Cicero's *Topics*, he wrote several commentaries.

Boethius was in fact logician-in-waiting to the medieval world, the transmitter of Aristotle's logic and Porphyry's introduction to it—and more, since in his commentaries he quotes from other works of Aristotle and from Plato too. He organized for logical philosophy a specialized vocabulary and definitions still important, not only to those who labor in the tradition of the Schoolmen, but to logicians of non-Aristotelian persuasion too.

Less important perhaps for medieval scholarship, but more significant for an understanding of the *Consolation*, are his five theological treatises. Four of these are vouched for by Cassiodorus, Boethius's good friend and like him counselor to Theodoric, but less involved politically or more skillful or more fortunate. Cassiodorus lived out his life long enough to retire to a monastery he had founded on one of his own estates. A great keeper of documents and recorder of literary, philosophical, and theological fact, he performed a valuable service for us in his authentication of Boethius's theological opuscula.

One of the most compelling of these treatises, the *De Trinitate*, was written for Boethius's beloved father-in-law, Symmachus, and only for the learned to read and to understand. It is not for the mob, Boethius says; he will not cast pearls before swine. The language is difficult because new. He will follow the promptings of reason—and St. Augustine. Those promptings elicit from him a masterpiece of prefatory rhetoric, a touching peroration and a definitive demonstration of how far philosophy can go in unlocking the mysteries. The treatise went far to establish the intellectual viability of the concept of tri-unity. Upon it St. Thomas built a masterful commentary.

In his treatise directed against the Nestorian and Eutychian heresies, he argues with a clarity that is still confounding to heretics. What is more important, in refuting the assertions that there had to be in Christ two persons if there were two natures (Nestorius's error) or if there was but one person then but one nature (Eutyches' mistake), he illuminates brightly the dogma of the hypostatic union. The work remains, though closely written and distinctly technical, a superb commentary on its theological materials: this is what it means to say of Christ that He is One Person with two natures.

In the course of answering the heretics, Boethius comes to his famous definition of the person, one long accepted, by Thomas, by the Schoolmen, and by modern theologians: "naturae rationabilis individua substantia"—"an individual substance of a rational nature." That is, he is saying, the human person is an individual intellectual substance complete in itself, not accidental to any subject, a rational individual existing for himself.

The little treatise *De Fide Catholica, On The Catholic faith*, which is not mentioned by Cassiodorus, can be argued to be Boethius's. It can also be rejected. Its terseness is reminiscent of the other theological tractates. Its scriptural tone is unique among Boethius's works. It fits well enough with the other works, however, and is certainly attractive enough to deserve much more attention than it normally receives. In its own small way it is a masterpiece of compression, of doctrinal precision and of eloquence. See, for example, the concise opening paragraph:

> The Christian Faith is proclaimed by the authority of the New Testament and of the Old; but although the Old scripture contains within its pages the name of Christ and constantly gives token that He will come who we believe has already come by the

birth of the Virgin, yet the diffusion of that faith throughout the world dates from the actual miraculous coming of our Saviour.[1]

And see its stately closing lines:

> All . . . that the faithful now expect is that the end of the world will come, that all corruptible things shall pass away, that men shall rise for future judgment, that each shall receive reward according to his deserts and abide in the lot assigned to him for ever and for aye; and the sole reward of bliss will be the contemplation of the Almighty, so far, that is, as the creature may look on the Creator, to the end that the number of the angels may be made up from these and the heavenly city filled where the Virgin's Son is King and where will be everlasting joy, delight, food, labor, and unending praise of the Creator.

A small divine office can be made of such writing.

The ending of the little work on the Catholic faith is, on the surface anyway, impersonal and detached. But there is in it more than a touch of the lovable individual rational substance that was Boethius. There is much more of this affecting but altogether unaffected tone in the dedications of his treatises to father-in-law and friends, and in his frequent personal asides and many personifications of argument and idea. Much of the consolation and the wisdom of the monumental *De Consolatione Philosophiae* is personal in exactly this way. For of all the great works of Christian humanism the *Consolation* is one of the most personal, so personal that it has eluded many who read it and almost as many who write about it. Rarely has anyone made an *exemplum*, an instructive moral tale, so completely out of his own life and labors and predicament.

To be understood, not simply to be classified, the *Consolation* must be seen as exemplary, not merely cautionary; it must be seen as illustrative in the several dimensions, and especially the great depth, of Christian allegory. There is clear enough meaning on the surface. There is more beneath it. It is not merely a philosophical exposition of the nature of sin, suffering, hope, and the true way, and their place in a providentially ordered world. It is certainly not a work of stiff-upper-lip Stoicism. It contains a fullness of literary device, and of a particularly rhetorical nature. For mathematician, musician, geometer, and logician that he was, Boethius was also a rhetorician, like the most considerable of his masters, Augustine, and the most considerable of his works, as a result, abounds in rhetorical figure.

Looking in his prison cell for fitting garments for his *Consolation*, Boethius went to an ancient pattern, that blending of verse and prose which goes by the name of *satyra Menippea*, after the work of the Roman poet Varro. From it he cut a new design, a Christian one, a hopeful one, a surpassingly elegant one. The *Consolation* consists of five books of alternating prose and verse, through almost all of which the narrative continues unblocked and unstopped. The exceptions are interludes in meter at the end of each of the first four books and at special moments throughout the work, poems of a commanding excellence in Latin, fit to stand alone, but also very much a part of the Boethian drama.

Into that drama we plunge with the first line of the opening verse of the first book. He had begun to write couplets, he tells us, on those subjects fitting for elegy, death, and old age, when a remarkable woman suddenly hovered over him, one "having a grave countenance, glistening clear eye . . . her color fresh and bespeaking unabated vigor, and yet discovering so many years that she could not at all be thought to belong to our times; her stature uncertain and doubtful, for sometime she exceeded not the common height of men, and sometime she seemed to touch the heavens with her head, and if she lifted it up to the highest, she pierced the very heavens, so that she could not be seen by the beholders . . ."

On her gown, which, he later learns, she herself had woven,

are engraved the Greek letters *pi* and *theta,* initials of the words *praktike* and *theoretike*, representing the practical and theoretical realms of speculation. For this is Philosophy personified, which is to say Wisdom itself—not the discipline of philosophy, of the investigation of problems through the employment of the rational faculties, as distinguished from the revelations and language of theology; the distinction, like the two vocabularies, was unknown in Boethius's time.

Seeing the muses gathered around Boethius's bed and encouraging his tears by providing words to go with them, Lady Philosophy erupts with anger. She chases from the cell the Sirens, as she calls them, the strumpets who feed grief with sugared poison. As his old nurse, his critic, philosopher, and friend, she will take over the duties of the attending physician. Now, then, she says, it is time to seek cures rather than to make complaints.

Boethius responds by reaching into his life for languishing looks and laments at his fortune and misfortune. Almost forcibly, Philosophy brings him back—not to earth but to her high heaven—to move step by step from despair to hope, through a soft serenity in the face of trial and suffering and detachment from worldly pleasures, to peace in the dual embrace of reason and virtue, united in the virtues of faith and hope.

In the course of his examination of the conflicts in his mind between Providence and free will, Boethius is first led to grievous complaint, Joblike complaint:

> why should punishments,
> Due to the guilty, light on innocents?
> But now the highest place
> Giveth to naughty manners greatest grace,
> And wicked people vex
> Good men, and tread unjustly on their necks;
> Virtue in darkness lurks,
> And righteous souls are charged with impious works . . .

"Now I know," says Philosophy, acting as surrogate for St. Augustine, ". . . perhaps the greatest cause of thy sickness: *thou hast forgotten what thou art.*" It is to the recovery of himself that the remaining four books of the *Consolation* are devoted, to the recovery of himself, and by the simplest of allegorical substitutions, of ourselves. The human person recovered, recollected, redirected is the end—in both senses of the word—of the book. That is Wisdom's true consolation, to help one to recover oneself, which is to discover what and who one is.

Perhaps the best known of all belayings of fortune—not even excepting Machiavelli's—is to be found in the second book of the *Consolation:* "I know the manifold illusions of that monster," Philosophy exclaims—for this is her enemy, Wisdom's enemy, man's enemy, "this blind goddess." "What else is fickle fortune but a token of future calamity?" She proposes to use "the sweetness of Rhetoric's persuasions" and all the blandishments of Music, "a little slave belonging to our house," to ease Boethius's condition.

One must not forget in what ways one is happy, when misfortune comes: Philosophy reminds Boethius of his noble father-in-law, his chaste wife, his distinguished sons—not to speak of all the honors granted him in his youth. "Wilt thou then reckon with fortune? This is the first time that ever she frowned upon thee." It is true: the worst misfortune is to have been too fortunate.

The main point remains: "This is the condition of man's nature, that then only it surpasseth other things when it knoweth itself, and is worse than beasts when it is without that knowledge. *For in other living creatures the ignorance of themselves is nature, but in men it is vice.*"

Philosophy pooh-poohs reputation and the attempt to get a stranglehold on posterity. The favors of fortune are no favors at all: "I think," she says, "that Fortune, when she is opposite, is more profitable to men than when she is favorable . . . prosperity with her flatterings withdraweth men from true goodness, adversity recalleth and reclaimeth them many times by force to true happiness."

A discerning Dominican, Père Gardeil, has called Book III "a literary monument raised to the glory of true blessedness." Certainly St. Thomas found it such and laid wreaths upon it with commensurate veneration. This is the book of remedies, the book with the great definition of that blessedness which all men naturally desire—"*an estate replenished with all that is good.*" Most men wander, however, go astray, in putting their trust in surfaces, in appearances, in shining and obvious lures: riches, honors, power, glory, pleasures. The end of all of these things is sorrow. Sufficiently convinced for the moment, Boethius invokes his Creator and prays for light in one of the most stirring of the meters of the *Consolation:*

> Let me behold the spring of grace and find Thy light,
> That I on Thee may fix my soul's well cleared sight.
> Cast off the earthly weight wherewith I am opprest,
> Shine as Thou art most bright, Thou only calm and rest
> To pious men whose end is to behold Thy ray,
> Who their beginning art, their guide, their bound, and way.

He follows this with a fine and concise example of his logic—a demonstration of the nature of true happiness: the imperfect supposes the perfect; imperfect good necessitates sovereign good; perfect good can be nothing else, no other, but God, the Good whom all seek and all desire, He whose substance consists in nothing else but goodness.

But still the wicked triumph here below, Boethius protests in Book IV. Yes indeed, agrees Philosophy, but order will be restored in the life to come, eternal order founded on merit and demerit, reward and punishment, the great order of Providence—

"This is the glorious land
Where I was born, and in this soil my feet forevermore shall stand.
Whence if thou pleasest to behold the earthly night which thou hast left,
Those tyrants which the people fear will seem of their true home bereft."

There are compensations and balances here on earth, too, to take the sting out of evil and to remove some of the tension it exerts among the good: "Whatsoever is at all is one, and that unity is goodness, by which it followeth that whatsoever is must also be good. And in this manner whatsoever falleth from goodness ceaseth to be, by which it followeth that evil men leave to be that which they were, but the shape of men, which they still retain, showeth them to have been men: wherefore by embracing wickedness they have lost the nature of men." The logic is inexorable: men are made miserable by their evil deeds, the more they persist in them the more miserable they must become. The wicked are truly the most unhappy of men; they may be thankful that death comes to bring an end to their wickedness and misery.

Finally, in the fifth book, Boethius and the reader are confronted with Divine Omniscience. Its great mercy is to have foreseen all things but not as a result to have obliterated human freedom. It is true that it is only with the greatest difficulty that we can grasp how these two truths can be reconciled. But however hard to understand, the principle is firmly asserted: there can be no rational nature without free will. Since God sees all things in an eternal present, His knowledge of future contingencies no more hinders their freedom than does the sight of free acts being performed before us, in the present, prevent those who do them from performing them freely. We understand things and events not by the forces within them, but by our own faculties of knowing.

Thus our knowledge–like God's–is outside events and does not in any way hinder their freedom. Reason and faith, then, may be reconciled, philosophy and religion shown to have the same end, once one can see the harmony in which foreknowledge and freedom of the human will co-exist, so ordered by Divine Providence.

An increasing and expanding consciousness on Boethius's part has produced an increasing realism. Hope has replaced despair; serenity, tension; and with a deeper knowledge of himself, of who he is, has come at last some indication of Who God is, and thus of where and how consolation is to be found.

The concluding words are those of a saint. It is not hard to understand why the Sacred Congregation of Rites confirmed the custom of the diocese of Pavia in honoring St. Severinus Boethius on October 23 of each year. The local cult is sanctioned, and so is Hope, by the words which conclude the *Consolation of Philosophy* and sum up its comfort:

> For this force of the divine knowledge comprehending all things with a present notion appointeth to everything its measure and receiveth nothing from ensuing accidents. All which being so, the free-will of mortal men remaineth unviolated, neither are the laws unjust which propose punishments and rewards to our wills, which are free from all necessity. There remaineth also a beholder of all things which is God, who foreseeth all things, and the eternity of His vision, which is always present, concurreth with the future quality of our actions, distributing rewards to the good and punishments to the evil. Neither do we in vain put our hope in God or pray to Him; for if we do this well and as we ought, we shall not lose our labour or be without effect. Wherefore fly vices, embrace virtues, possess your minds with worthy hopes, offer up humble prayers to your highest Prince. There is, if you will not dissemble, a great necessity of doing well imposed upon you, since you live in the sight of your Judge, who beholdeth all things.

This is the great amen of wisdom, a high expression of the highest hope and faith. Some of its meaning must be low, however, if we have not come to this height from the depths in which the book begins. For this is a literary work, carefully constructed in its entirety. None of its lines, none of its passages is adventitious. None stands altogether alone. All hang together with that unity so dear to Boethius and Augustine. To lose any of it is in a sense to lose all. For as we make the laborious ascent from despair to hope, sharing with Boethius the guidance of Wisdom, we must recognize the meaning of this Christian allegory: what is enacted here is man's pilgrimage. If in the unfolding of that drama we come, in a heightened state of consciousness, to know ourselves well enough and something at least of the design revealed in creation, then we may attain to that endless present which is Boethius's definition of eternity, where we have not yet reached tomorrow, but have lost yesterday forever.

CHAPTER V

Gregory the Great: "And No Man Wonders"

One of the handsomest of early printed books is Hartmann Schedel's *Weltchronik*, published in Latin and German editions in 1493. One of the most arresting of its 645 woodcuts is devoted to Gregory the Great. It shows the first of the popes of the name of Gregory, on his head the triple tiara emblematic of his office, at his lips a dove's beak. The picture illustrates a legend firmly attached to Gregory's name, one that accounts for his being known in the Middle Ages as Gregory the Golden-Mouthed.

The story is short. One day, while dictating his *Homilies on the Book of Ezekiel,* a veil was drawn between Gregory and his secretary. The pope continued to dictate, but in fits and starts. He was silent for long periods. The secretary could not contain his curiosity; he made a hole in the curtain, peeked in and there saw a strange sight: a dove was perched on the pope's head with its beak between his lips. When the dove withdrew, Gregory spoke and the secretary wrote. When Gregory was silent, the secretary returned to the hole in the curtain and once again saw the dove's beak between the pope's lips.

The dove was Gregory's emblem, the Holy Spirit his devotion. It is to the role of the Third Person of the Trinity that Pope Gregory particularly calls our attention. For he is not only firmly persuaded that truth has a mouth, but that he can hear its utterances. In his letters of spiritual counsel and of pastoral care he speaks as its representative. In his commentaries on Scripture, he writes as surrogate for other inspired prophetic voices.

Gregory's work is not based on the assumption that he was uniquely chosen to be the voice of truth and special representative in the sixth century of the Holy Ghost. Indeed, he despaired of ever being equal to the task of unravelling the words of biblical history in their allegorical senses, he explains to St. Leander of Seville in the dedicatory epistle of his largest commentary, the *Magna Moralia* on the Book of Job. But, he says, he took comfort, remembering the real power of the Lord:

> in a strait between my alarms and my devout aspirations, I lifted up the eyes of my mind to the Bestower of all gifts, waiving my scruples, I fixed my thoughts on this, that what an affection flowing from the hearts of my brethren enjoined upon me, could not certainly be impossible. I despaired, indeed, of being a match for these things, but, stronger for my very despair of myself, I forthwith raised my hopes to Him, by Whom the tongue of the dumb is opened, Who *maketh the lips of babes to speak eloquently*, Who has marked the undistinguished and brute brayings of an ass with the intelligible measures of human speech. What wonder, then, that a simple man should receive understanding from Him, Who whenever He willeth, utters His truth by the mouths of the very beasts of burden?[1]

The central underlying assumption upon which all of Gregory's work is based is that one can always go to one place to find the word of God, to Sacred Scripture. Directly inspired by the Holy Ghost, it is from that Person that Scripture achieves its holiness, which is revealed again and again, not in the letter of its histories, but in the spirit. The spirit is hidden under so many coverings, it often has to be teased from the text. And so Gregory, like Augustine before him, goes through Scripture, at all speeds—now carefully and calmly, now racing—following wherever the spirit leads:

be it known that there are some parts, which we go through in a historical exposition; some we trace out in allegory upon an investigation of the typical meaning; some we open in the lessons of moral teaching alone, allegorically conveyed; while there are some few which, with more particular care, we search out in all these ways together, exploring them in a threefold method. For first, we lay the historical foundations; next, by pursuing the typical sense, we erect a fabric of the mind to be a stronghold of faith; and moreover as the last step, by the grace of moral instruction, we, as it were, clothe the edifice with an overcast of coloring.

It is not hard to serve the various foods, the different "viands of discourse," by "the alternate application of different methods." Gregory is quite up to the demands of each of the techniques of Scripture; he proves as much by the beauty and simplicity of his own rhetoric, fashioned to conform to the crunchy Latinity of the Vulgate text:

as the word of God, by the mysteries which it contains, exercises the understanding of the wise, so usually by what presents itself on the outside, it nurses the simple-minded. It presenteth in open day that wherewith the little ones may be fed; it keepeth in secret that whereby men of a loftier range may be held in suspense of admiration. It is, as it were, a kind of river, if I may so liken it, which is both shallow and deep, wherein both the lamb may find a footing and the elephant float at large. Therefore as the fitness of each passage requires, the line of interpretation is studiously varied accordingly, in that the true sense of the word of God is found out with so much the greater fidelity, in proportion as it shifts its course through the different kinds of examples, as each case may require.

Gregory's difficulties clearly are not those of rhetoric. He has a much cruder problem, he explains to Leander: he has suffered for years from stomach aches. But even these may be ordered to a divine purpose:

many a year's circuit has gone by, since I have been afflicted with frequent pains in the bowels, and the powers of my stomach being broken down, makes me at all times and seasons weakly; and under the influence of fevers, slow, but in constant succession, I draw my breath with difficulty; and when in the midst of these sufferings I ponder with earnest heed, that according to the testimony of Scripture, *He scourgeth every son whom He receiveth;* the more I am weighed down by the severity of present afflictions, from my anticipations for eternity, I gather strength to breathe with so much the better assurance. And perchance it was this that Divine Providence designed, that I, a stricken one, should set forth Job stricken, and that by these scourges I should the more perfectly enter into the feelings of one that was scourged.[2]

Gregory's was very much the literary temperament. To the gnawings of his stomach, he added the twinges of the gout, from which he suffered for a fine round biblical term—seven years. Whether directly as a result of these aches and pains or for more elevated reasons, he did enter easily into the feelings of the stricken man of Uz.

Gregory was trained to a life of suffering, real and vicarious—or at least we may assume as much of the sainted son of a sainted mother and the sainted nephew of two sainted aunts. His mother is honored in the calendar as St. Silvia on November 3 and his Aunts Tarsilla and Aemiliana are also canonized by tradition. Only his father Gordianus, a patrician of great wealth, escaped the dignity.

The major suffering of Gregory's youth of which we have record is of the threats and privations visited upon the Romans by the Goths, who were in and out of Rome many times between 546 and 552, that is, between Gregory's sixth and twelfth years. All his life he had to deal with the barbarians: when he was sent as special ambassador to Byzantium by the pope in 579, his particular task was to get help from the Byzantines in repulsing the advancing–and repulsive–Lombards. This was in the years of Roman decline, according to Gibbon, "the lowest period of her depression." No wonder that Gregory could write at the beginning of the *Magna Moralia*, "now that the end of the world is at hand," and assume that he would not be contradicted.

But even under Goths and Lombards, Gregory's spirit quickened. At the age of thirty, he attained the highest civil rank in Rome, that of prefect. Within a year, he relinquished his rank to become a monk. He deeded a half-dozen of his estates in Sicily to as many monasteries and founded a Benedictine community in his home on the Celian Hill under the patronage of the Apostle Andrew. There he spent, he says, the happiest years of his life. Against his will he was ordained one of the seven deacons of Rome by the pope in 578, and sent to Constantinople the next year. In Constantinople he took on the Patriarch Eutychius in controversy over the palpability of the risen bodies of the elect. The Patriarch insisted they were lighter than air and hence impalpable. Not at all, said Gregory, basing his case on the palpability of Christ's risen body. The Emperor upheld Gregory and burned the book in which Eutychius had perpetrated his palpable errors, but not in time to save both men great sickness, the Patriarch's unto death. On his death-bed, Eutychius recanted.

For the rest, Gregory's mission to the Empire of the East was not successful, at least in worldly terms. He did not obtain aid for Rome against the Lombards. What is even more remarkable, this noble Roman learned no Greek in the six years he spent in Byzantium. But he did meet Leander, sainted brother of two sainted brothers, Fulgentius and Isidore, the encyclopedist who succeeded Leander in the see of Seville. The learned Spanish bishop became his close friend and the benefactor of all those to whom the *Moralia* was dear. It was he who asked Gregory to write it, which Gregory promptly did.

The rest of Gregory's writings fit neatly into the context of his active life, the one from which he constantly fled. The homilies on Ezekiel and the Gospels were written for his monks at St. Andrew's and for his own contemplative exercises. The *Liber Pastoralis Curae*, *The Book of Pastoral Care*, was published for the instruction of bishops at the beginning of his pontificate–from which too he had fled. "I wished to avoid this burden," he says, "lest I should fail in the pastoral rule through my imperfect discharge of its duties. But as it is impossible to resist the ordinances of God, I have obediently followed what the merciful hand of the Lord has been pleased to work out for me."

He himself led a life of monastic simplicity. In his *Pastoral Care*, he directs bishops to the same regimen. Their primary task is the cure of souls. To it they must order their lives, learning how to teach and, if necessary, to reprove those under them, remembering at all times their own weaknesses and the fact that the better the work one does, the more danger one runs of excessive self-confidence:

Whence it is needful, when we are flattered by the abundance of our virtues, that the eye of the soul should come back to her own weak points, and should put herself down in a wholesome manner; and look not at the right things which she hath done, but at those which she hath neglected to do; to the end that the heart, being broken by the remembrance of her weakness, may be the more strongly embellished in virtue before the Author of lowliness. For in general also, the Almighty God, though He perfect in great measure the souls of rulers, yet for this cause leaveth them imperfect in some small measure, that while they shine with wondrous virtues, they may be wearied with the irksomeness of their own imperfectness, and may in no wise set themselves up on account of great things, when they still toil in their strife against the smallest; but since they have not strength to overcome the lowest difficulties, they may not dare to boast themselves upon their principal actions.[3]

Gregory is anxious not to fall prey to the same temptation. See, he directs the Bishop of Ravenna, to whom the treatise is dedicated, see how "I, a foul painter, have portrayed a fair person and direct others to the shore of perfection while I am still tossing on the waves of transgression. But I beseech thee, in this shipwreck of my life, to sustain me with the plank of thy prayers, that since my own weight makes me sink, the hand of thy merit may lift me up."

Gregory's style in the *Pastoral* verges on the sententious, partly because he is a moralizer, partly because what once must have seemed fresh ways of putting his maxims and reflections have by repetition become hackneyed and dull. But the short treatise never becomes tiresome to read; there is too much of Gregory in it for that. The details of Church government presented in the first part come from a large experience of almost every kind of administration, civil and ecclesiastical. The portrait of the pastor, preacher, and ruler of men in the remaining three parts is also drawn from Gregory's life. No pope before and few afterward ever gave such serious consideration to the problems of papal administration as they arise from spiritual concerns. It is the kind of consideration that prompted Gregory's liturgical reforms and that forever links him, either as sponsor or approving administrator, to the blessed music of the chant that goes by his name. It was this same sense of pastoral responsibility that led him to create the stations of the Roman missal: he used to meet some of the faithful and the clergy at a church previously agreed upon and then with them proceed to the church of the station. There Mass was solemnly celebrated and a sermon delivered. This was a pope who stayed close to the people. This was a native Roman who never forgot one small element of the greatness of Rome. What Augustine did for the meaning of Babylon and Jerusalem, forever associating them with the cities of man and of God, Gregory achieved for the meaning of Rome as the defining center of the Church, and on just as firm a scriptural basis.

Gregory's was a hierarchical mind, with a profound respect for the defining authority of Holy Scripture and the Holy See. His letters regularly demonstrate that cast of mind, as he administers and admonishes, accepts and rejects ideas, encourages and discourages the wise and the foolish, the learned and the untutored, the holy and the worldly. Long trained in Roman ways, Gregory gave especially to the organization of the spiritual life the attention of a hierarchical Roman mind. His teaching on the union and interdependence of the contemplative and active lives is, as Dom Cuthbert Butler has demonstrated with copious quotations, "characterized by a practicality and good sense, essentially Roman, that make it a truly valuable guide for the shaping of life." The substance of Gregory's position is contained in a series of comments on Job 5:26, "Thou shalt enter into the grave in abundance, as a heap of wheat is brought [*i.e., comes in*] in its season."

> For what is denoted by the name of the grave, saving a life of contemplation? which as it were buries us, dead to this world, in that it hides us in the interior world away from all earthly desires. For they being dead to the exterior life, were also buried by contemplation, to whom Paul said, "For ye are dead, and your life is hid with Christ in God." An active life also is a grave, in that it covers us, as dead, from evil works; but the contemplative life more perfectly buries us, in that it wholly severs us from all worldly courses.
>
> . . . It is hence that the Redeemer of mankind in the day-time exhibits His miracles in cities, and spends the night in devotion to prayer upon the mountain, namely, that He may teach all perfect

preachers, that they should neither entirely leave the active life, from love of the speculative, nor wholly slight the joys of contemplation from excess in working, but in quiet imbibe by contemplation, what in employment they may pour back to their neighbors by word of mouth.

. . . The converted soul may neither so delight in repose for the sake of the love of God, as to put aside the care and service of our neighbor, nor busying itself for the love of our neighbor, be so wedded thereto, that entirely forsaking quiet, it extinguish in itself the fire of love of the Most High.

. . . It is above all things necessary to know, that the compositions of souls are infinitely varied one with another, for there are some of such inactivity of mind, that, if the labors of business fall upon them, they give way at the very beginning of their work, and there be some so restless, that if they have cessation from labor, they have only the worse labor, in that they are subject to worse tumults of mind, in proportion as they have more time and liberty for their thoughts. Whence it behoves that neither the tranquil mind should open itself wide in the immoderate exercising of works, nor the restless mind stint itself in devotion to contemplation. For often they, who might have contemplated God in quiet, have fallen, being overcharged with business; and often they, who might live advantageously occupied with the service of their fellow-creatures, are killed by the sword of their quiescence. It is hence that some restless spirits, whilst by contemplation they hunt out more than their wits compass, launch out even to the length of wrong doctrines, and, whilst they have no mind to be the disciples of Truth in a spirit of humility, they become the masters of falsities.[4]

All through his writings on the contemplative life, Gregory remains practical. However much more merit the contemplative life may offer to the soul than the active, the soul cannot be heightened in love of God until it has been broadened in love of neighbor. With a fine show of the rhetoric of antithesis, he sums up his practical advice to aspiring souls: "Even though they already scale the heights in contemplation, in compassion they share the needs of the weak; for charity wonderfully rises to the heights when it mercifully draws itself to the lowliness of its neighbors; and the more kindly it descends to the weak, the more mightily it returns to the heights." And remember, Gregory says in one of his finest cautionary passages, if you are fortunate enough to "have made ever so small a beginning in spiritual conversation," do not lament the fact that others must bear the burdens of this world and do not affect to despise those who "in order that the tender minds of spiritual men may be released from worldly cares . . . the more willingly . . . employ themselves in worldly anxieties." Gregory's allegorical, administrative, and apologetic skills are marvelously intertwined in the paragraph that follows. It is a beautifully sustained piece of rhetoric. It is also a tightly reasoned argument for the union of contemplative and active lives, particularly in the conduct of Church affairs:

And how properly this is ordered in the Church by Divine appointment is signified by the very construction of the tabernacle. For Moses is commanded by the voice of God to weave curtains of fine linen, and scarlet, and blue, for the covering of the Holy of Holies within. And he was ordered to spread, for the covering of the tabernacle, curtains of goats' hair, and skins, to sustain the rain, and wind, and dust. What then do we understand by the skins and goats' hair, with which the tabernacle is covered, but the gross minds of men, which are sometimes, hard though they be, placed on high in the Church by the secret judgment of God? And because they are not afraid of being employed in worldly concerns, they must needs bear the winds and storms of temptation which arise from the opposition of this world. But what is signified by the blue, scarlet, and fine linen, but the life of holy men, delicate, but brilliant? And while it is carefully concealed in the tabernacle under goats' hair and skins, its beauty is preserved entire. For in order that the fine linen may shine, the scarlet glitter, and the blue be resplendent with azure brilliance, the skins and the goats' hair endure the rains, the winds, and the dust from above. They then who advance in great excellence within the bosom of holy Church, ought not to despise the doings of their rulers, when they see that they are engaged in the business of the world. For that they penetrate in safety into secret mysteries, is owing to the help of those who buffet with the storms of this world from without. For how would the fine linen retain the grace of its brightness, if the rain were to touch it? Or what splendor and brightness would the scarlet or blue display, should the dust light on, and defile them? Let the strong texture of the goats' hair, then, be placed above, to resist dust; the brightness of the blue, fitted for ornament, be placed beneath. Let those who are engaged in spiritual pursuits alone, adorn the Church. Let those guard her, who are not wearied even with the labors of the world. But let not him who now gleams with spiritual brightness within Holy Church, murmur against his superior, who is employed in worldly business. For if thou glitterest securely within, like scarlet, why dost thou blame the goats' hair with which thou are protected?[5]

This is writing of a very high order, as almost every line of the *Moralia* is. Nonetheless, Gregory does not enjoy a large reputation as a stylist. His most considerable biographer in English, F. H. Dudden, sees him as a writer "inferior to Augustine," upon whom Gregory modelled himself most of the time. "The construction of his sentences is often clumsy and involved. The natural order of words is frequently tampered with, certainly without any advantage in euphony or force. The words themselves are sometimes unclassical, or used in an unclassical sense or with unclassical constructions." But Dudden grants him a language that is often "dignified and expressive" and that "in moments of passion or excitement . . . rises even to eloquence. Sound sense and good feeling are the characteristics of his writing." That is a 1905 judgment by an Englishman to whom classical form had something resembling unction. Twenty-five years later, the French medievalist Gustave Bardy had similar reservations about Gregory's style:

> We must not seek for great regard to form in St. Gregory's works. The Latin spoken and written by this great Pope is such as we should expect to find at that time when the old world was crumbling to pieces. But it is simple and homely, and the new words and barbarous expressions need not be taken into account. And why, indeed, should St. Gregory seek to compose works of art, seeing that both he and his contemporaries were possessed with the idea that the world was speedily coming to an end?[6]

Other judgments, more recent in time, are no more flattering. According to Etienne Gilson, who yields Gregory a scant page and a quarter and four footnotes in his *History of Christian Philosophy in the Middle Ages*, it was really his "genius for organization [that] caused him to be called Gregory the Great." According to M. L. W. Laistner,

> Gregory was neither a profound nor an original thinker. His spiritual master was Augustine whose teaching and doctrines he assimilated with rare thoroughness, yet without sounding completely the depths of Augustine's thought. Compared wih Boethius or Cassiodorus, or with the great theologians of the fourth century, he lacks distinction as a writer, as well as width of culture. The Bible, which he must have known wellnigh by heart, is almost the sole source from which he introduces citations into his writings, and he does so constantly.[7]

Professor Laistner, it is true, recognizes that Gregory could write a thoroughly polished, rhetorically precise Latin and offers the reader a fair example of such writing in a passage "in which each half sentence perfectly balances the other." But Gregory consciously rejects classical elegance, and for good reason; he explains why near the end of the dedication of the *Moralia* in words that were famous in the Middle Ages, as they should have been:

I beg that in going through the statements of this work, you would not seek the foliage of eloquence therein: for by the sacred oracles the vanity of a barren wordiness is purposely debarred those that treat thereof, in that it is forbidden to plant a grove in the temple of God. And doubtless we are all of us aware, that as often as the overrank crop shows stalks that abound in leaves, the grains of the ears are least filled and swelling. And hence that art of speaking itself, which is conveyed by rules of worldly training, I have despised to observe; for as the tenor of this Epistle also will tell, I do not . . . avoid the confusion of barbarisms, and I slight the observing of situations and arrangements, and the cases of prepositions; for I account it very far from meet to submit the words of the divine Oracle to the rules of Donatus.

Gregory's major source of edification is the Holy Spirit. He will not refer the inspired word of God to the rules of the grammarian for approval. He has no patience with those who choose pagan models, even of the rarest and noblest kind, rather than Scripture. He scolds Bishop Desiderius of Vienne, as everyone who writes about Gregory is careful to point out, for "expounding grammar to certain persons," that is, for lecturing on secular literature: "The same mouth cannot sing the praises of Christ and of Jupiter." He is uneasy with those who worry overmuch about the human authorship of the books of Scripture:

He then Himself wrote them, Who dictated the things that should be written. He did Himself write them Who both was present as the Inspirer in that Saint's work, and by the mouth of the writer has consigned to us his acts as patterns for our imitation. If we were reading the words of some great man with his Epistle in our hand, yet were to enquire by what pen they were written, doubtless it would be an absurdity, to know the Author of the Epistle and understand his meaning, and notwithstanding to be curious to know with what sort of pen the words were marked upon the page. When then we understand the matter, and are persuaded that the Holy Spirit was its Author, in stirring a question about the author, what else do we than in reading a letter enquire about the pen?

One must turn to Scripture for examples of enlightenment, Gregory says:

Amongst these marvellous works of the Divine Providence it yields us satisfaction to mark, how, for the enlightening the night of this present life, each star in its turn appears in the face of heaven, until that towards the end of the night the Redeemer of mankind ariseth like the true Morning Star; for the space of night, being enlightened by the stars as they set and rise in their courses, is passed with the heavens in exceeding beauty. Thus in order that the ray of stars, darting forth at its appointed time, and changed in succession, might reach the darkness of our night, Abel comes to show us innocency; Enoch, to teach purity of practice; Noah, to win admittance for lessons of endurance in hope and in work; Abraham, to manifest obedience; Isaac, to show an example of chastity in wedded life; Jacob, to introduce patience in labor; Joseph, for the repaying evil with the favor of a good turn; Moses, for the showing forth of mildness; Joshua, to form us to confidence against difficulties; Job, to show patience amid afflictions. Lo what lustrous stars see we in the sky, that the foot of practice may never stumble as we walk this our night's journey; since for so many Saints as God's Providence set forth to man's cognizance, He, as it were, sent just so many stars into the sky, over the darkness of erring man, till the true Morning Star should rise, Who, being the herald to us of the eternal morning, should outshine the other stars by the radiance of His divinity.[8]

If to the reader the order and method of Scripture do not, in themselves, seem marvelously to enlighten "the night of this present life," then Gregory's performance will of necessity seem dim to him. "To us," Beryl Smalley writes, his "is a most annoying system. Everything in St. Gregory's teaching is attached, however loosely, to the thread of the text, which precludes any attempt at coherence or logical arrangement." She does see "how suitable it was for educational purposes. In two or three addresses, or hours of study, St. Gregory's hearers or readers would get a series of lessons on doctrine, prayer and ethics, in a well arranged and carefully varied time-table." But we "miss in Gregory," she says, the "spirit of intellectual curiosity." But do we? Because he did not "seek to compose works of art," as Abbé Bardy suggests, did he not in fact create them? Is it really, as M. Gilson concludes, "one of the numerous ironies of history that this adversary of *belles lettres* should be the one to start the immense movement of literary culture which was to invade the West progressively through the rise and spread of Anglo-Saxon civilization"?

For Gregory and others of his naive persuasion, "the numerous ironies of history" are nothing but the orderings of Providence. Of course he composed works of art, works of considerable quality, and naturally enough these offered impetus to the development of medieval culture. To writers like the Venerable Bede, Alfred the Great, and Dante, and to all the painters and sculptors and designers of churches who found the letter or the spirit of their iconography in Gregory's work, his was inspired art. To those of us who still read him with love and respect, the only wonder is that his influence has ever ceased. For whether on the subject of Church government or the contemplative life, considering the levels of meaning of Scripture or the rules of grammar to be followed in expounding it, Gregory's writing has felicity as well as fervor, incisiveness as well as delicacy. For all the intensity of his devotion to Augustine—and it was boundless—he was altogether an individual, a highly personable man and a warm one who could and did think for himself.

All of Gregory's life was dedicated to a seeking after God, and as his writings constantly reveal, a finding of Him. The language of seeking and finding in Gregory is sometimes homely, often exalted, always absorbing—if the seeking and finding of God is to the reader as to the writer the all-consuming devotion of his days. Now his is a very small view to the light of God, Gregory reports, through a very narrow slanting window (Ez 40:16), but the reception within is wide:

> In slanting, or splayed, windows that part by which the light enters is narrow, but the inner part which receives the light is wide; because the minds of those that contemplate, although they have but a slight glimpse of the true light, yet are they enlarged within themselves with a great amplitude. For even the little they see, they are scarcely able to hold. It is very little indeed that those who contemplate see of eternity; but from that little the fold of their minds is extended unto an increase of fervor and love.[9]

Perhaps there are no visible things to be seen at all—for often these things, "from their constant contact with us, turn away the eye of our mind from self consideration." Distracted by outward things, we forget what is going on within our own mind. That is why, in some of our most intimate colloquies with God, it is not we who bring ourselves to Him, but He who comes to us. And still we do not understand, even with every aid of revelation. We cannot penetrate to the center of things, but we can come close enough to the limitlessness of God to recognize our own limitations. This brings us to another center, the core of the teaching of the Book of Job and Gregory's exposition of it. What follows is not merely spiritual counsel, but the sort of psychological therapy that only those who have the dark knowledge of God can offer. From the depths of his own physical suffering and from the harshness of his struggles with the barbarians, Gregory draws aid and comfort that is rational and realistic and as practical today as in the sixth century. The passage that follows is also a significant reading of the peremptory summoning to his senses that out of the whirlwind the voice of the Lord addresses to Job: "Who can declare the order of the heavens?" (38:37):

> To know the course of heaven, is to see the secret predestinations of the heavenly disposals . . . Which certainly no one can do who is placed in this life . . . Who can understand why one man, who plots for the deaths of his neighbors, survives, and another, who would be likely to preserve the lives of many, dies? One man, who is only eager to do hurt, attains the height of power, another only desires to defend the injured, and yet he himself is lying under oppression . . . One both wishes, and is able, to aim at the loftiness of holy living; another is neither willing nor able. One wishes, and is not able; another is able, and is not willing. Who then can examine into these secrets of the heavenly judgments? Who can understand the secret balance of hidden equity? For no one attains to understand these recesses of secret judgments. Let this be said then to a man, that he may learn his own ignorance; let him know his own ignorance, that he may fear; let him fear, that he may be humbled; let him be humbled, that he may not trust in himself; let him trust not in himself, that he may seek for the assistance of his Creator, and that he who is dead from trusting in himself, may seek the assistance of his Maker, and live.[10]

The understanding that Gregory seeks is not of this world. It is presented only in vision, in the sort of blinding light which Dante accepts as a fair approximation of the confrontation of the Creator by the creature. It is this vision that Gregory reports of St. Benedict in the second book of his *Dialogues*, that part of Gregory's hagiology which is given over entirely to the sweet narrative of the life and miracles of his father in religion, "who, from his younger years, carried always the mind of an old man; for his age was inferior to his virtue . . ." The experience as described by Gregory adds much to the stature of Benedict:

> The man of God, being diligent in watching, rose early up before

the time of matins (his monks being yet at rest) and came to the window of his chamber, where he offered up his prayers to almighty God. Standing there, all of a sudden in the dead of the night, as he looked forth, he saw a light, which banished away the darkness of the night, and glittered with such brightness, that the light which did shine in the midst of darkness was far more clear than the light of the day. Upon this sight a marvellous strange thing followed, for, as himself did afterward report, the whole world, gathered as it were together under one beam of the sun, was presented before his eyes, and while the venerable father stood attentively beholding the brightness of that glittering light, he saw the soul of Germanus, Bishop of Capua, in a fiery globe to be carried up by Angels into heaven.

How can the world be seen by one man? Gregory's answer defines the limits of his own mystical theology: if we see God at all, we see Him at a remove. As Ezekiel did (2:1), we may see a "vision of the likeness of the glory of the Lord," but no more. The semblance of the Lord is enough, however. It throws Ezekiel onto his face. Afterwards, it makes all created things seem little and insignificant. The world is not made any smaller, but the soul of a man like Benedict is made much larger by mystical experience of this stunning kind:

All creatures be as it were nothing to that soul which beholdeth the Creator: for though it see but a glimpse of that light which is in the Creator, yet very small do all things seem that be created: for by means of that supernatural light, the capacity of the inward soul is enlarged, and is in God so extended, that it is far above the world: yea and the soul of him that seeth in this manner, is also above itself; for being rapt up in the light of God, it is inwardly in itself enlarged above itself, and when it is so exalted and looketh downward, then doth it comprehend how little all that is, which before in former baseness it could not comprehend. The man of God, therefore, who saw the fiery globe, and the Angels returning to heaven, out of all doubt could not see those things but in the light of God: what marvel, then, is it, if he saw the world gathered together before him, who rapt up in the light of his soul, was at that time out of the world? But albeit we say that the world was gathered together before his eyes, yet were not heaven and earth drawn into any lesser room than they be of themselves, but the soul of the beholder was more enlarged, which, rapt in God, might without difficulty see that which is under God, and therefore in that light which appeared to his outward eyes, the inward light which was in his soul ravished the mind of the beholder to supernal things, and showed him how small all earthly things were.[11]

It was to the life of vision that Gregory directed himself, his monks, and the Church. But it was a direction that conformed to the nature of man and the world here below. It was never a truncating sort of counsel that he gave. He would not in any way trim the dimensions of human existence in order to make it superhuman, any more than he would have rearranged the chapters and verses in Ezekiel or Job in order to make more systematic his homilies and moralizations. He is content to accept the sense of Job 5:6, "Nothing upon earth is done without a cause, and sorrow doth not spring out of the ground." He is happy to accept the several senses of the verse spoken by Job's comforter Eliphaz, and the next verse and the next and the next—"Man is born to labour and the bird to fly. Wherefore I will pray to the Lord, and address my speech to God: Who doth great things and unsearchable and wonderful things without number." Those "unsearchable and wonderful things" can be seen, but only with the eyes of faith. What we see we may not understand, but we can marvel, and we can wonder. But do we?

Who may see to the bottom of the marvellous works of Almighty God, how He made all things of nothing, how the very framework of the world is arranged with a marvellous mightiness of power, and the heaven hung above the atmosphere, and the earth balanced above the abyss, how this whole universe consists of things visible and invisible, how He created man, so to say, gathering together in a small compass another world, yet a world of reason; how constituting this world of soul and flesh, He mixed the breath and the clay by an unsearchable disposal of His Might? A part, then, of these things we know, and a part we even are. Yet we omit to admire them, because those things which are full of marvels for an investigation deeper than we can reach, have become cheap from custom in the eyes of men. Hence it comes to pass that, if a dead man is raised to life, all men spring up in astonishment. Yet every day one that had no being is born, and no man wonders, though it is plain to all, without doubt, that it is a greater thing for that to be created, which was without being, than for that, which had being, to be restored. Because the dry rod of Aaron budded, all men were in astonishment; every day a tree is produced from the dry earth, and the virtue residing in dust is turned into wood, and no man wonders. Because five thousand men were filled with five loaves, all men were in astonishment that the food should have multiplied in their teeth; every day the grains of seed that are sown are multiplied in a fulness of ears, and no man wonders. All men wondered to see water once turned into wine. Every day the earth's moisture being drawn into the root of the vine, is turned by the grape into wine, and no man wonders. Full of wonder then are all the things, which men never think to wonder at, because, as we have before said, they are by habit become dull to the consideration of them . . .[12]

Simply as a rhetorical outburst, this passage is Gregory's mightiest. But it is more than that. It is a likeness of the vision that we may all enjoy, even those of us who are no mystics, no saints, no Benedicts, no Gregorys, even we.

CHAPTER VI

St. Bernard: The Rhetoric of Mysticism

ONE OF THE MOST ENGAGING OF THE MANY LEGENDS THAT surround the life of Bernard of Clairvaux suggests the power of his personality and the magnetism of his oratory. Whenever he came to a new town, according to the tale, wives and mothers hurried to hide their men. All that Abbot Bernard had to do, they feared, was to talk to a man to turn him into a monk. Had he not spirited his uncle Gaudry from his wife and children, his brother Guido from his family, his brothers Andrew and Gerard from knighthood and the profession of arms? Did not his apostolate to his family remove to the cloister his brother Bartholomew at sixteen and his brother Nivard at fifteen? Did not his father Tescelin, an old man, become his own son's subject at Clairvaux? Did he not so successfully scold his sister for her worldly vanities, when she came to visit her family at the monastery, that within five years she entered the convent of Jully, where her sister-in-law, Guido's wife Elizabeth, was superior? There was good reason to believe Bernard could spirit away people.

One of the least attractive of the legends is that Bernard was the behind-the-scenes ruler of the Church of the twelfth century, more powerful even than the pope. Did he not journey back and forth on papal business, making political decisions as often as religious? Did he not rebuke bishops and archbishops? Did he not cause to be elected pope one of his own monks, abbot of the Cistercian monastery of the Three Fountains just outside Rome? Was it not he, Bernard of Clairvaux, who maintained this monk, Bernard of Pisa, on the papal throne as Eugenius III? Did he not preach the Crusades? Was he not, in fact, elected commander-in-chief of the armies of the cross that were being gathered together in 1150 for another holy war? Was this a suitable role for a cloistered monk? The answer to all these questions, including the last, is yes—for this monk was not more powerful than the pope, and did not direct papal or any other affairs from a place of concealment behind the arras. Nor was he the most powerful man in Europe in the twelfth century, but he was surely the most persuasive.

For proof of Bernard's persuasiveness, we must turn away from political affairs, away from the councils of the Church in which his words were heard and heeded, even from the dispute with Peter Abelard, whom he defeated in open combat, as it were, merely by standing in his white Cistercian robes and reading a list of the black Benedictine's heterodoxies and heresies. It is to the works of love we must turn, the written works, in which he courts and wins exaltation, not only for himself but for his readers. This is persuasion, as St. Bernard intended it. Fittingly enough for a man who was out of his monasteries almost as much as he was in them, it is a suasion to which we may all be swayed. It is not directed to Cistercian monks exclusively. But neither they nor we, neither religious nor lay people, will be moved by all that there is within Bernard's works of love to move them if they fail to recognize their literary dimension, which makes them so immediately accessible, even to a modern reader, utterly untrained in and unprepared for the procedures of twelfth-century monasticism.

Let me hasten to add here that I am not talking about the doctrines of courtly love discovered by some scholars in St. Bernard's language of the love of God. Of all the dubious accusations of weakness of mind and corruption of soul to which the Middle Ages have been subject, this one of organized courts of love is at once the least likely and the most offensive. It translates delicate rhetorical figures into literal-minded readings of the utmost grossness, which accept as honorable fact what, with wonderful wit and not so very subtle indirection, the writers of "courtly love" were pointing to as dishonorable fancy. The failure to recognize literary devices for what they are turns sour the essential sweetness of the medieval mind and makes the wit and ingenuity of mature writers seem like little more than the products of an adolescent itch. One understands this urge to single entendre on the part of the prurient, resulting in the translation of the multifaceted literature of the Middle Ages into a literature of surfaces designed to fit a doctrine of sensuality. It is more difficult to understand a similar literalness in the readings of some of those who really know the period.

The allegorical method is not easily understood if one treats it mechanically. If one looks, in Bernard or Dante or Chaucer or Shakespeare or anywhere else, for simple substitutions of an algebraic kind, the results must be simple and the literature thus arrived at somewhat crude. If one recognizes that distinctions of the sort that Augustine makes in his rhetorical works are involved, then at least one finds the right direction. Where it leads is where Bernard goes: through a narration of events, states of being or behavior, to a proposed pattern of meaning and moral improvement which will ultimately show us eternal truths.

To the extent that such a pattern is always to be found in the Christian allegorists of the Middle Ages, their method is mechanical. But the design is an intricately worked one; the fact that one can immediately identify its leading colors does not mean that all its twists and turns are either obvious or hackneyed or inflexible. The method is predicated upon clear convictions about the natural order: because of the overseeing of Divine Providence, nature necessarily leads to supernature, the human serves the divine, and the literature of allegory moves quite normally from this world to the next. In that movement, nothing known to man need be by-passed. Every discipline, every experience can be productive of revelations. The chaff, when husked, always reveals the wheat.

An excellent summary of the allegorical method is contained in the prologue to the first book of the *De Sacramentis*, the inspired encyclopedic work of Hugh of St. Victor, Bernard's contemporary. His immediate concern is the design of Scripture, but his description fits all creative works—which certainly includes everything of Bernard's:

> it is clear that all the natural arts serve divine science, and that the lower wisdom, rightly ordered, leads to the higher. Accordingly, under the sense of the significance of words in relation to things history is contained, which, as has been said, is served by three sciences: grammar, dialectic, and rhetoric. Under that sense, however, consisting in the significance of things in relation to mystical facts, allegory is contained. And under that sense, consisting in the meaning of things in relation to mystical things to be done, tropology is contained, and these two are served by arithmetic, music, geometry, astronomy, and physics. Besides these, there is above all that divine science to which the Divine Scripture leads, whether in allegory or in tropology; one division of this which is in allegory, teaches right faith, the other, which is in tropology, teaches good work. In these consist knowledge of truth and love of virtue; and this is the true restoration of man.[1]

Such are the terms in which one must understand Bernard. He was, like Augustine and Gregory, a scriptural commentator in everything he wrote—it would not be wrong to say in everything he thought as well. The restoration of fallen man was the consuming interest of his life, the text of all his sermons, the basis of his own call to the religious life and the motive with which he lured others to it. Any effort to understand or to aid in the work of restoration had to be grounded in Scripture. Hence, all of Bernard's work springs from scriptural soil. It was with a plenitude of biblical quotations that he recalled the Cistercian order to a strict observance of the Benedictine rule and made rigorous additions to it. With ample assistance from Scripture, he provided a continuing means of restoration for the Church, its prelates and its pontiffs, in his monolithic *De Consideratione.*

The five books *On Consideration*, addressed to the pope and through him to the whole hierarchy, illustrate Bernard's method very well. The work starts by considering the pope's own person. It sweeps upward, as all works that move from nature to supernature do, from the lower wisdom to the higher. In it, Bernard offers Pope Eugenius very practical advice, not untouched by worldly considerations, some administrative, some political, most of them concerned to preserve the dignity of the highest of all offices on earth. The pope is enjoined to keep that office pure, and particularly free of the stains of simony. His greatest weapon is the wisdom that the universal church has to offer. Wisdom will come with counsel, with advisers drawn from all nations, men of prudence and selflessness, cardinals who are, in St. Paul's phrase, true "ambassadors for Christ." Surrounded by such men, with his own spiritual life in order, the pope will be worthy of such titles as model of justice, mirror of sanctity, doctor of nations and guide of Christians, friend of the Bridegroom, paranymph of the Bride and pastor of the people, and finally, in resounding scriptural terms, "priest of the Most High, vicar of Christ, anointed of the Lord."

Having examined the person of the pope and the things beneath and around him, Bernard turns to the things above him, to the angels and to God. He takes us through each of the ranks of angels–Angels, Archangels, Virtues, Powers, Principalities, Dominations, Thrones, Cherubim, and Seraphim–to reveal the attributes of God. The angelology brings him to his great concluding litany on the nature of God. What is God? he asks again and again. He answers in great eloquent phrases, with recourse to the Book of Wisdom, to John and Jeremiah, to Romans and Ephesians, and necessarily, of course, as one steeped in Benedictine liturgical practice, to the psalms. What is God? What is the Highest of things? It is Length, because of Its eternity, Breadth because of Its charity, Height because of Its majesty, and Depth because of Its Wisdom.

The same impassioned rhetoric blows through the little treatise *De Diligendo Deo, On the Love of God*, written at the request of Cardinal Haimeric, chancellor of the Holy See: "You want me to tell you why and how God should be loved. I answer that the reason we should love God is God Himself and that the way to love Him is without measure."

The spirit which animates the *De Diligendo* is that of the most precious of scriptural books to Bernard, the *Song of Songs*. The fifteen little chapters are given over to commentaries on biblical texts, but never to mere technical exegesis. This is explanation through rapture, commentary through poetry. Here, for example, is an excursus on texts from the *Song of Songs*, with supplementary material from John's Gospel, from Ephesians, Philippians, Genesis, and the twenty-seventh psalm. The Church speaks, and says—

I am wounded with charity; and again: *Stay me up with flowers; compass me about with apples: because I languish with love.* She [the Church] sees *King Solomon in the diadem wherewith his mother crowned him;* she sees the Only-begotten of the Father *bearing His own cross;* she sees the Lord of Majesty struck and spat upon; she sees the Author of life and glory held fast with nails, pierced with a lance, overwhelmed with reproaches, finally laying down that precious Life of His for His friends. She sees all this and the sword of love pierces her soul the more and she says: *Stay me up with flowers, compass me about with apples: because I languish with love.* These *apples*, to be sure, are the pomegranates which the bride, led into the garden of her Beloved, plucks from the tree of life; they have borrowed their own peculiar savour from the Bread of Heaven, their color from the Blood of Christ. She then sees death itself struck dead and the Author of death led in triumph. She sees captivity led captive from hell [limbo] to earth, from earth to heaven, *that in the name of Jesus every knee should bow of those that are in heaven, on earth and under the earth.* She perceives that the earth which under the ancient curse had brought forth thorns and thistles, has sprung into blossom again at the grace of a new benediction. And in all this recalling that verse: *And my flesh hath flourished again, and with my will I will give praise to Him,* she longs to add to the fruits of the Passion which she has plucked from the tree of the cross, some of the flowers of the resurrection whose fragrance especially allures the Beloved to visit her again and again.

The language is erotic. Bernard's love is passionate. He is a wildly passionate man, madly in love with God. He has looked and longed and found himself unworthy: "What shall I render to God in return for Himself? For even if I were able to give myself back a thousand times, what am I in God's sight?" Unworthy, yes, but not of looking and longing and loving without measure. His life is circumscribed by God. So must all life be: it is our nature to be surrounded by Him. See, see how logical I am, Bernard says:

I said above: The cause of loving God is God. I spoke the truth, for He is both the efficient and final Cause. It is He who gives the occasion, it is He who creates the affection, He consummates the desire. It is He who wrought, or rather, was *made* [i.e., is what He is] in order that He might be loved; He, it is hoped, will be so fruitfully loved as not to be loved in vain. His love makes our love ready and rewards it. He goes before more graciously than any other, He is repaid more justly, He is awaited more sweetly. He is *rich unto all who call upon Him;* still He has nothing better than Himself to give. He gave Himself to merit for us, He retains Himself, to be our reward, He offers Himself as the food of saintly souls, He gives Himself as the price of the redemption of those [i.e., of every individual soul] in captivity. You are *good*, O Lord, *to the soul that seeketh* Thee: what, then, to one who finds? But in this is the wonder that no one can seek Thee save him who first has found Thee. Therefore You wish to be found in order that You may be sought, to be sought in order that You may be found.[2]

This logic brings Bernard to the four degrees of love. To begin with, man loves himself for his own sake; as a fleshly being he sees all and knows all only through himself. When he finds that he requires more than himself, that he is not self-sustaining, he rises to the second degree of love, a love of God not for Himself, but for man's own sake. At this level, he comes to know God a little, to think about Him, to read about Him, to pray to Him, even to obey Him: "Little by little God becomes known to him through experience, in a sort of familiarity, and consequently He grows sweet; and thus by tasting how sweet is the Lord he passes to the third degree." Now he no longer loves God selfishly, but for Himself. And here, Bernard says, a man rests for a long time. Perhaps no one in this life has ever risen beyond this third degree. For the last, the fourth, degree brings a man to that exalted state where he loves even himself only for the sake of God. At that point, one will be out of time and in eternity. One will be joined to God in that heavenly country which is the land for which man was destined, where there is neither suffering nor sorrow, no occasion for misery, no opportunity for pity or compassion or mercy, for justice and love alone remain in the mind there.

Again and again in his biblical commentaries—whether in the form of sermons or short treatises or long—Bernard follows the numerical pattern dear to all trained in the spirit of Augustine and Boethius. Thus does he establish a sense of proportion in his analysis of good or evil: there are four classes of Christians who walk in the procession of the Saviour, seven species of spiritual leprosy, six ascensions of Christ which we ought to imitate. He establishes seven degrees in the sacrament of Confession: self-knowledge, penitence, sorrow, confession of the mouth, mortification of the body, purification of conduct, and perseverance. He names seven degrees of obedience: to obey with a good heart, to obey with simplicity, to obey with cheerfulness, to obey promptly, to obey with fortitude, to obey with humility, to obey with perseverance. Commenting on the line in Isaiah (12:3), "You shall draw waters with joy out of the Saviour's fountains," Bernard identifies these as the four fountains of truth, wisdom, power, and charity, from which are derived, respectively, the waters of judgment, of counsel, of helpfulness, and of charity.

Let any who would reduce these distinctions to a facile, or worse, factitious, numerology, be warned. The numbers are useful in the spiritual life, as all who have practised devotions so ordered can testify. But they are only means to an end, surface narrations which mean little until they have been applied, in good conscience. They must be interpreted allegorically, even these allegorical interpretations of Scripture, and then applied. Their ultimate significance is, in Hugh's words, "in relation to mystical things to be done." In such a way, one draws from Bernard's four symbolic fountains waters, or graces, that permit us to distinguish between what is lawful and what is not (the waters of judgment), graces that tell us what it is advisable to do and what not (the waters of counsel), graces that overcome fear (the waters of helpfulness), and graces that overcome concupiscence (the waters of charity). Similarly, see what he means by two of the spiritual leprosies, preaching on the text, "Go, wash seven times in the Jordan, and thou shalt be made clean" (4 Kgs 5:10):

Pride, my brethren, has infected us with a sevenfold leprosy, in the proprietorship of earthly goods, in the glory of vesture, in bodily gratifications, in two ways with regard to the mouth, and in two ways with regard to the heart. The first may be called the "leprosy of the house" (Lev 14:36). From this we may be purified by bathing in the Jordan, that is, by steeping our souls in the thought of the descent of Christ. For we shall thus realize how He Who was so rich became so poor for our sakes; how He descended from the unspeakable riches of His heavenly home, and, appearing upon earth, would not have even the wealth–such as it is–of this world, but came in such utter poverty that immediately after His birth He had to be laid in a manger, "because there was no room for Him in the inn" (Lk 2:7). In short, who does not know that "the Son of man had not where to lay His head" (Mt 8:20)? How can the riches of earth become an object of desire to him who bathes himself thoroughly in this mystery by assiduous meditation? Surely it must seem to be a great abuse, yea, a most monstrous perversity, that a vile little worm wants to be wealthy, when, for its sake, the God of Majesty and the Lord of Hosts has willed to make Himself poor.

By the leprosy of the garments (Lev 13:47) I mean all the foolish pomp and vanity of the present life. From this also thou shalt be cleansed by washing in the Jordan, that is, by pondering how Christ the Lord was wrapped in poor swaddling clothes, was made "the reproach of men and the outcast of the people" (Ps 12:7).[3]

The same sense of numerical order runs through the first of Bernard's treatises, the *De Gradibus Humilitatis*, *The Degrees of Humility*. It is a little work full of definitions. Humility "is that thorough self-examination which makes a man contemptible in his own sight." Humility offers its pursuers a banquet to begin with–"the bread of sorrow and the wine of remorse." This is the first of the three foods of truth, its taste bitter, its purpose purgative. The second food is "sweet and consoling": it consists of "honey-sweet sips of love." The last, the food of contemplation, is "solid and strengthening."

As with all who labor in the Augustinian tradition, and for

the same ends, the beginning is that self-knowledge which makes one meek and merciful to others. Bernard's advice is shrewd. It is also incisive:

I do not say make yourself what you are not, but observe what you are, that you are wretched indeed, and so learn to be merciful, a thing you cannot know in any other way. For if you regard your neighbor's faults but do not observe your own, you are likely to be moved not to ruth but to wrath, not to condole but to condemn, not to restore in the spirit of meekness but to destroy in the spirit of anger.

Now you can go on to know your neighbor, and having been purged of ignorance, weakness and willfulness, can turn to the contemplation of God. The language has an admirable precision: we ascend to the three degrees of truth by the labor of humility, the emotion of compassion, and the ecstasy of contemplation. We find truth harsh at the first level, loving at the second, pure at the last. That purity "snatches" us up to "invisible heights." On the first level, truth "instructs, as a teacher; on the second it consoles, as a friend or brother; on the third it draws close, as a father to his children."

The third degree is equivalent to St. Paul's third heaven. It is the peak to which grace alone can lift one. This elevation is the *anagoge*, the great ascent to which all Christian allegory is directed, and for which the moralizing that goes by the name of tropology is intended. Once again Bernard resorts to literary language; once again his source and resource is the *Song of Songs:*

The Father unites this soul to himself as a glorious bride, so that neither the reason can think of itself nor the will of its neighbor, but that blessed soul delights only in saying, *The King hath brought me into his chamber*. And it is worthy, coming from the school of humility, where it first learned from the Son's teaching to enter into itself, taking heed of the warning, *If thou know not thyself, go feed thy kids.* It is worthy to be led by the Holy Ghost from that school of humility and brought by affection into the storerooms of love, by which are meant the hearts of its neighbors. Thence, stayed with flagons and comforted with apples, namely good habits and holy virtues, it is finally admitted to the chamber of the King, of love for whom it is sick. There for a little while, about half an hour, there being silence in heaven, it rests sweetly in the longed for embrace, and sleeps itself; but its heart waketh, with which it searches out the secrets of truth, that it may feed on the memory of them when it returns to itself. There it sees invisible things, hears unspeakable words, which it is not lawful for a man to utter. They surpass all that knowledge which night showeth unto night; but day unto day uttereth speech, and it is lawful to speak wisdom among the wise, and to compare spiritual things with spiritual.

But why, Bernard asks himself, am I "running with idle chatter rather than quickness of spirit through the two upper heavens, when in fact I am laboriously crawling on all fours beneath the lowest?" There is a way down as well as a way up: "Jacob saw the angels ascending and descending on the same ladder. What does all this mean? Simply that if you desire to return to truth, you do not have to seek a new way which you know not, but the known way by which you descended." Thus the twelfth step of pride going down becomes the first step of humility going up, and so forth through each of these degrees, through curiosity, levity, a foolish gaiety, boastfulness, and the like.

The monks who illustrate each of the different kinds of pride are among Bernard's most memorable sketches. The writing is delightful; the figures are almost comic. A series of short bold lines fills in the pictures. Curiosity:

If you shall see a monk, whom you formerly trusted confidently, beginning to roam with his eyes, hold his head erect, prick up his ears, wherever he is standing, walking, sitting; you may know the changed inner man from the movements of the outer.

Boastfulness:

He must either talk or burst . . . An occasion for talking having been found, if mention of literature arises, ancients and moderns are brought forth. Opinions fly around, weighty words resound. He interrupts a questioner, he answers one who does not ask. He himself puts the questions, he himself solves them, he cuts short his fellow speaker's unfinished words . . . He does not care to teach you, or to learn from you what he does not know, but to know that you know that he knows.

Singularity:

At dinner he keeps constantly looking around the tables, and if he sees anyone eating less than himself, he grieves that he is beaten and begins mercilessly to deprive himself of even that food which he had planned to allow as indispensable, fearing the damage to his reputation more than the pangs of hunger. If he discovers anyone more haggard, anyone more cadaverous, he despises himself, he gets no rest. And since he cannot see his own face as others see it, he looks at his hands and arms which he can see, he pokes his ribs, he feels his shoulders and loins, so that he may guess the pallor or color of his face according as he finds the limbs of his body satisfactorily emaciated or not. Zealous for himself, indifferent to the community, he keeps vigil in bed, he sleeps in the choir. Although he sleeps the night out while the others are saying psalms at matins, when the others are resting in the cloister after matins he alone remains in the oratory. He spits and coughs; from his corner he fills the ears of those outside with groans and sighs.[4]

And so on, step by step, through conceit and audacity, making excuses for one's own sins, hypocritical confession and defiance, to expulsion from the monastery and a life of habitual sin.

It does not require much schooling in the allegorical method to adapt this work to the lay life. One need not have sat at a refectory table to find oneself guilty of singularity, determined to show the intensity of one's devotion to a cause by the constant outdoing of rivals, volunteering for extra duties while neglecting one's regular and normal but less conspicuous assignments. One need not be a religious to recognize oneself in the monk who must either talk or burst, who "hungers and thirsts after hearers." And surely it is not difficult to identify the monastery as this world and expulsion from it as a sign of the loss of closeness to God—of a fall from the state of grace to that of sin.

Identifications and substitutions of the same sort follow the reader through the course of Bernard's letters, not for the purposes of easily procured, quickly enjoyed vicarious experience, but for the restoration and recovery of spiritual integrity which always motivated Bernard's writing. He is a moralizer, no doubt about it: pious mottos abound in his letters as in his more deliberately organized religious treatises. He is also a craftsman. It is impossible not to be caught up in his correspondence, not to be snatched, as he himself might say, back to twelfth-century quarrels and friendships, the high hopes and low doings of churchmen and laymen, the life—almost all of it—lived in Bernard's Europe.

Some of the life of Bernard's time was edifying, much of it was not at all. His letters reflect both sorts of performance, by religious and laity alike, by men of high station and low. Some are written with anger, a few with forbearance, most with love. He pleads many causes, intercedes for many friends. He laments the demands on his time that make it impossible for him to spend time with his friends:

> But by punishment for my sins it has come about that regretfully I find that I am not able to do so, I acknowledge this not as a fault, but as a punishment for my faults . . . I am troubled

enough on other accounts but, I must confess, on none so much as on this. It vexes me more than all the labors of my journey, than the discomfort of the heat, than the anxiety of my responsibilities.

Christian friendship was very much on Bernard's mind. It was at his request that the English Cistercian St. Ailred of Rievaulx wrote his beautiful work on spiritual friendship, translating into Christian terms Cicero's *De Amicitia*, a classic long treasured by monks like Bernard and Ailred.

Nothing so inspired this angry man, this gruff man, this loving one to proffers of friendship as the open recovery of grace by one who had fallen from it. Among all those to whom the joyous restoration of God's friendship led to the eager offer of Bernard's, none elicited a warmer response than Suger, Abbot of St. Denis. Suger actually played the part at the Court of France that historians so often assume Bernard did at Rome. He was a definitive example of a worldly churchman. Chief of the ministers of Louis the Fat, he was a lover of luxury who created at St. Denis one of the most sumptuous establishments of his time, in or out of the Church. Suger may have been converted by the words of Bernard's *Apologia*, that stern defense of the saint's restoration of the Benedictine rule in all its austerity at Cîteaux; or his conversion and the great changes he worked as a result of it at his abbey may have come about more tortuously. But reform was in the air in France, breathed boldly, gustily into it through the lungs of Bernard and his Cistercian brethren. St. Denis moved from ostentation to simplicity; Bernard wrote its abbot joyfully:

The good news of what God has done in your soul has gone forth in our land encouraging all the good people who hear it. To be sure all those who fear God and have heard of it are amazed and full of joy at this great and sudden change of the right arm of the Most High . . . Who suggested this perfection to you?

I must confess that although I much desired to hear such things of you, yet I hardly dared hope that I ever would . . . It was your fault, not those of your monks, that good and zealous people censured. It was against you and not against the whole community that they murmured . . . But you have done more than satisfy your critics, you have earned their praise, although this sudden change of so many great things should be deemed more the work of God than of yourself. In heaven the conversion of one sinner arouses great joy, but what about the conversion of a whole community, and a community such as yours?

This reform moves Bernard to hope that Suger's great friend Stephen, the Archdeacon of Notre Dame and Dean of Orleans, will be led to take the same steps. "Two unheard-of and detestable improprieties" had recently arisen in the Church, Bernard says. One was the "arrogance" of Suger's "way of life." The other was the immensely proud and intolerably worldly behavior of Stephen—"the stench of which is in everyone's nostrils. I dare not hold my own nose against such a bad smell." In friendship, speak to your friend Stephen, Bernard pleads with Suger, and "prove yourself a true friend to him by doing what you can to make him a friend of truth. True friendship is only possible between two who are united in the love of truth."

To the dying Suger, Bernard later sent another letter of friendship, bidding him not to fear "to put off the earthy man," for "the joy of the Lord awaits you." But, Bernard says, he will miss the reformed abbot. He will try, he promises, to come to see him to receive the dying man's blessing:

But no man can arrange his life just as he wishes, and so I cannot dare to promise what I am not sure of being able to perform; yet I will try my best to do what I am not yet able to see my way to doing. Perhaps I shall come, perhaps I shall not. But whatever happens I, who have loved you from the first, shall love you without end. I say with all confidence that I can never lose one whom I have loved unto the end: one to whom my soul cleaves so firmly that it can never be separated, does not go away but only goes before. Be mindful of me when you come to where I shall follow you, so that I may be permitted soon to come after you and come to you. In the meantime be sure that I shall never lose the dear memory of you, although to my sorrow I lose your dear presence.[5]

The greatest of friendships—if this is not too facile a way to describe Bernard's relationship with God—was the subject of Bernard's greatest work, his eighty-six sermons on the first two chapters and the opening four verses of the third chapter of the *Song of Songs*. The circumstances under which these sermons were written are not altogether clear. They may have been delivered to his monks over some eighteen or nineteen years of conferences and transcribed by one of them or simply circulated among them in manuscript. Whatever the means, the purpose is clear: it was to teach the monks to scale the heights of love, as Bernard had.

Love is the end; love is the means; love and lose alone will lift one to the level of this song which is so far beyond all other songs: "Love speaks in it everywhere; if anyone would understand the things he reads in it, then let him love! . . . the cold heart cannot grasp its burning eloquence. It is with love as with . . . Greek or Latin; just as, unless you know the tongue yourself, you will not understand it when you hear it spoken, so to the man who loves not, love's language appears crude, and will be only sounding brass and tinkling cymbal in his ears." Love alone, love especially consecrated, will guide one through the *Song*. It is not a work, Bernard might be saying, for the anthropologists and the sociologists, the practitioners of the higher criticism, those biblical scholars who find in the *Song of Songs* only a collection of Jewish marriage songs, the burden of which is the physical love between man and woman:

The anointing of grace alone can teach a canticle of this sort; experience only, can unfold its meaning. Let those who have had experience of it recognize it; let those inexperienced in it burn with a longing not so much of knowing as of actually experiencing it. For, it is not a noise of the mouth, but a shout of the heart; not a sound of the lips, but a tumult of internal delights; a harmony of wills, not of voices. It is not heard outside, for it does not cry out in public. Only the one who sings hears it, and the one to whom it is sung.[6]

It is not heard outside; it does not cry out in public. The *Song of Songs* is composed in figurative language. To its hearing, says Bernard, "You must bring chaste ears . . . and when you think about the Lovers in it, you must not understand by them a man and a woman, but the Word and the Soul. And if," he continues, "I say 'Christ and the Church' instead of Word and Soul, the difference is only this: that by the Church is meant the unity—or rather unanimity—of many souls."

It is not Bernard's aim to break the tension created by the language of sexual love, but to exalt it. He never turns with exaggerated modesty from the passionate appeal to the senses of the biblical text. Neither does he welcome it with exaggerated pleasure. He establishes in his commentary what might be called a decorum for mystics. Those capable of misinterpreting him in either unbecoming way are incapable of reading the *Song of Songs* itself. But Bernard speaks best for himself. He is commenting on the verse, "Nightlong on my little bed I sought Him Whom my soul loveth" (3:1):

There is one more thing I should like to point out to you about this verse; and that is the modesty which the Bride shows in it. I do not think that there is any virtue lovelier than modesty; and I should like to take it in my hands like a beautiful flower, and present it to each of our young brethren here. Not that we elders do not need it too; but it is a jewel specially befitting both the life and the demeanor of the young; it is the sister of self-control, a certain index of good character, and a sure token of greater holiness to come. The Wise Man says, "There is a shame that bringeth sin, and there is a shame that bringeth glory." That the Bride's shamefastness is of the latter kind is indicated by the time and place of her quest for the Word—"nightlong on my little bed." Nothing is so congenial to a modest mind as privacy; and this the night-time and the couch ensure. For we are bidden to enter our chamber when we want to pray, doubtless for the sake of privacy. And though this is enjoined partly as a measure of precaution, lest if men see us praying their praise may hinder our prayer's effect and rob us of its fruit, there is a lesson of modesty in the injunction too. For nothing is more integral to modesty than its avoidance of praise and display; and nothing is more unfitting than ostentatious piety . . .

One of the most illuminating of the explications of Bernard, this is also one of the last in the cycle of sermons on the *Song of Songs*. Other comments soar more or say more, at least on the surface seem to ascend higher or to probe more deeply. But as with these nearly final words of Bernard, written perhaps in the last year of his life, so with all of them in this work and all the others with the same theme: they are gathered in love and given in love that others may receive as much and return as much. This is the love of the mystics; this is the love of the Bride; this is the love of Bernard and the index to all his accomplishments, monastic, theological, political, intellectual, spiritual, poetic:

Rightly, then, does the Bride renounce all other affections and devote herself wholly to love and love alone, since love is the one thing she can reciprocate. But when she has poured out her whole being in love, what does it amount to, beside that inexhaustible and ever-flowing Fount? The stream of Love Himself, of the Word Who is the Bridegroom, and the stream of her who loves Him, the soul who is the Bride, flow not with equal volume; you might as well compare a thirsty man to the spring at which he drinks! What then? Are her hope of perfect union, her yearning and her longing, her confidence and ardor, to perish and fail of their purpose because she cannot keep up with the Giant Who runs apace, or equal the Honey in His sweetness, the Lamb in His meekness, the Lily in His dazzling purity, the Sun in His splendor and Love's own Self in love? No! For though she loves less than the Word, because she is a creature and is less, yet, if she loves with her whole being, nothing is lacking, for the whole is there. And to love like that is, as I said, to wed; for it is not possible for a soul to love thus and not to be beloved, and it is this reciprocity of love between the two that constitutes complete and perfect marriage.[7]

CHAPTER VII

Thomas Against Thomas

WITH EACH OF THE MEN I HAVE DISCUSSED SO FAR, certain images are indelibly associated. With Augustine, it may be one of many, such as the boy stealing pears, or the moment in the garden when he heard the command to "Take up and read, Take up and read," or the all-night discussion that ended up with the cockfight in front of the public baths. With Boethius, it is inevitably his prison cell, the condemned consul stretched on his bed, in earnest confabulation with the heavily gowned personification of wisdom. With Gregory, it is almost certainly the image out of the Nuremberg Chronicle—the dove dictating to the Pope behind a veil. With Bernard, it must be a man on a journey, stopping to make recruits for the Cistercian cloister or the armies of the Crusades or to receive a dying abbot's blessing.

With Thomas Aquinas, there are pictures too that come to mind. But the link is the tenuous one of anecdote, anecdote much closer to folklore than established biographical fact. There is the child Thomas of pious legend asking his Benedictine instructors at Monte Cassino, "What is God?" There is the attempt by his family to dissuade him from his Dominican ambitions by giving him a naked girl as a companion in the fortress where this same family had made him a prisoner for more than a year—or so at least one colorful tradition has it. There is the lovely tale of his pining away for lack of a herring—literally pining away, on his deathbed—in a part of the world where herrings had never been seen, much less eaten, when *mirabile dictu* a wandering hawker of viands showed up with herrings in his basket. And then there are all the quite authentic pictures one has of his size, beautifully rounded pictures of a beer-barrel-shaped medieval monk.

But these images lack substance. They are merely incidental to the life of St. Thomas and quite irrelevant in any consideration of his theological and philosophical achievement. No, like it or not, the primary association the mind makes with Thomas is of *Questiones disputatae* or of such bird-tracks across the page as *S.T., IIa, IIae, 33, 3, ad 3*—the *Secunda Secundae,* the second part of the second part, of the *Summa Theologica,* question 33, article 3, in the reply to the third objection. For some, this kind of investigation and arrangement is the peak of man's analytical accomplishments and the definitive demonstration of the ability of the human mind to find its way to the truth in tranquil certainty. For others it is a grim caricature of scholastic method. For most, even those soaked in it through years of Catholic education, it is a world apart, like chemistry, where truth is known and always spoken about, but in complicated formulas understood only by the initiate. Such mysteries simply cannot be translated into the language of the common man—or even the uncommon one, unless he happens to be a Thomist and has the key.

It is no small affront to the dignity of the saint and no small cruelty to his readers that Thomas should thus have been set against Thomas. The reduction of his accomplishment to the methodology and the manner of the *Summas* has resulted in the slighting of his other works or their publication in popular or severely truncated versions that cannot and do not do justice to their method, manner, or matter. The result of the Thomists' insistence upon a jargon, for which they more than Thomas are responsible, has been the exclusion of Thomas from the world of secular modern philosophy. What is far worse, for both those of Christian and of secular persuasion, Thomas has become not a writer, but a dealer in esoteric philosophical doctrines; not a humanist, but a highly recondite theologian; not even a saint, but an oracle to whose pronouncements Catholic officialdom repairs with monotonous regularity.

From this approach, one would never gather that Thomas was in fact a literary craftsman of considerable skill and a gifted poet. One might not quite understand that it was thought quite natural to give him the assignment of composing the Divine Office and the Mass for the Feast of Corpus Christi, when it was instituted in 1264. True, the Dominicans have never been shy about this masterpiece of Thomas's. How could they be? Among its parts is the majestic sequence *Lauda Sion Salvatorem,* with its precise, doctrinal, and yet thoroughly poetic exposition of "the living bread," the Eucharist. At First Vespers, the hymn is the *Pange lingua,* the perfectly chiseled beauty of which no translation can possibly convey. But even this masterpiece is little respected or even thought about. For most of us, it exists only in its last two verses–those that begin "*tantum ergo sacramentum*" and "*genitori genitoque*"–in dismal performances at the Benediction of the Blessed Sacrament which have succeeded in effacing from outer or inner ear awareness of the meaning of the words or the larger work which they bring to a conclusion.

One should add to these the poem *Adoro te devote.* In it, as in the *Pange lingua* and the *Lauda Sion,* there is the tell-tale austerity of Thomas and the music of his verse too. For anyone with any feeling for the relationship of sound and meaning in poetry, the pattern of vowel tones and nasal consonants in at least one pair of couplets is superb. One not only sees the allegorical representation of Jesus as the pelican, one hears it:

> pie pellicane Iesu domine,
> me immundum munda tuo sanguine;

cuius una stilla salvum facere
totum mundum posset omni scelere.

An attempt to give this side of St. Thomas wider fame, although not for literary purposes, was made by Monsignor Martin Grabmann, who never descended to the level of jargon, on the subject of Thomas or anything else. The book is *Das Seelenleben des heiligen Thomas von Aquin*, excellently translated as *The Interior Life of St. Thomas Aquinas* by an American Dominican, Nicholas Ashenbrener. The occasion for the volume was the six hundredth anniversary of the canonization of Thomas—and it is Thomas the saint that Monsignor Grabmann was determined to reveal in his work. This is never easy to do with any figure: sanctity does not appear from behind a curtain on cue. It is particularly difficult to do with Thomas, whose spirituality is rarely summoned forth, even by his most zealous admirers. As for his humanity—between the exaggerations of pious hagiographers and the eviscerations of jargon-writing Thomists, it has become almost hopelessly remote.

The great merit of the Grabmann book is to remind us why a saint is canonized, by calling attention to "the basic features of St. Thomas's soul"—wisdom, charity, and peace. Monsignor Grabmann makes these more than just verbal integers in a spiritual arithmetic: they come alive in a fresh culling of Thomas's works. It is the kind of reading of Thomas that made him the inevitable choice of Renaissance painters when they looked for one whose intellectual penetration had raised him to what might be called face-to-face contemplation of God. He filled that ecstatic role as logically as Catherine of Siena did the part of the bride in representations of the mystical marriage. It is a science of wisdom that Thomas practised, not for any love of the intricately woven surface, but for the sake of the wisdom beneath:

The scientific formation and the order, so admired and worthy of admiration, of the thought and of the works of St. Thomas, are not merely an external arrangement and an exact assembling of material, not merely a function and result of logical classification. Rather it is an internal evolution, in which lofty metaphysical and theological thoughts and views, in their conclusions, applications, and relations, pervade and govern, as dominating principles, the whole intellectual structure, giving it a perfectly unified style. The external arrangement is only the appearance, the garment of this inner order, which grows by organically developing and forming a central idea.[1]

Who sees this begins to see Thomas. For in his work, exactly as in Augustine's, the balancing of outer mode and inner dispositions follows the harmony of the natural and supernatural orders: "The testimonies of the canonization process and the canonization bull of John XXII proudly state that Thomas maintained a complete equilibrium of soul . . ." In that balance, Thomas regularly weighed his own work. After his last experiences of mystical conversation, he had little more to say to man. He could not finish the *Summa Theologica:* "Reginald, I cannot. All that I have written is as straw compared to what I have seen." The words are justly famous.

He longed for an end to his life and teaching, he told his good companion in religion, Reginald of Piperno. When he came to his deathbed, he expressed that longing as Bernard did, in terms of the *Song of Songs*. To an exposition of it he devoted his very last days. Grabmann sums up the longing in doctrinal terms: "For this life on earth, St. Thomas proposes the principle that the love of God is better and more valuable than the knowledge of God, and teaches us the comforting doctrine that we can love God more than we can know Him." This is a teaching presented with some subtlety by Thomas; for those not used to reading Thomas as a devotional writer, it requires some searching. But in all the passages in his work where he holds Christ up for our emulation as well as our adoration, the point is clear enough. There is, for example, this trenchant series of statements in his commentary on the Creed:

St. Augustine says that the passion of Christ can bring about a complete reformation of our lives. Whoever wishes to live perfectly need do nothing other than despise what Christ despised on the Cross, and desire what Christ desired. There is no virtue that did not have its example on the Cross.

So if you seek an example of charity, then, "greater love than this no man hath, that a man lay down his life for his friends." And this Christ did upon the Cross. If, therefore, He gave His life for us, we ought to endure any and all evils for Him . . . If you seek an example of patience, you will find it in its highest degree upon the Cross. Great patience is exemplified in two ways: either when one suffers intensely in all patience, or when one suffers that which he could avoid if he so wished . . . If you seek an example of humility, look upon Him who is crucified; although He was God, He chose to be judged by Pontius Pilate and to be put to death . . . If you seek an example of obedience, imitate Him who was obedient to the Father unto death . . . If you seek an example of contempt for earthly things, imitate Him who is the King of kings, the Lord of rulers, in whom are all the treasures of wisdom; but on the Cross He was stripped naked, ridiculed, spat upon, bruised, crowned with thorns, given to drink of vinegar and gall, and finally put to death. How falsely, therefore, is one attached to riches and raiment, for: "They parted My garments amongst them; and upon My vesture they cast lots." How falsely to honors, since "I was covered with lashes and insults"; how falsely to positions of power, because "taking a crown of thorns, they placed it upon My brow"; how falsely to delicacies of the table, for "in My thirst they gave Me to drink of vinegar." Thus, St. Augustine, in commenting on these words, "Who, having joy set before Him, endured the Cross despising the shame," says: "The man Christ despised all earthly things in order to teach us to despise them."[2]

There is more of the same incisive writing in Thomas's little work on the defense of the faith against Moslems, Greeks, and Armenians, delivered as a letter to the Cantor of Antioch. The substance of the section on the death of Christ is the same as that in the commentary on the Creed just quoted. But there is more; there is a meditation on the voluntary abasement of Christ that has the incandescence of a document by one of the Greek fathers on the same subject. It lights up the pages of the opusculum and illumines for us the mind and soul of Thomas:

If Christ had lived in wealth, power, and great dignity, it could be believed that His doctrine and miracles had been received by reason of human ingenuity and favor. And so that the work might manifestly be of divine power, He chose what was abject and lowly in the world: a poor mother and a needy life, uneducated Apostles and disciples; to be despised by the great men of the world, and eventually to be condemned to death. In this way He manifestly showed that the acceptance of His miracles and of His doctrine ought to be attributed to divine rather than human power.

Therefore in all that He accomplished and suffered, human infirmity is simultaneously conjoined with divine power. In His nativity, wrapped up in swaddling clothes, He was placed in a manger—but gloriously praised by angels and adored by the Magi. He was tempted by the devil, but ministered to by angels. He lived in need and poverty, but raised the dead to life and gave sight to the blind. He died fixed to a Cross, numbered among thieves, but at His death the sun was darkened, the earth trembled, the stones were shattered, the graves were opened, and the bodies of the dead arose. If, therefore, from such a beginning, one sees the fruit which followed, namely the conversion of nearly the whole world to Christ, and still seeks other signs for believing, he can be regarded as harder than a rock, for at His death the rocks burst asunder.[3]

Thomas is not always so eloquent. His is usually rather the rhetoric of understatement. He sought reality unadorned and usually hesitated to impose upon the fruits of his speculation even the barest hint of enthusiasm, or of contempt, or of any personal response in-between, no matter how mild. As a result, most of the time he reads as one unmoved and unmovable, a humorless investigator of such colorless objectivity as to seem part of the object itself. This is a procedure entirely consonant with that humility of his to which so many of his contemporaries testified. It does not always make for an engrossing or even amiable style. But there is a trick to the procedure. Once perceived, it considerably lightens the examination of Thomas, in English or Latin, and makes far more understandable the contrasting performances of the hymn-writer and the composer of *Summas*, the poet of the Corpus Christi Mass and the author of the *Quodlibets*, the master of the meditations on Christ as a model of human behavior and the maker of *Questiones Disputatae*.

Thomas's personality emerges in his style not through rhetorical ornament, but through example. He amplifies by specifying. Aristotle writes in the *De Anima* on the subject of smell:

> man smells but feebly, discerning nothing odorous save with some special pleasure or disgust, as though our organ for the perception of smells were defective. It is arguable indeed that, as hard-eyed animals see color, yet so that delicate differences are not sharply defined to them, except as these cause fear or not, so are smells to the human species.

Thomas expands Aristotle's statement by just a few words—but how valuable they are:

> Man smells weakly—indeed only what is strongly odorous and

causes pleasure or disgust; and this because his sense of smell is lacking in a keen and exact discernment of its object. Hence one may reasonably opine that human beings stand with respect to odors in the same case as hard-eyed animals, such as locusts and certain types of fish stand with respect to colors; for these animals on account of their weak vision and ill-disposed organs, see only what is very obviously visible and as such is apt to frighten them, or the contrary.[4]

He has explained, by his additions, that only strong odors can cause pleasure or disgust; he has described the defect in man's sense of smell; he has given examples of hard-eyed animals and shown why they cannot perceive delicate distinctions. This is the handsomely practised art of Thomas. It is never entirely absent from his pages, but it must always be looked for. The way to find it is to remember at all times that Thomas was by profession a teacher, a university professor, which in medieval terms as in modern means a commentator, one continually composing glosses on other men's texts. It is to his commentaries that one must look for an understanding of the commentator.

The dimensions of Thomas's spirit were as large as those of his flesh. As with any teacher of quality, particularly in the humanities, he knows the texts upon which he comments so well that he seems at times to have written them himself or to think he has. But this is a process of clarification, not of appropriation. In his exposition of the *De Trinitate* of Boethius, which is almost as much a commentary on Augustine's work of the same name, what he accomplishes is expansion of Boethius's little work, confirmation of Augustine's, and the development of his own thinking on the vexing question of the materials and methods proper to philosophy and theology. The achievement is all the more impressive when one discovers that Thomas's commentary does not get beyond the beginning of the second of the six sections which follow the preface of Boethius's treatise. This is enough, however, to furnish him with the matter for a tidy epistemology and some of his clearest and most significant metaphysical distinctions. It also reveals a remarkable awareness of the meaning of words and the function of style in developing and communicating knowledge among human beings.

Simply as a *tour de force*, St. Thomas's elaboration of the two hundred and forty words of Boethius's preface into brief commentary and extensive debate is impressive. To begin with, he analyzes the structure of the preface: its threefold general division; the four causes of the work, material, efficient, formal, and final; its intended audience—that is, Symmachus, the wise man who was Boethius's father-in-law; the manner in which one must write to reach such a man; and the inevitable difficulties of the project. He then goes on to consider the major questions which arise from the compendious preface concerning the knowledge of divine things and the ways that such knowledge is made manifest.

The substance of Thomas's approach to these questions is contained in a quotation from Augustine's *De Trinitate:* "I shall not be without zeal in seeking out knowledge of God, whether through Scripture or creatures." Since "knowledge of God through creatures is given in philosophy," Thomas reasons, "it is not unfitting that in sacred doctrine one should make use of philosophical reasoning." But reason has only its allotted place, and no more: "It is possible by natural reason to know that God exists, but not that He is a Trinity, and one God." We ought to take from the philosophers what Augustine says in the *De Doctrina Christiana* they may have uttered by chance, "truths helpful to our faith"; these truths "ought to be taken from them as from unjust possessors and used to our advantage." In the same way, Thomas says, sign and symbol may be helpful when they are so converted by sacred use that their very nature changes. Thomas too recognizes the nourishment to be found in the figurative language that was meat and drink to Augustine, Gregory, and Bernard:

> It may be said: No conclusive argument can be drawn from figurative speech, as the Master [Peter Lombard] says. Dionysius also says in his letter to Titus that symbolic theology has no weight of proof, especially when such interprets no authority. Nevertheless it can be said that when one of two things passes into the nature of another, the product is not considered a mixture except when the nature of both is altered. Wherefore those who use philosophical doctrines in sacred Scripture in such a way as to subject them to the service of faith, do not mix water with wine, but change water into wine.

Language is very much on Thomas's mind in the last of the four articles that make up his discussion of Question II. Here he examines that sentence of the preface in which Boethius speaks of veiling his ideas "in new and unaccustomed words" that only he and his father-in-law will understand: "The rest of the world I simply disregard: they cannot understand, and therefore do not deserve to read." Now, Thomas asks, should divine truths be concealed by new and obscure words? His answers are Augustine's and Gregory's, the answers of all those to whom sacred things ought to be concealed in order to be more ardently sought and venerated when found. Several scriptural texts establish Thomas's position, as earlier they had Augustine's: from Matthew (7:6), "Give not that which is holy to dogs"; from Luke (8:10), "To you it is given to know the mystery of the kingdom of God, but to the rest in parables." Because these things are true, Thomas concludes, "one ought by obscurity in speech conceal some sacred truths from the multitude."

These are blunt answers to those who object to obscurity in the language of divine science. Thomas continues, once more through the words of Augustine and Gregory, to offer not only a defense of obscure figurative language, but also a psychology of censorship, one perhaps more subtle in its distinctions than the thinking of many followers of Thomas. First of all, in this context, he cites Gregory's gloss on the text of Exodus 21:33, "If a man open a pit, and dig one, and cover it not, and an ox or an ass fall into it . . ." Gregory says:

He who in sacred eloquence now understands lofty things should cover over these sublime truths by silence when in the presence of those who do not comprehend them, lest through some scandal of mind he cause the loss of some little one among the faithful or of an infidel who otherwise might have come to believe. Those truths, therefore, ought to be hidden from those to whom they might do harm; but a distinction can be made as regards speaking, since these same truths may be privately revealed to the wise, though publicly silence is kept regarding them.

Then, on the same subject, he quotes Augustine, who points out in the *De Doctrina* that certain ideas are so difficult to explain to an unspecialized audience that one rarely attempts to speak about them or even to mention them. But, when one writes, says Augustine,

the same distinction cannot be adhered to, because a book, once published, can fall into the hands of anyone at all, and therefore some truths should be shielded by obscuring words so that they may profit those who will understand them and be hidden from the simple who will not comprehend them.

Following such reasoning, Thomas concludes, we can see that "no harm is done to anyone, because those who understand are held by that which they read, but those who do not understand are not compelled to continue reading." This leads him to a typically concise and persuasive summary:

These authorities speak of hiding truths which ought to be made manifest; wherefore it is previously said in Ecclesiasticus 4:28,

"Refrain not to speak in the time of salvation." By this, however, there is no denial of the fact that there are mysteries which ought to be concealed by obscuring words. The doctrine of Christ ought to be taught publicly and openly to this extent: that the truths expedient for each one to know be made clear. Things that are not expedient, however, need not be publicly taught. The doctors of sacred Scripture are not debtors to the wise and to the foolish in such a way that they must propose the same truths to both, but that they propose to each what is to the advantage of each. Subtle truths are not concealed from the multitude on account of envy, but rather out of due discretion.

There are few better introductions to Thomas's method, matter, and style than this *Expositio super librum Boethii De Trinitate*. The method is that of the *Summa Theologica*. The matter is that covered in many places by Thomas. The style is his familiar one too: bare bones piled on top of each other to make a heap, a shining heap. As the heap shines, so does the matter, which is to a large extent the method as well. Nowhere else does Thomas discourse at quite such length or with quite such lucidity on the nature of his own disciplines of learning, philosophy, and theology. Furthermore, he emulates the neat and succinct arrangement of Boethius's *De Trinitate:* the bones are not only piled and shined, they are fitted together in perfect order.

The last article of Question III is a transparently clear and simple elucidation of the dogma of the Trinity, to which all that has gone before contributes. In the course of a discussion of the causes of plurality in Question IV, Thomas explains technically, but without many difficulties for those used to philosophical language, the principle of contradiction. In so doing, he establishes what he means when he calls a proposition "non-intelligible": it is either because of a defect in the proposition itself or on the part of the one attempting to understand. This, in turn, leads Thomas, by way of a brief discussion of numerical diversity, to the opening sentences of Part II of Boethius's tractate and a consideration of the division of the modes of speculative knowledge—natural science, mathematics, and divine science—and their separate and related functions. Very early in this last discussion, Thomas makes a set of distinctions of historic importance on the three degrees of abstraction to which the speculative sciences conform. Again, his perceptions are presented with exemplary simplicity and clarity.

The practical intellect, Thomas points out, is concerned with the truth as a means to action; the speculative, with the truth as an end in itself. Objects of speculation are therefore not in the realm of the accidental but of the necessary: the speculative sciences are distinguished "according to the order of abstraction from matter and from motion." That order is threefold, and not made up of two or four or any other number of parts but three. Thomas's organization is definitive here for matter, method, and style. It is worth following in its entirety—and closely:

First degree of abstraction. There are certain objects of speculation which are dependent upon matter as to their existence, since they cannot exist except in matter, and these are distinguished because they depend on matter both really and logically, such as things whose definition posits sensible matter. Hence, they cannot be understood without sensible matter, as, for example, in the definition of man it is necessary to include flesh and bones; and with things of this kind physics, or natural science, is concerned.

Second degree of abstraction. But certain other things, although they depend upon matter as to their existence, do not so depend as far as the intellect is concerned; because in a definition of them sensible matter is not included, as in the case of lines and numbers with which mathematics deals.

Third degree of abstraction. But there are still other objects of speculation that do not depend upon matter for existence, because they can exist without matter: either they are never found in matter, as God and the angels, or they are sometimes in matter and in other cases not, as substance, quality, potency, act, one, and many, and things of this sort.

With these things theology treats, that is, divine science, because the most important of its objects is God. By another name, it is called metaphysics, that is, *transphysica*, because it is fitting for us to study it after physics, as it is natural for us to arrive at knowledge of the nonsensible by means of those things that are sensible.

It is also called first philosophy, inasmuch as other sciences, receiving their principles from it, follow upon it.

Moreover, it is not possible for there to be other things which, according to the intellect, are dependent upon matter, but not so with respect to their real existence; because the intellect, inasmuch as it is considered in itself, is immaterial; wherefore there is no fourth division of philosophy over and above those named.

In Question VI, the last of the divisions of Thomas's exposition of Boethius, he is concerned with "the most important" of the objects of theology or metaphysics, God, or what he prefers to call for the purposes of this discussion, "divine things." We are in the order of intellectual speculation now, but we have not relinquished the judgment of the senses or the imagination, for both sense and imagination are "principles or starting points of our speculation." The procedure is that established by St. Paul, through visible things to the invisible—"For the invisible things of him, from the creation of the world, are clearly seen, being understood by the things that are made; his eternal power also, and divinity" (Rom 1:20). We follow too the principle that divine truths are shown to us "under the figure of sensible things in order that our intellect should . . . from these things . . . mount up to such as are invisible: wherefore use is made of things most common, that there may be even less occasion for remaining at their level, as says Dionysius."

We go far, following the logic of Thomas's authorities. The procedure outlined by Paul is corroborated for Thomas by Gregory's gloss on Genesis 32:30, in which Jacob reports, after wrestling with the angel, "I have seen God face to face," and by Dionysius:

> "Unless a man, in some way did, indeed, behold [divine truth], he would not feel himself incapable of beholding it"; but we do feel that we cannot perfectly know the divine essence; therefore in some way we have intellectual vision of it.
>
> Further, Dionysius says that the human mind tends to be elevated through visible things to supermundane heights, which means nothing other than to a knowledge of separated forms; therefore in some way we are capable of knowing separated forms.

Can we know the divine essence itself or the form of any other separate substance by means of speculation? The answer of course is, no, not here below. Man's happiness is of two kinds, the imperfect one of this world and the perfection of Heaven by which "God Himself will be made visible to us through His essence, and other separated substances will be known; but . . . not through any of the sciences of speculation, but through the light of glory." The truth has served its purpose, however, even in the imperfect way of the world. It has acted as a compelling motive to draw man toward salvation, by preparing him in an orderly way for the gift which will elevate him to it. Thomas's method has been once again the method of the allegorists: a development from the letter to the spirit; from signs to things; from something sensed, perhaps, to a glimpse of larger significations; from something witnessed to something performed; and finally, with divine aid, a rise to the grace of true understanding. The third degree of abstraction and the level of the allegorists called "the anagogical" are united in purpose and power. The concluding words of Thomas's *Expositio* could just as well describe the patterns of knowledge unfolded by Augustine in the *De Doctrina Christiana* and the *De Magistro* and by Gregory in his *Magna Moralia:*

> There are inscribed upon our minds certain inherent principles by means of which we can prepare ourselves for perfect cognition of separate substances even if [in this life] we cannot attain to it by means of them. For although man naturally tends toward his ultimate end, he cannot gain possession of it by purely natural means or powers, but only by grace. And this is so because of the [supernatural] eminence of that end.[5]

In all of Thomas's work there is demonstrated a deep respect for the authority of the Fathers and Doctors of the Church, as well as Scripture, the popes, philosophers ancient and modern, the ecumenical councils and provincial synods. The index of authorities quoted in the *Summa Theologica*, for example, runs in one edition to almost three hundred pages. In all his reasoned answers to theological and philosophical questions, Thomas relies on authority stated and firm: he never replies "On the contrary" or concludes "I answer that" without a full supply of teachers and guides at his side. At no point, however, does he display his knowledge and affection for these good friends of his so thoroughly as in his collection of passages from the Fathers and their followers commenting on and glossing the four Gospels, a collection which the Renaissance called by the name of *Catena Aurea, The Golden Chain.*

There are many links in Thomas's *Golden Chain*—Augustine and Ambrose and Jerome, of course; Bede and Leo the Great and Isidore of Seville; all the great Gregorys; Alcuin and his disciple Rabanus Maurus, and Origen and the Greek

Fathers. Many learned men and many good ones first discovered the dimensions of the Greek Fathers, their color and craft, in this bursting bouquet of Thomas's. And yet the book itself is today almost unknown. What a loss that is! For this is an anthology incomparable among the world's collections. It provides at once the most reliable guide to Patristic thinking and its principal source, the Gospels. It offers nearly endless material for meditation, and leads the reader with words that leap from the page to the unearthly encounter which was probably Urban IV's aim in asking Thomas to compile the work and certainly Thomas's in doing so.

Like the *Summas*, the *Golden Chain* is a work of synthesis, and like them too, a massive and a noble one. In the *Summas*, the nobility is the result of Thomas Aquinas's meditation on the resources of the human reason. In the *Golden Chain*, the nobility is the product of St. Thomas's contemplation of the sources of revelation. It is right that the marks made by the imperfect human reason across the page should resemble birdtracks, and just as proper that the chain that ties the contemplating soul to its object should be golden. It was the special genius of Thomas to see the need for both. It was his special grace to find appropriate ways of saying so.

Those whose knowledge of Thomas is limited—if "limited" is the word—to his great works of theological and philosophical synthesis cannot fully grasp the size of the saint's achievement, much less hold on to it. But there is no need for us to have and to hold a mental picture of Thomas—his writing is enough when there is this much to say. How much? Thomas's architectonic *Summas* indicate how much. How much? Thomas's prayers suggest how much:

O God, in whom is every consolation, who discern in us nothing that is not your own gift, grant me, when the term of this life is reached, the knowledge of the first Truth, the love of the highest Good. Give my body, most generous Giver of rewards, the beauty of clarity, the swiftness of agility, the aptness of subtility, the strength of impassibility. Add to these the affluence of riches, the influence of delights, the confluence of good things; that so I may rejoice; above, in your consolations; below, in the pleasantness of the place; within, in the glory of soul and body; about me, in the delightful company of angels and of men. With you, most merciful Father, may my mind discover the illumination of wisdom; my desires, the winning of all desirable things; my efforts, the praise of triumph; there where, with you, is the escaping of all dangers, the distinction of mansions, the concord of wills; where reigns the amenity of spring, the lucidity of summer, the richness of autumn, the quiet silence of winter. Grant me, lord God, life without death and joy without sorrow; there where reign supreme freedom, free security, secure tranquillity, joyful bliss, blissful eternity, eternal beatitude, the vision, and the praising, of Truth, yourself. Amen.[6]

How much? The tale told by Thomas's first biographer, William of Tocco, tells how much. According to William, the sacristan of St. Dominic's church in Naples saw the saint one day kneeling in ecstasy before a crucifix and heard a voice speak from the cross: "You have written well of me, Thomas. What reward do you ask for your work?" Thomas answered: "Nothing less than Thyself, O Lord." How much? All.

CHAPTER VIII

Dante: The Sacred Poem

THERE ARE TWO WAYS TO TAKE UP THE *Divine Comedy*. One is to make a life-long study of it. The other is to turn to it as to a book of meditations, drawing from it in many readings, in small portions, the great weight of wisdom with which it is infused. Neither way excludes the other, but the first does require the equipment, the dedication, and the energy of a scholar, while for the second a small degree of devotion is enough.

It is true that in the course of any attentive reading of Dante one must become something of a scholar. One cannot read the opening canto of the *Inferno* without being thrown into the midst of several circling histories, revolving grandly around each other. For Dante, in this hundredth part of the work alone, has linked his personal history to biblical events and events in his own lifetime, to the Creation, to the Trojan War, to Aeneas and his creator Virgil. Upon all of this he has superimposed an allegory, sometimes personal, sometimes universal, always obscure, which is the despair of the literal-minded and the delight of the imaginative, but for all full of meaning.

There is in this same first canto a repletion of medieval astronomy, about which one must know something in order to fix the narrative in time and space. The references to Virgil are of no small account, for the Latin poet will be Dante's guide, and the reader's, through two thirds of the *Comedy*. And even in translation, one must pay some attention to Dante's prosody, for in the structure of his verse he has placed the essential parts of his system of values, of his modes of thought, of the convictions which possessed him in the living and writing of the *Divine Comedy*.

Devotion to the *Comedy* begins with the disentangling of its formal elements. One must recognize, to begin with, the high place accorded number in such systems as Dante's. Convinced by the reasoning of such thinkers as Augustine and Bonaventure, and inspired, like the saints, by the opening chapters of Genesis, Dante turned to numbers as objective signs leading directly to God. Beauty, as we know, was for the thinking medieval mind the result of a series of balances, of a science of proportion pursued assiduously to achieve a rhythmic arrangement of parts, a small order reflecting however inadequately the larger one of God.

In the sixth book of his *De Musica*, Augustine traces seven steps of ascent from sensible things to the Creator of all things. From the first apprehension of numbers by our senses, through all their translations into gesture, judgment, learning, and art, some elements of beauty remain. This, Augustine says, has been so ordained by God's Providence:

> He has created and rules all things, so that even the sinful and miserable soul may be moved by numbers. Set numbers are moving even to the lowest corruption of the flesh. These numbers can be less and less beautiful, but they cannot lack beauty entirely. God, most good and most just, grudges no beauty, whether fashioned by the soul's damnation, retreat, or perseverance.[1]

Thus, even in that part of the *Comedy* that deals with corrupt souls, even in Dante's *Inferno*, there is order and therefore beauty.

For Bonaventure, in the *Itinerarium Mentis ad Deum, The Mind's Road to God*, this reasoning leads to a sweeping generalization about the nature of beauty and delight. It is closely allied, like St. Thomas's system, to the Pauline formula—*per visibilia ad invisibilia:*

Since, therefore, all things are beautiful and in some way delightful, and beauty and delight do not exist apart from proportion, and proportion is primarily in number, it needs must be that all things are rhythmical (*numerosa*). And for this reason number is the outstanding exemplar in the mind of the Maker, and in things it is the outstanding trace leading to wisdom. Since this is most evident to all and closest to God, it leads most directly to God as if by the seven differentiae. It causes Him to be known in all corporeal and sensible things while we apprehend the rhythmical, delight in rhythmical proportions, and through the laws of rhythmical proportions judge irrefragably.[2]

In Dante's verse, this small cosmos of order is made up first of all of an interlocking series of three-line stanzas, in which the first and third lines always rhyme and the end of the second line always becomes the rhyme of the first and third lines of the following tercet, until the scheme and the canto come to an end with a single line. Unfortunately, this pattern cannot be translated into English without an effect either of doggerel or of a pompous monotony. The music is in the Italian original to stay. Nonetheless, the theology that underlies the invention by Dante of *terza rima* is clear enough, and it is so well reinforced by what might be called the trinitarian or triune construction of the poem that there is no missing Dante's point—or Augustine's or Bonaventure's.

There are one hundred cantos in the *Comedy*, an introductory one, followed by thirty-three designed to carry Dante down through Hell, thirty-three in which he mounts to the peak of Purgatory, and thirty-three which reach across the heavens to confront that stunning light which reflects *l'amor che move il sole e l'altre stelle*, the Love that moves the sun and the other stars. Each of the three sections of the work ends in the stars, literally and figuratively. Each follows an elaborate scheme of persons, places, and events. Each carries a little farther the narrative which begins with Dante lost in the brambles of the dark forest of this world and ends with Dante found in the spectacular illumination of outer space. Each uncovers in its own way the apposite principles of moral theology and of one or another of the branches of speculative and practical philosophy. Each is caught up, in greater or lesser detail, in that geography of eternity which Dante fashioned out of the earth-centered universe of the second-century astronomer Claudius Ptolemaeus. And each too turns upon some moment or moments in Dante's life, in Dante's Florence, in Dante's Italy, in Dante's Europe, which have the effect of bringing alive with startling vividness the closing years of the Middle Ages and the inaugural ones of the Renaissance.

History moves with stately motion through the *Comedy*. It also erupts from time to time in a rhetoric angry enough to communicate the treachery of a Brutus and Cassius or a Judas Iscariot, the murder of a brother, a nephew, or a father-in-law, or the terrifying experience of Ugolino, a man so desperate with hunger that he ate his own children:

> "When I awoke, before the dawn, I heard my sons moaning in their sleep and asking for bread. Cruel thou art indeed, if already thou grievest not, at the thought of what my heart was foreboding: and if thou weepest not, at what art thou wont to weep? They were now awake, and the hour was approaching at which food was wont to be brought to us, and each one of us, because of his dream, had misgivings. Then I heard the door below of the horrible tower being nailed up; whereupon I looked into the faces of my sons and spoke not a word. I was not weeping. I was turned to stone within me, but they were weeping and my dear little Anselm said: 'Thou lookest so, father, what ails thee?' I shed no tear, however, nor did I answer all that day or the next night, till another sun came forth upon the world.
>
> "When a faint ray had penetrated into the prison of woe and when I perceived upon their four faces the aspect of my own, I

bit my hands for grief. And they, thinking that I did it from desire to eat, suddenly rose up and said: 'Father, it would give us less pain, if thou wouldst eat of us; thou didst clothe us with this wretched flesh, do thou despoil us of it.' I calmed myself then, so as not to make them more sad, and that day and the next we were all mute. Ah, cruel Earth, why didst thou not open? When we had come to the fourth day, Gaddo flung himself outstretched at my feet, saying: 'My father, why dost thou not help me?' Then he died; and even as thou seest me, so did I see the three fall one after another between the fifth and the sixth day; then, already blind, I began to grope among them, and for two days called them after they were dead; then starvation, more effective than grief, did its work."[3]

It is easy to forget the stateliness for the anger. Nothing that follows upon the betrayals in the concluding three cantos of the *Inferno* in any way diminishes the intensity of emotion displayed in those verses. But the emotion is balanced by a mind and spirit marvelously recollected and disciplined to an adamantine edge by the use of reason.

This balance of reason and emotion is Dante's own prescription in the *Convivio*, the august set of treatises on the design and purpose of his work; and he follows it. His argument is simple and clear, in the best scholastic manner: things should be named by their most noble attributes, as man should be by his reason, and not by his senses or anything less noble. When we say that man lives, it ought to mean that man uses his reason, that which gives him his particular purpose in life and his ultimate nobility. He who forsakes his reason and lives only by his senses, lives not as a man but as a beast, just as Boethius says: *asino vive*—he lives the life of an ass. "And when I speak of animals," Dante says, "I do not refer to the lower animals only, but I mean to include also those who in outward appearance are men, but spiritually are no better than sheep or any other equally contemptible brute."

Man is destined for the sweet order of heaven. This is his beatitude. This is the bliss to which Dante is dedicated. The miracle of the *Commedia* is that Dante has been able to translate man's beatitude into man's works and man's words. This, he explains to St. James, in the midst of his catechism in Paradise on the theological virtues, is what hope means: to have some certain instinct on earth of the bliss to come in heaven. With the aid of the psalms of David, Dante has developed such an instinct:

> "Hope," I said, "is a sure expectation of future glory, and it springs from divine grace and precedent merit. This light comes to me from many stars, but he first distilled it in my heart who was the sovereign singer of the Sovereign Lord. In his divine song he says: 'Let them hope in thee that know thy name'; and who does not know it that holds my faith? Besides his showers, thou didst shower on me in thy epistle, so that I am full and in turn rain your rain on others."[4]

With the aid of the *Commedia*, we may hope to do as much, to rain Dante's and James's and David's rain on others.

Dante's central hope, the muscle of his will, is to pass on to others what he has learned. All of us, he says, must leave some such legacy to posterity. This is, for him, the necessary obligation of our nature, redressing balances, and imposing upon society, across generations, a constructive order:

> It behoves all men on whom a higher nature has impressed the love of truth to labor for those who are to come after them, in order that posterity may be enriched by their labors, even as they themselves have been enriched by the labors of their predecessors. For he is far from fulfilling his duty, let him not doubt it, who, after being instructed in public affairs, is not careful to contribute in some measure to the public welfare. Such an one is no "tree by the waterside bringing forth fruit in due season," but rather a devastating whirlpool, which is for ever engulfing, but never gives back what it has swallowed.[5]

This is the political system asserted in the *De Monarchia* and defended in the *Commedia*.

Order is Dante's path to beauty. Two orders in particular animate his life and works: outer and inner order, the serenity of the life of the spirit when ordered in conformity with the will of God, matched by an order at least ambitioned in society, and manifestly achieved in the hierarchical structure of the Church. There is far more to this in Dante's view than the mere paralleling of microcosm and macrocosm. It is not simply a matter of concentric circles, of spheres that fit neatly into each other after the design of Ptolemy's astronomy. It is rather a question of the multiplicity of perfections which form the pattern of creation, and may, with the appropriate graces, impose order on our imaginations, on our intellects, on our memories and understanding, and finally on our wills, when judgment shall have been transmuted and given permanence and perfection.

This is the point of the *Commedia*, which a critic long after Dante's lifetime properly enough crowned with the adjective *Divina*, "divine." It is an allegory of that multiplicity of perfections to which our understanding is debtor and our charity creditor. In Hell we see perfection in the breach. In Purgatory we see it painfully being reconstructed. In Paradise we see it once more attained. We learn about the perfect moral system by which our desires are met and—even at their most excessive or defective or perverted—granted. This is the doctrine of *contrapasso*, of the step-by-step matching of punishment to sin, by which the wrathful tear each other to pieces forever and the violent spend their Hell immersed in blood; by which flatterers are covered with filth and hypocrites are masked in leaden cloaks and the makers of discord tear each other to pieces; by which Paolo and Francesca, having been brought together by tempestuous passion, are at the mercy of violent winds, helplessly clasped in each other's arms for all time and whatever may come after; by which Count Ugolino, in whom hunger had more power than love, sets his teeth—forever—in the head of the man responsible for the imprisonment and starvation of the Count and his sons and his grandsons.

In the extraordinary construction, coherent and cohesive, which is Dante's Purgatory, we are given the full perfection of the artist to watch, to hear, to touch and taste and smell. It is by art that Dante must proceed. He has only the broadest outlines of doctrine to guide him, only the most meagre suggestions of the theologians to give body to the soul in Purgatory and substance to the place it inhabits. It is fitting then—orderly, and quite consciously directed to this order—that it is in the *Purgatorio* that the arts find their special places and play their particular roles. Here it is that music accompanies each of the purgations on each of the terraces; here it is that Dante meets painters and poets and musicians; here that he discusses with another poet his own "sweet new style," the *dolce stil novo* copied by others in such number. Dante explains to his fellow poets that he learns from Love's presence within him what to write and how to write.

In Purgatory, Dante discovers the purpose of his literary labors in the compliments he directs toward himself through the mouths of Virgil and other writers of stature. But he also describes his own sins and their tempering in these cantos devoted to arts and artists. He is purged of lust, in "the fire that refines," along with the great Provençal poet, Arnaut Daniel. He is purged of anger by a searing, engulfing, and cleansing smoke. He stoops with a painter, like him a penitent on the terrace of pride, tied "side by side with that burdened soul, as oxen are yoked together." Pride is the worst of Dante's sins, as it is the worst of all sins; and one, he seems to say, to which artists in particular are prone.

On this terrace, the first of Purgatory proper, Dante sees

a remarkable pavement figured with thirteen classical and scriptural examples of pride. He sees Satan, "him that was created nobler than any creature, fall as lightning from heaven." He sees "Nimrod at the foot of his mighty work, as if bewildered . . . looking at the peoples in Shinar that shared his pride." Four of those he sees he addresses in round vocatives:

O Niobe, I saw thee traced on the roadway, with what tearful eyes, between thy seven and seven children slain!

O Saul, how thou appearedst there dead on thine own sword in Gilboa, which never after felt rain or dew!

O mad Arachne, so did I see thee already half spider, wretched on the shreds of the web thou wroughtest to thy hurt!

O Rehoboam, thine image here does not seem now to threaten, but a chariot bears it off full of terror when no one gives chase![6]

Finally, he sees Troy, the epitome of a proud civilization: "O Ilion, how abased and vile the design showed thee that we saw there!" In Dante's design, astonishingly detailed in its allegorical order, the first letters of the thirteen tercets that describe these figures spell out *UOMO,* Italian for "man," the prideful creature, the fallen one.

On the terrace where pride is purged, Dante rejects the claims of that earthly fame to which his name is so many times linked in Purgatory: "The world's noise is but a breath of wind which comes now this way and now that and changes name because it changes quarter." In this place too he hears sung a scholastic elaboration of the Lord's Prayer. It is exactly the same sort of expansion and delineation of the original as St. Thomas made of Aristotle and it is a splendid example of the influence of Thomas on Dante:

"O Our Father who art in Heaven, not circumscribed, but through the greater love which Thou hast for Thy first works on high [the heavens and the angels]; praised be Thy name and

Thy power, by every creature, even as it is meet to render thanks to Thy sweet effluence. May the peace of Thy kingdom come upon us, for if it come not we cannot of ourselves attain it, with all our striving. As Thine angels, singing Hosanna, make sacrifice of their will to Thee, so many men make sacrifice of theirs. Give us this day the daily manna without which in this rough desert he goes backward who most toils to advance. And as we forgive everyone the evil we have suffered, do Thou graciously forgive and regard not our deserts. Put not our virtue, which lightly is subdued, to trial with the old adversary but deliver us from him who so assails it. This last prayer, dear Lord, we make not for ourselves, for it is not needed, but for those who have remained behind us."[7]

The dominant note of Purgatory, to which arts, artists, and sinners of all sorts contribute, is that of human perversity. Virgil's sorrowful reflections at the end of the fourteenth canto sum it up in marvelously mournful Italian, much of the meaning of which is in the sound of the words:

> "Chiamavi'l cielo e 'ntorno vi si gira,
> mostrandovi le sue bellezze etterne,
> e l'occhio vostro pur a terra mira;
> onde vi batte chi tutto discerne."

> "Heaven calls to you and wheels about you,
> showing you its eternal beauties,
> and your eyes gaze only on the earth;
> therefore He scourges you who sees all."

Nonetheless, in spite of the perversity, it is here, in Purgatory, that Paradise is regained and the vague adumbrations of hope which have darted into the poetry grow from suggestion to fulfillment. The first perfection reached in Purgatory is that of the active life. Later it will be transcended but not forgotten or debased; it too is seen as a vision, and to it Dante lifts some of his loftiest poetry. He meets the spirit of this vision of perfection on earth. The passage is a supreme example of Dante's use of the rhetoric of similitude:

As a lady turns in the dance with feet close together on the ground and hardly puts one foot before the other, she turned toward me on the red and yellow flowerets like a virgin that veils her modest eyes and gave satisfaction to my prayer, approaching so that the sweet sound came to me with its meaning. As soon as she was where the grass was just bathed with the waves of the beautiful river she did me the grace to lift her eyes; and I do not believe such light shone from beneath the lids of Venus when, through strange mischance, she was pierced by her son. Erect, she smiled from the other bank, arranging in her hands many colors which the high land puts forth without seed.

She tells him exactly where he is now in his vision—in Eden:

"Those who in old times sang of the age of gold and of its happy state perhaps dreamed on Parnassus of this place; here the human root was innocent, here was lasting spring and every fruit, this is the nectar of which each tells."

It is in the fragrance of Eden's eternal spring that he meets his blessed intercessor in heaven, Beatrice:

I once saw at the beginning of the day the eastern parts all rosy and the rest of the sky clear and beautiful and the sun's face come forth shaded so that through the tempering vapors the eye could bear it long; so, within a cloud of flowers which rose from the angels' hands and fell again within and without, a lady appeared to me, girt with olive over a white veil, clothed under a green mantle with the color of living flame. And my spirit, which now so long had not been overcome with awe, trembling in her presence, without having more knowledge by the eyes, felt old love's great power.

He turns to Virgil to cry out with joy at the sight. But Virgil is gone; human wisdom cannot lead where Dante is going now. As he moves from action to contemplation, from Purgatory to Paradise, he must be given revelation. This Beatrice brings him, but first she hands him "another sword," a list of Dante's failures, his falls from grace after her death, with which she reproaches him and to which he must sadly admit. Finally he is ready for purgation in the river Lethe, to take away the memory of sin, and in the waters of Eunoè, to restore the recollection of virtue.

A pageant precedes and follows the meeting with Beatrice, a pageant of colors and textures and meanings of a depth and breadth beyond the categories of description, Dante tells us. But he has been remade. He has for the second time come forth into the effulgent light of the stars. He is ready now to mount them.

The trip into Paradise is an ascent beyond words with words. It is into a region where being can only be and never more become, but can only—so close to Being Itself, in contemplation of Being—can only, only, only blessedly be:

> Looking on His Son with the Love which the One and the Other eternally breathe forth, the primal and ineffable Power made with such order all that revolves in mind or space that he who contemplates it cannot but taste of Him. Lift up thine eyes with me then, reader, to the lofty wheels, directing them on that part where the one motion strikes the other, and from that point take thy pleasure in the art of the Master, who so loves it in His heart that His eye never leaves it.

Thus do Power and Wisdom exhibit Love in Creation. Or at least this is one way, much more adequate than most, of trying to describe it. This is the way that Dante finds as he enters the heaven of the Sun, fourth of the ten concentric spheres which make up Paradise. This is the way of the theologians, who flame with light as they dance and sing their song of wisdom, circling around Dante and Beatrice three times in honor of Power and Wisdom and Love, the Blessed Trinity. Dante selects twelve of them for special comment. One of them introduces the others:

"I was of the lambs of the holy flock that Dominic leads on the path where there is good fattening if they do not stray; he that is next beside me on the right was my brother and master, and he is Albert [the Great] and I Thomas of Aquino. If thou wouldst be thus informed of all the rest, follow after my words with thine eyes, going round the blessed wreath. That next flame comes from the smile of Gratian, who served the one and the other court [civil and canon law] so well that it gives pleasure in Paradise; the other who next adorns our choir was that Peter [Lombard] who, like the poor widow, offered his treasure to Holy Church. The fifth light [Solomon], which is the most beautiful among us, breathes from such a love that all the world below hungers for news of it; within it is the lofty mind to which was given wisdom so deep that, if the truth be true, there never arose a second of such vision. Beside it see the light of that candle which below in the flesh saw farthest into the nature and the ministry of the angels [Dionysius the Areopagite]. In the little light that is next smiles that defender of Christian times of whose treatise Augustine made use [Paolo Orosio, the historian]. If now thou art bringing thy mind's eye from light to light after my praises, thou art already left eager for the eighth. Within it rejoices in the vision of all good the holy soul who makes plain the world's deceitfulness to one that hears him rightly [Boethius]; the body from which he was driven lies below in Cieldauro, and he came from martyrdom and exile to this peace. See, flaming beyond, the glowing breath of Isidore [of Seville], of Bede, and of Richard [of St. Victor] who in contemplation was more than man. This one from whom thy look returns to me is the light of a spirit to whom, in his grave thoughts, death seemed slow in coming; it is the eternal light of Siger [de Brabant], who, lecturing in the Street of Straw, demonstrated invidious truths."

Once introduced, these figures come alive. St. Thomas tells the story of St. Francis, St. Bonaventure the story of St.

Dominic—the Dominican paying tribute to the Franciscan, the Franciscan to the Dominican. All rivalries end in Paradise; Siger the Averroist is lauded by Thomas, his most vigorous opponent; competing religious orders recognize each other's merits and their own limitations.

Somehow in the translation of being into words that must by their very nature continually change in meaning, Dante is able to answer the demands of mutability, to create conflict and resolve conflict in the time-honored way of the drama and still to hold to the contemplative order which is his special concern in the journey through the ten heavens to that strange sight, that high fantasy, that still point of light in a turning world which is God. It is light painted with our likeness: it is Christ: it is the Love that moves the sun and the other stars. Through appointed representatives Love adds all unto us, answers all our questions. Dante suggests the kind of light that will be shed in eternity by a scholastic puzzle about light. If at the resurrection of their bodies, souls shine with their dazzling unearthly brightness, how will they be able to endure looking at each other with bodily sight? Solomon answers Dante's question:

I heard in the divinest light of the lesser circle a gentle voice, such perhaps as the angel's to Mary, reply: "As long as the feast of Paradise shall last, so long our love shall radiate this vesture about us. Its brightness answers to our ardor, the ardor to our vision, and that is in the measure each has of grace beyond his merit. When the flesh, glorified and holy, shall be put on again, our person shall be more acceptable for being all complete, so that the light freely granted to us by the Supreme Goodness shall increase, light which fits us to see Him; from that must vision increase, the ardor increase that is kindled by it, the radiance increase which comes from that. But like a coal that gives flame and with its white glow outshines it so that its own appearance is preserved, so this effulgence that now surrounds us will be surpassed in brightness by the flesh which the earth still covers. Nor will such light have power to trouble us, for the organs of the body shall be strong for all that can delight us."

Light it is that Dante sees in Paradise, the light of being, the light of the soul and far removed from the earthly body. But always in the *Paradiso*, in this world beyond personality as we normally understand it, personality is revealed too; and light is shed upon us here below. Love constrains Dante to teach with love, with Him who loves, and through whom He loves—the human person. It is, Dante never fails to remind us, a human being, Beatrice, *che'mparadisa la mia mente*, who "imparadises" his mind. It is she whose appearance in his life at the age of nine remade it, made it a new life. It is she whose death gave Dante a personal representative in the courts of heaven. It is she whose beauty, now that she is in heaven, is so shattering to the human eye that she dare not smile:

"Were I to smile" she began to me "thou wouldst become like Semele when she was turned to ashes; for my beauty, which thou hast seen kindle more the higher we climb by the stairs of the eternal palace, is so shining that if it were not tempered thy mortal powers in its blaze would be like a branch split by a thunderbolt."

It is she, who is at once a figure of wisdom and the most persuasive portrait of an idealized woman in literature, whose intercessory power he gratefully acknowledges two cantos before the summit of the *Commedia:*

"O Lady in whom my hope has its strength and who didst bear for my salvation to leave thy footprints in Hell, of all the things that I have seen I acknowledge the grace and the virtue to be from thy power and from thy goodness. It is thou who hast drawn me from bondage into liberty by all those ways, by every means for it that was in thy power. Preserve in me thy great bounty, so that my spirit, which thou hast made whole, may be loosed from the body well-pleasing to thee."

Dante had hoped at the end of his journey to see Beatrice once more, to question her further on things about which his mind was still in suspense. He sees instead an old man, his eyes and cheeks glowing with gladness, his face filled with the tenderness of a father. It is St. Bernard. And it is he, of all the glorious company of heaven, whose prayer leads Dante to the final mediation, to her whose analogue Beatrice is, and through her to the final assertion of that order to which all Dante's work on earth has been directed—from the first shadowings of the new life in his verse and the earliest speculations about their meaning in his elaborate glosses on it right up to the hundredth canto of the *Commedia*. Bernard speaks for Dante to the Virgin:

"*Vergine madre, figlia del tuo figlio*, Virgin Mother, daughter of thy Son, lowly and exalted more than any creature, fixed goal of the eternal counsel, thou art she who didst so ennoble human nature that its Maker did not disdain to be made in its making. In thy womb was rekindled the love by whose warmth this flower has bloomed thus in the eternal peace; here thou art for us the noonday torch of charity, and below among mortals thou art a living spring of hope. Thou, Lady, art so great and so prevailing that whoso would have grace and does not turn to thee, his desire would fly without wings. Thy loving-kindness not only succors him that asks, but many times it freely anticipates the asking; in thee is mercy, in thee pity, in thee great bounty, in thee is joined all goodness that is in any creature."

What greater testament is there to Providence, to order, purpose, and design in all things, in all being and becoming, than this final tribute of Dante's to the power of intercessory prayer? He has moved, in "the sacred poem to which both heaven and earth have set their hand," from Virgil to Beatrice, from Beatrice to Bernard, from Bernard to Mary, and from Mary to the Supreme Light, to Order, to Purpose, to Love Itself:

Now my speech will come more short even of what I remember than an infant's who yet bathes his tongue at the breast. Not that the living light at which I gazed had more than a single aspect —for it is ever the same as it was before—, but by my sight gaining strength as I looked, the one sole appearance, I myself changing, was, for me, transformed. In the profound and clear ground of the lofty light appeared to me three circles of three colors and of the same extent, and the one seemed reflected by the other as rainbow by rainbow, and the third seemed fire breathed forth equally from the one and the other. O how scant is speech and how feeble to my conception! and this, to what I saw, is such that it is not enough to call it little. O Light Eternal, that alone abidest in Thyself, alone knowest Thyself, and, known to Thyself and knowing, lovest and smilest on Thyself! That circling which, thus begotten, appeared in Thee as reflected light, when my eyes dwelt on it for a time, seemed to me, within it and in its own color, painted with our likeness, for which my sight was wholly given to it. Like the geometer who sets all his mind to the squaring of the circle and for all his thinking does not discover the principle he needs, such was I at that strange sight. I wished to see how the image was fitted to the circle and how it has its place there; but my own wings were not sufficient for that, had not my mind been smitten by a flash wherein came its wish. Here power failed the high fantasy; but now my desire and will, like a wheel that spins with even motion, were revolved by the Love that moves the sun and the other stars.[8]

Thus has Dante brought himself and his readers to the highest of the four levels of meaning which his work is intended to convey. Three of the levels are clear enough: he has taken the letter of the narrative and given it allegorical breadth and moral depth by substituting people and events for ideas, and making all—people and events and ideas—yield judgments of value. Finally, at the end, he has lifted all to the anagogical level, the level of grace. *He* has lifted all? No, not Dante, he would say, and we must say with him, since only the source of grace can give grace, not Dante but Christ in him. If we do not see this, if we do not say this, then we have not ourselves reached the fourth level of meaning and we do not understand what makes Dante's *Comedy* divine.

CHAPTER IX

The Renaissance Assimilation

NO SUCCESSFUL ATTEMPT CAN BE MADE TO OUTLINE THE texture of Renaissance thought that does not take into consideration the complexity of traditions which entered into the diction, affiliations, and derivations of the circle of poets and philosophers that Lorenzo de' Medici gathered around him in Florence in the late fifteenth century. The exact shade of influence and derivation in any one case is not important. What matters is the balance in almost all these writers of almost every known pagan philosophical position and Christian theology. Three of the most revealing, most artful, and most appealing of the group are its chairman, Lorenzo; its theologian, Marsilio Ficino; and its youngest member, Giovanni Pico della Mirandola.

Like the others in the circle, Ficino, Pico, and Lorenzo were much influenced by the Schoolmen. By their readings in scholastic philosophy, they were moved to make their own attempts at systems of thought of a highly complex nature not always readily accessible to the modern mind, even to one sympathetic to their thought. Fortunately for us, all were gifted writers and men of taste. Their summas are, on the whole, brief. That they are also persuasive is due not only to the brevity, but to the straightforward, almost naive way their authors kept before themselves their central aim, to make thoroughly Christian the obviously good and wise pagans, such as Plato and Aristotle.

Theirs was a mining operation, following the blueprints of Augustine. Marsilio Ficino, the most determined of Lorenzo's group to turn pagan sources into Christian resources, and the best equipped, at least as a theologian, uses a figure based on Augustine's in the *De Doctrina Christiana* to indicate the necessary procedure. There is in Plato, he points out, a rich vein of doctrinal gold to be extracted from the rock and sand of his intricate form. This was what was accomplished by the men we call the Neo-Platonists, by Philo and Numenius, Plotinus, Porphyry, and Iamblichus. The result was that they opened up to Christians not only Plato but "the primitive theologians" whom he had absorbed:

> The primitive theology of the Gentiles in which Zoroaster, Mercury, Orpheus, Aglaophemus, and Pythagoras are at one is to be found entire in the books of our Plato. In his letters Plato prophesies that these mysteries can be made plain to mankind only after many centuries. And that was what happened. For it was first in the time of Philo and Numenius that the thought of the primitive theologians, embodied in Plato's writings, began to be understood. That is to say, it was directly after the preachings of the apostles, and their writings. For the Platonists used the divine light of Christians for the interpretation of the divine Plato. This is the reason why Basil the Great and Augustine affirm that the Platonists plagiarized the mysteries of John the Evangelist. I myself have certainly found that the chief mystic doctrines of Numenius, Philo, Plotinus, Iamblichus, and Proclus were borrowed from John, from Paul, Hierotheus, and from Dionysius the Areopagite. All the magnificent things they said of the divine mind and the angels and other theological topics, were plainly borrowed thence.[1]

One cannot labor too much the significance of this conviction of Ficino's. Upon it rests the intellectual desire which transformed his life and Pico's, to synthesize a workable philosophy and theology out of pagan and Christian elements, in which reason occupies a position equal with faith, and religion is as a result made natural to man. This desire gives structure and depth, as well as an apologetic tone, to each of

Ficino's major works, his *Theologica Platonica* and *De Christiana Religione* and his commentaries on Plato's *Symposium* and *Philebus* and the *Enneads* of Plotinus.

Reason holds a high place in Ficino's synthesis, but it is only by an effort of the will that the ascent of mind and soul which is his goal is achieved. It is an ascent reminiscent of the soul's progress along Diotima's Ladder of Love in Plato's *Symposium,* of Dante's mounting to Paradise, and St. Paul's enraptured flight to the third heaven. In Ficino's life, a similar ascent may be traced, starting with the recapture of lost faith—aided, according to Ficino, by St. Augustine—rising through illness and recovery—with the help of the Virgin Mary, according to his own testimony—and ending in his ordination as a priest.

It is the guiding light of philosophy that makes such ascents possible:

> Since it is impossible to approach the celestial seats with a corporeal bulk, the Soul, taking thought as its guide, by the gift of philosophy, transcends through contemplation the nature of all things. So says Aristotle. Finally, to speak comprehensively, since philosophy is a celestial gift, it drives earthly vices far away, bravely subdues fortune, admirably softens fate, safely uses mortal gifts, abundantly offers immortal gifts . . . O sure guide of human life, who first defeats the monsters of vices entirely with the club of Hercules, then with the shield and spear of Pallas avoids or overcomes the dangers of fortune, and finally takes human Souls upon the shoulders of Atlas, frees them from this earthly exile, and returns them truly and happily to the celestial fatherland.
>
> To sum it up in a few words, philosophy is the ascent of the Soul from lower to higher things and from darkness to light; its cause is the instinct of the divine mind, its means and faculties the disciplines we have mentioned, its end the possession of the highest good, its fruit at last the right guidance of men.[2]

The function of the artist is essentially the same as that of the philosopher, to move from lower to higher things, and so to control his materials and himself that he rises from craftsmanship to contemplation. What the true artist achieves is, in the fullest sense of the word, proportion. An aesthetic constituent becomes an ontological one; the experience of the aesthetic object involves the true. Form is what pleases in beauty, proportion what pleases in form, number what pleases in proportion. This is Ficino's aesthetic doctrine, as it is Augustine's and Dante's, a doctrine of particular proportion based on universal number. The search for beauty becomes a quest of numerical proportion in all things until the mind of the artist has been freed from matter. Art is, then, the product of a contemplative activity which ends with the liberation of the soul.

In his *Oration on the Dignity of Man*, Pico entreats man to fulfill the contemplative function Ficino has outlined, to follow the rhetorical figure of the ladder to its logical end:

> let us fill our well-prepared and purified soul with the light of natural philosophy, so that we may at last perfect her in the knowledge of things divine. And lest we be satisfied with those of our faith, let us consult the patriarch Jacob, whose form gleams carved on the throne of glory. Sleeping in the lower world but keeping watch in the upper, the wisest of fathers will advise us. But he will advise us through a figure (in this way everything was wont to come to those men) that there is a ladder extending from the lowest earth to the highest heaven, divided in a series of many steps, with the Lord seated at the top, and angels in contemplation ascending and descending over them alternately by turns.

With "the art of discourse or reasoning" to equip us, we may become nothing less than "companions of the angels going up and down Jacob's ladder." Philosophical exercises, those of analysis, can bring us to the center of things. Theological activities, those of synthesis, can make us perfect:

using philosophy through the steps of the ladder, that is, of nature, and penetrating all things from center to center, we shall sometimes descend, with titanic force rending the unity like Osiris into many parts, and we shall sometimes ascend, with the force of Phoebus collecting the parts like the limbs of Osiris into a unity, until, resting at last in the bosom of the Father who is above the ladder, we shall be made perfect with the felicity of theology.

The dignity of man is Pico's concern. One approaches that dignity through many paths, he says; and all, if they bring us rest "at last in the bosom of the Father," are commendable. Approach through all those paths was the triumphant achievement of Pico in the nine hundred theses he published in Rome in December, 1486, along with an open invitation to scholars to public debate on any of them. Pico was only twenty-three then, but a marvelously learned and fearless young man, tutored in Ferrara, Padua, and Paris. Trained as philosopher and mathematician, skilled not only in the classical languages and in Hebrew but also in Arabic and Chaldean, he felt able to take on anyone in any of several dozen disciplines.

The reigning pope intervened; the debate was not held and Pico's theses were subjected to the scrutiny of a papal commission. He was found heretical in three of his nine hundred theses and variously unorthodox in ten others, no great failure on his part when one remembers that his searching geography of the mind of man had reached far beyond Christian lands to Islam, ancient Greece and Rome, Chaldea and the several countries in which the Hebrew of the Cabala was written.

The *Oration* is Pico's self-apologia. It was written as a speech to introduce the projected disputation and not published until after Pico's death. Its text is "the saying of Hermes

Trismegistus: 'A great miracle, O Asclepius, is man.'" Its purpose is a challenge to scholars, a call to battle: "Let us now join combat"—and "not," he adds, "without great pleasure." But it is a work of many parts, for all its brevity. The bellicose is only one of several tones Pico adopts in the course of his rhetorical masterpiece. He cozens. He wheedles. He pleads. He prays. He argues from authority. He appeals to the wisdom and learning of his listeners. He displays, "not without great pleasure," his own wide reading, demonstrating as he does so "the value and the dignity of the liberal arts" as they have been practised in non-Christian and Christian cultures. For chameleon man, as Pico calls him, under the generosity of God is graced with a self-transforming nature, the result of his free will:

> O supreme generosity of God the Father, O highest and most marvelous felicity of man! To him it is granted to have whatever he chooses, to be whatever he wills. Beasts as soon as they are born (so says Lucilius) bring with them from their mother's womb all they will ever possess. Spiritual beings, either from the beginning or soon thereafter, become what they are to be for ever and ever. On man when he came into life the Father conferred the seeds of all kinds and the germs of every way of life. Whatever seeds each man cultivates will grow to maturity and bear in him their own fruit. If they be vegetative, he will be like a plant. If sensitive, he will become brutish. If rational, he will grow into a heavenly being. If intellectual, he will be an angel and the son of God. And if, happy in the lot of no created thing, he withdraws into the center of his own unity, his spirit, made one with God, in the solitary darkness of God, who is set above all things, shall surpass them all.

Pico's tribute to the nature of man leads him through the ranks of the angels, each one of which he asks us to emulate: "Let us disdain earthly things, despise those of heaven, and abandoning everything of this world, hasten to that court which is beyond the world and closest to God." This in turn brings him, through Jacob and Job—for Pico's purposes companion figures—to the conflicts and contrasts of the life to which we are all heir: now up, now down, with only the branches of philosophy to soothe our troubled, our tumultuous, or angry nature:

These, reverend Fathers, are the considerations that have not only inspired but compelled me to the study of philosophy. I should certainly not set them forth were I not answering those who are wont to condemn the study of philosophy, especially among men of rank or even of a mediocre station in life. For this whole study of philosophy has now (and it is the misfortune of our age) come to despite and contumely rather than to honor and glory. Thus this deadly and monstrous conviction has come to pervade the minds of well-nigh all—that philosophy either must be studied not at all or by few persons, as if it were absolutely nothing to have clearly ascertained, before our eyes and before our hands, the cause of things, the ways of nature, the plan of the universe, the purposes of God, and the mysteries of heaven and earth; unless one may obtain some favor, or make money for one's self. Rather, it has come to the point where none is now deemed wise, alas, save those who make the study of wisdom a mercenary profession, and where it is possible to see the chaste Pallas, who was sent among men as the gift of the gods, hooted, hissed, and whistled off the stage; and not having anyone to love or to befriend her, unless by selling herself, as it were, she repays into the treasury of her "lover" even the ill-gained money received as the poor price of her tarnished virginity.

The harmony of ideas, to which the second half of the *Oration* is devoted, is not the vagabond assemblage of the uncommitted open mind of our time. Pico is no man's disciple, no school's follower, only wisdom's servitor. Is it possible that he can speak authoritatively of Schoolmen and Moslems, of Greeks of all epochs, of early Christians and earlier Chaldeans and Hebrews? "I have wished," Pico says, "to show by this contest of mine, not that I know many things, but that I know things of which many are ignorant." He knows beyond all else that "nothing moves one to religion and to the worship of God more than the persistent contemplation of the wonders of God." Always, these wonders, no matter where one finds them, are "the confirmation of the inviolable Catholic faith." Among such wonders, for Pico, are the books of the Cabala:

> When I had purchased these books at no small cost to myself, when I had read them through with the greatest diligence and with unwearying toil, I saw in them (as God is my witness) not so much the Mosaic as the Christian religion. There is the mystery of the Trinity, there the Incarnation of the Word, there the divinity of the Messiah; there I have read about original sin, its expiation through Christ, the heavenly Jerusalem, the fall of the devils, the orders of the angels, purgatory, and the punishments of hell, the same things we read daily in Paul and Dionysius, in Jerome and Augustine. But in those parts which concern philosophy you really seem to hear Pythagoras and Plato, whose principles are so closely related to the Christian faith that our Augustine gives immeasurable thanks to God that the books of the Platonists have come into his hands. Taken altogether, there is absolutely no controversy between ourselves and the Hebrews on any matter, with regard to which they cannot be refuted and gainsaid out of the cabalistic books, so that there will not be even a corner left in which they may hide themselves. I have as a most weighty witness of this fact that very learned man Antonius Chronicus who, when I was with him at a banquet, with his own ears heard Dactylus, a Hebrew trained in this lore, with all his heart agree entirely to the Christian idea of the Trinity.

Thus, Pico insists, all works of merit demonstrate the unity of truth, as all, one way or another, testify to the dignity of man. The argument is Augustine's and Boethius's and Gregory's and Thomas's, as well as that of the ancient Egyptians and of Pythagoras, of Plato and of Aristotle:

to make public the occult mysteries, the secrets of the supreme Godhead hidden beneath the shell of the Law and under a clumsy show of words—what else were this than to give a holy thing to dogs and to cast pearls before swine? Therefore to keep hidden from the people the things to be shared by the initiate, among whom alone, Paul says, he spoke wisdom, was not the part of human deliberation but of divine command. This custom the ancient philosophers most reverently observed, for Pythagoras wrote nothing except a few trifles, which he intrusted on his deathbed to his daughter Dama. The Sphinxes carved on the temples of the Egyptians reminded them that mystic doctrines should be kept inviolable from the common herd by means of the knots of riddles. Plato, writing certain things to Dion concerning the highest substances, said: "It must be stated in riddles, lest the letter should fall by chance into the hands of others and what I am writing to you should be apprehended by others." Aristotle used to say that his books of *Metaphysics*, in which he treated of things divine, were both published and not published. What further? Origen asserts that Jesus Christ, the Teacher of life, made many revelations to his disciples, which they were unwilling to write down lest they should become commonplaces to the rabble . . .[3]

It was Pico's great ambition, after having penetrated the mysteries and unravelled the knots, to bring all into accord. Ficino, playing on Pico's feudal title as Count of Concordia (Latin for "harmony" or "union"), wrote, "He is not only Count of Concord, he is its Lord and ruler, since he reconciles Jews with Christians, Aristotelians with Platonists, Greeks with Romans." Pico made his first attempt to reconcile Plato and Aristotle in his *De Ente et Uno*, *On Being and Unity*, the introduction to a massive work he did not live to complete. In one of his *Conclusiones*, he had already stated his thesis: that Plato and Aristotle did not differ in sense or substance on any question of philosophy or theology, however different their words might be.

No less than any of the Fathers, Pico was intent on lifting the veils of allegory, in Scripture and pagan works alike, to uncover the mystic senses of rhetorical figures and to show the unity concealed in them. His assimilation was wider and broader than the Fathers', if not so deep. He did not hesitate, for example, to use Cabalistic techniques along with traditional Christian exegesis in the *Heptaplus*, his commentary on the six days of creation as narrated in Genesis. The result is a work which brings everything of any significance in the world to root in the first twenty-seven verses of the first chapter of the first book of the Bible. All of nature, all of history, all of mystery—all is there. For justification of his method, Pico points to the large and illustrious numbers of hermetic works—to the Pythagoreans; to the myths, mathematical images, and other enigmatic veils with which "our Plato" hides his thoughts; to the indirections and obscurities of Scripture, which Scripture itself explains: "Thy words have I hidden in my heart," Psalm 118 sings, "that I may not sin against thee."

None of Pico's remaining works possesses the gusto and grandeur of the *Oration* or the breadth of the *Heptaplus*, except perhaps the symphony of sentences with which he offered to take on the whole world of scholarship. The world of scholarship? It was more, it was existence itself which this prodigious youngster, who died at the age of thirty-one, tried to embrace. He earnestly believed man's reach extended that far.

In the hierarchy of being which he describes in the fifth *expositio* of the *Heptaplus*, Pico makes man the unifying creature, linking heaven and earth, bringing peace or chaos to both as he finds one or the other in himself. When man falls from his proper place by sin, he says, the universe itself is shaken. That is why every creature abhors the crimes of men. That is why every angel exults with joy at the repentance of one sinner. When, in the last paragraph of the fifth part of the

Heptaplus, Pico writes that in our cause the Son of God became man and was crucified, he records not a pious sentiment but an awesome fact. Once again, his text is, "A great miracle, O Asclepius, is man."

Angelo Poliziano, the brilliant poet and scholar who was tutor to Lorenzo's sons, called Pico "the phoenix who rested in the laurel." To "the laurel," Lorenzo, Pico paid compliments just as felicitous and a good deal more obsequious. In several dedications and in a famous letter, Pico praises his great patron and protector for his wisdom, his versatility, and his fidelity to literature, discourse and meditation, even when most occupied in affairs of state. To these compliments, courtly but not unconventional, one cannot take exception. But when, in a letter written after receiving some poems from Lorenzo, he declares Dante and Petrarch Lorenzo's inferiors, one wonders if he has not moved from honest admiration to unbecoming flattery. If one disregards the more outrageous superlatives, however, one may find substance and good sense in Pico's praise. It is the modernity of Lorenzo's style that most impresses him, his economy of words, and his vigor. These things still impress one in Lorenzo's verse, and one must also still be impressed, as Pico and Poliziano and Ficino were, by the accomplishment of so much writing of quality on the part of so busy a statesman.

Lorenzo inherited his position as ruler of Florence. His grandfather Cosimo had established the city as Medici territory by creating city-wide prosperity. Lorenzo secured his position by a diplomacy of discourse and donation, talking some states out of war, bribing others, and surrounding Florence with powers so ingeniously balanced that war between them was unthinkable. Those whose confidence in Lorenzo was not won by his statesmanship were diverted by the entertainments he produced for the Florentines. And scholars and poets, librarians and linguists, philosophers and theologians, painters and sculptors and musicians were his most devoted followers. For he befriended them with a largesse appropriate to a *Magnifico;* he understood them; he admired them.

The intellectual life had always appealed to Lorenzo. At the age of sixteen he struck up a friendship with another gifted prince, Frederick of Naples. Before both had reached their majority or their thrones, they compiled together a collection of poems, the *Raccolta Aragonese.* As a youngster Lorenzo was instructed by the most versatile of men, Leon Battista Alberti, architect and architectural theorist, painter and painting theorist, moral philosopher and sociologist, athlete, military strategist, mathematician, musician, naturalist, inventor, and papal secretary. As a young man—but never an old one, for he died at the age of forty-three—Lorenzo surrounded himself with men of like quality and made Florence the center of art and philosophy, unequalled in its time except by the group Lorenzo's son, Pope Leo X, gathered around him in Rome thirty years later. To his country villa at Careggi or a monastery in the forest of Camaldoli, Lorenzo took his circle of intimates for discussions, disputations, and deliberations. The level of speculation was not always the highest, but the brows were, for the speculators included Pico, Poliziano, and Ficino, Luigi Pulci and Matteo Palmieri, Alberti and Christoforo Landino. In his garden in Florence, Lorenzo gathered together a representative set of plaster casts of classical sculpture and organized an atelier for the study of the art, to which Michelangelo came as a boy. Verrocchio did much of his major sculpture and Botticelli a fair portion of his painting for Lorenzo. And he commissioned, as well, paintings by Ghirlandaio, Filippino Lippi, Luca di Signorelli, Andrea del Castagno, Baldovinetti and the Pollaiuoli.

With such men around him, Lorenzo could have been pardoned for limiting his performances to appreciations or imitations. But far from being a writer of the second rank, he was a master of clipped and concise statement, a virtuoso versifier, a natural poet. He produced no long poem of any kind, no epic, no sonnet sequence. But he did lift his voice in loving verses to a blessed intercessor, Lucrezia Donati—interestingly enough, a descendent of Dante's wife. And he did write a gloss on forty-one of his 163 love poems, the *Comento del Magnifico Lorenzo de' Medici sopra alcuni de' suoi sonetti,* which compares favorably with the work which inspired it, Dante's celebrated exposition of his own verses called *La Vita Nuova, The New Life.*

Several kinds of new life, linguistic and literary, philosophical and theological, are examined thoughtfully and defended at length in Lorenzo's *Comento.* To begin with, the Tuscan tongue spoken in Florence is proposed as the right and natural one for Italian writers. It possesses all the marks, he says, of a literary language of dignity. It is adaptable to conceptual thinking. It has "sweetness and harmony" and has been used by such great writers as Dante, Guido Cavalcanti, Petrarch, and Boccaccio for the expression of ideas at once "subtle, grave, and necessary to human life." It has an honorable past and deserves the support of "good citizens" that it may have as auspicious a future. Whether it was Lorenzo's patriotic appeal, the good sense of his argument, or the intrinsic merits of the language itself, his view prevailed. After him, no one again questioned the propriety of writing in the Italian vernacular.

In defense of the sonnet form, Lorenzo lists the qualities which recommend his own verse. At its best, he points out, the sonnet has an epigrammatic brevity. It can be used for either serious or light subjects, but preferably should be restricted to one idea at a time, expressed simply, clearly, and without harshness or obscurity. Finally, the fact that its rhyme scheme makes it the most difficult of vernacular forms makes it also the most worthy of praise.

Language and verse-form occupy Lorenzo only as a preface to his *Comento*. The bulk of the work is concerned with the development of his sonnets after the death of a gentle lady and his own subsequent growth in the life of the spirit. The development of both the poetry and the poet makes an absorbing tale and a fresh one. Whatever it owes to Dante's *Vita Nuova*, it is a work of considerable profundity and very much Lorenzo's own.

The *Comento* is in substance a meditation on death. All of the verses upon which Lorenzo constructs his first gloss deal with the lady *in morte*, in death. None is a poem written *in vita*, during the life of the *gentildonna*, as in Dante's sequence. Lorenzo's love, and thus his poetry, lead him as far as possible from the things of this world: "The beginning of a true life is the death of an untrue one." With these words, Lorenzo comes to the four sonnets with which he mourns the passing of the lady and establishes the principle of his whole work, that death marks a beginning, not an end.

For the purposes of Lorenzo's allegory, death is made an unmistakable beginning and not an end: the first lady is replaced by a second and even more fetching one, whom Lorenzo meets at one of the entertainments he himself instituted for the delectation of the Florentines. But actually both ladies are personifications. The first represents the beauty of this world, of which one must take leave; the second, the beauty of the next, to which one should look forward. To attempt to fit either figure literally into Lorenzo's life, as so many commentators on the *Comento* have done, is to reduce the work unjustifiably to commonplaces. Through both sonnets and commentary, Lorenzo does everything possible to establish the spiritual combat as the subject, not only of these verses, but of all his writing. He does so by adding to all the other levels of meaning of his commentary one in which the poems themselves, as poems, stand for his retreats from pomp and vainglory. Thus at the very center of the *Comento* appears this sonnet of Lorenzo's:

Let him who wishes seek pomp and honor, follow
  Bright esplanades and temples and great halls,
  Seek precious things, gold, everything that calls
  For thousand worries, thousand-fold of sorrow.
A verdant meadow full of lovely flowers,
  A rivulet that bathes the grassy earth,
  A little bird who pours love's lament forth,
  These win much rather all my deepest ardors:
The shady woods, the rocks, some lofty hill,
  The darksome caves, the wild beasts fugitive,
  Some light-foot nymph who trembles in her fear.
There with my wandering thoughts I see at will
  Beautiful lights that shine as though alive;
  Something or other drives them from me here.[4]

The point of these lines, well enough known to Italians, though usually out of context, is made clear by Lorenzo's commentary: the sweetness of the imagination has something in common with man's true beatitude, which leads the soul to eternity, but only through the direct contemplation of divine goodness. This, Lorenzo says, is the significant contemplation, the true one, not that vain use of the imagination which whets only mortal appetites. But any innocent exercise of the contemplative faculties may have in it an abiding sweetness and something of perfect happiness. That is the meaning of Lorenzo's seeking refuge in the country.

The pre-eminent image in Lorenzo's poetry is the fleeing poet. In the *Comento*, he moves from one lady to another, from one love to another, from one world to another. In one sonnet, he casts himself as Lot fearfully retreating from Sodom. In other works, sometimes with only the faintest allegorical meaning, sometimes with a blatant one, he leaves the city for the country, relinquishing humdrum human cares for the beauties of nature, and replacing empty exercises of the imagination with the direct contemplation of divine goodness. The descriptions of nature are handsome enough in themselves: the change of seasons, the life of the peasant, the colors and sounds and movements of the people, the animals, the flowers and the trees of the Tuscan landscape.

There are few complications, though many beautifully turned lines, in Lorenzo's pastoral poetry, in his miscellanies of love, and in his carnival songs. There are few puzzles but much pleasure in such classical effusions as the *Amori di Venere e Marte*, *The Loves of Venus and Mars*, or in the country feast which Lorenzo makes of a day's falconry in *La Caccia col Falcone*. There are some consistent themes of a minor order in all these poems, such as the plaintive nocturne which opens his first eclogue, *Corinto*, or the *carpe diem* note which Lorenzo rings so authentically in the last line of the same work,

> *Cogli la rosa, o Ninfa, quando e il tempo.*
> Gather ye rosebuds, O Nymph, while ye may.

The full blossom of his philosophical flower is not visible in such writings, however. That is the function of the six *capitoli* or "chapters" of *L'Altercazione*.

A fine mixture of philosophical disputation and contemplative calm gives *L'Altercazione* its affecting tone. The poem moves with Lorenzo from "the rough tempest" of city life to a pastoral scene, where he meets a shepherd who is astonished to see him there. So is Marsilio Ficino, whom he meets next.

Lorenzo asks Marsilio to identify true happiness for him and to tell him where he may find it. Ficino sends him far beyond this world, away from the caprices of cruel Fortune, away from all worldly professions and even from "the spectacle of beautiful heavenly sights," for these are not the highest good. Ficino explains that man's beatitude lies in the separation of the soul from the body, not in order to reach the circles of the angels, but to fly to God. This is achieved, as those who know Ficino might expect, by an effort of the will rather than of the intellect:

> The soul intent on knowing God
> profits little by long quest;
> he who loves Him soon finds joy.

Lorenzo does find joy in Ficino's words:

> My heart was so filled with sweetness,
> that hearing him I felt drawn
> to the Good that his words described.

Finally, in the last *capitolo*, Lorenzo offers up a prayer to God, like the concluding tercets of Dante's *Paradiso*, rich in plays on the words for light—"*lume*," and "*luce*,"—and the effects of light—"*vista*," "*splende*," and "*splendor*." The prayer continues for 205 lines, illuminating concepts and dogmas as it goes—immortality, amplitude, sublimity, strength, the *summum bonum*, joy, wisdom, grace, charity, mercy, the Trinity.

In Lorenzo's other *capitoli*, the points of departure vary, but in each case the measure is *terza rima* and the message is to prepare for the celestial ascent by putting off the encumbrances of the body. In one, he bids himself

> Think of the dignity of thy intellect,
> not given you to pursue earthly things,
> but because it has heaven for its object.

In another he offers a friend comfort on the death of his young daughter:

death is the mortal road
to the spotless age, the pure, the clean;
life is in leaving every confinement of life.

In the five *capitoli* which are invocations to God, he praises God's eternal government, describes the chain of being, pictures God's power, and sings two sacred songs of the exultant kind he wrote as lauds to the Virgin and to Christ. The tone of these *rime spirituali* is that of his *Rappresentazione di San Giovanni e Paolo*, a tender, sometimes agreeable, sometimes tedious morality play based on the lives of two brothers martyred in Rome under Julian the Apostate. The best of Lorenzo is more indirect, as in the *Comento*, or the country poems, or *L'Altercazione*, or that strange, not quite successful but haunting satire, *I Beoni*. The full title of the work, *Simposio ovvero I Beoni*, *The Symposium, or the Drunkards*, indicates what it is, a satire directed at the Florentine Platonists. The poem opens with a description of the time of year, autumn. Lorenzo is returning to Florence. As he approaches the Faenza gate, he notices great crowds rushing along the road. Among them he finds a good friend, Bartolino, whom he asks to explain the hurrying crowd. Bartolino tells him that all are going to the bridge at Rifredi, where a cask of wine has been tapped.

Bartolino identifies several companions for Lorenzo, all united in their thirst. Lorenzo asks, "Who is the one with the rosy cheeks? And the two with him, with the long gowns?" Bartolino answers, "The fattest is the rector of Antella . . . The other in back, with the sweet smile and the strange pointed nose, is from Fiesole; he has made of drink his paradise." The third, he explains, is the Fiesolan's curate, Ser Antonio.

Lorenzo meets another friend, Adovardo, and greets him, but Adovardo protests, "I am no longer Adovardo, but

Thirst . . ." Adovardo offers a scholastic argument for his metamorphosis, concluding:

> and as Antaeus renewed his strength
> by falling onto the earth—so the story goes—
> so does my thirst, through drink, become greater thirst.

Adovardo is a humanist and a courtier: he has "*un bel dubbio*," a lovely puzzle, to offer; and pleases himself by making his neat classical reference to Antaeus. The *Symposium* becomes, as Plato's banquet finally does too, a drunken revel, in which all the Florentine company turn from the wine of the chalice to the wine of the barrel. Lorenzo pokes vigorous fun at doctrinaire Platonists who take too literally Plato's description of the infusion of matter with form in a passage describing the violent sneeze of a drunkard:

> When the humor of that fiery spittle
> reached the ground, in the dry dust
> moisture and heat were united as one:
> and then that perfection that comes from on high
> gave the dust spirit, and a frog was born,
> and right before our eyes it leaped.

Bartolino describes the company in detail:

> The third of those that you saw here
> had some beginnings of theology anyhow,
> and put on learned airs with his friends;
> he had learned that the greatest punishment
> that our Saviour suffered on earth
> was when upon the cross he cried, "I thirst!"

This is astringent satire, not blasphemy—except on the part of the man thus described. It is a thrust delivered at the vanity of the intellect, the target of most of the satire in *I Beoni*. This is the wine at the banquet turned sour. These are men who have lost all sense of direction. Where are they going?

To Rifredi, to drink. And why? Because they thirst. But their thirst is entirely of the flesh—or at least so they think; they have no concept of spiritual thirst.

Finally, the crowd is assembled at the bridge. Lorenzo pictures a considerable variety of the men who are there: lame, halt, one-legged, bleary-eyed, some with dropsy, some with faces rosy as cherubim, some with twisted eyebrows, some with diseased noses. At the end they turn to each other, but to no avail:

> There were some disposed
> to talk to their neighbors; but the rising and
> swelling of the crowd dragged them off to separate points.

There the manuscript breaks off; some commentators think that the rest of it is lost, more think Lorenzo never returned to it after this point. My suggestion is that the irony here was intended, that this is the final irony: they have turned from everything to wine, and now they have nothing. Driven by physical desire, they are physically unable to communicate, even with their nearest neighbor. All that is left is thirst. Their greatest punishment is to thirst, and all the more the more they drink.

For Lorenzo and his circle, too, all that was left was thirst, but their thirst was of a different kind, and there is every indication in their works that their thirst was appeased.

CHAPTER X

Shakespeare and St. John of the Cross: De Contemptu Mundi

Sometime in the middle of the twelfth century, Bernard, a monk of Cluny, addressed a series of verses to his abbot on his contempt for the world, *De Contemptu Mundi.* Packed with interior rhymes and charging to banging couplet endings, the long poem seems almost cheerful as it records the iniquities of this world. Judgment is at hand; heaven or hell lies in wait:

> Hora novissima, tempora pessima sunt, vigilemus,
> Ecce minaciter imminet arbiter ille supremus . . .
>
> The world is very evil; the times are waxing late;
> Be sober and keep vigil; the Judge is at the gate.

There are signs of doom enough, Bernard laments vigorously, auguries of all sorts. The sky lights up with ugliness; monsters are born among us. Society is sick from top to bottom; every order, every estate, men and women, laity and clergy. Learning is corrupt. Our bishops spend more time hunting than praying, and in Rome everything is bought and sold. There is nothing left but to get down on your knees and pray: it is later than you think.

Shakespeare is not often quite so simple-minded in his denunciation of the sins of men. But if one seeks a single frame into which all his pictures fit, this is it, the frame of disorder. For him, too, *tempora pessima sunt,* the time is out of joint. And he too, much of the time, seems to take pleasure in listing all the "foul and pestilent congregation of vapours" he finds in the air about him. Shakespeare was a Renaissance man, a sixteenth-century man, and like Lorenzo de Medici and many of his own most gifted contemporaries, an uneasy man. He did not like his own world, not at least what he saw was happening to it. He urged his audiences to meditation on their losses. He urged them as an artist urges: by example, the example of his own meditation, the parables provided by his musings; by his allegories: the amusements, and the debilitating, depressing, debauching tragedies that could turn one bitter, as from time to time they seemed to turn Shakespeare. But there is hope in Shakespeare as well as contempt, hope for the world, hope for man. It is not to be found, however, by those who come to Shakespeare merely to admire. Hope prevails in Shakespeare, as in the world, only after patient search and painful experience and often at the edge of despair.

In reading Shakespeare, with that special vigilance that is the corollary of humility, we must refuse to hold him up as the mirror of our own nature or of our own time. He was describing his time, not ours. We must not make Shakespeare over into Sigmund Freud or Karl Marx, on the one hand, or into a defender of all that is brave and bright and pure in a Christian democracy, on the other. He was a Christian, but hardly a democrat. But he was devoutly concerned to probe the inner workings of society, even as Marx; and he was at least as discerning a destructive analyst. And the insides of human psyches interested him at least as much as they do a modern psychoanalyst. What is more, even as Freud, he found a cesspool beneath the cranium and, like the Viennese commissioner of insanitation, he described at length what he found floating there.

But he did all of this in a different way from the moderns; his tools were very different from ours. Whatever his education—and it seems fairly clear from the plays and the few documents we have that it was not much more than seven years of study at the Stratford Grammar School—his tools had to be those of the late Middle Ages. He learned his letters with a hornbook, matching his grasp of the alphabet with the knowledge that he, like all children, was full of the devil. He probably learned his Latin from sixteenth-century grammars and collections of sententious phrases based on medieval sources. He undoubtedly found his rhetoric and logic in Cicero, his numbers in Boethius, his geometry in Euclid, his moral philosophy in Seneca, and his theology in Peter Lombard, or in redactions and recensions of these masters as well as Aristotle, Augustine, and Thomas Aquinas. He certainly found his share of entertaining classical tales in Aesop and Ovid and Homer and neo-classical narratives at least as amusing in Boccaccio and Chaucer. He may have dipped into the Greek New Testament; he certainly knew Jerome's Vulgate. He may have studied some Plato; he certainly had at least that passing knowledge of the Fathers and the Schoolmen that compilations like Erasmus's *Adagia* would provide.

How much of this do we have to know to understand Shakespeare? Enough to protect ourselves from that remorseless philistinism that almost pridefully misunderstands the allegorical or emblematic conception of nature of Shakespeare, of the Elizabethans, and of the Renaissance. Theirs was a somewhat fuller, slightly more scientific version of medieval cosmology, natural philosophy, and metaphysics. But all the disciplines, for them as for their medieval predecessors, were founded on the palpable unity of the design of nature, of all things, of all creatures, of the universe itself.

It is not a difficult cosmology to understand. Essentially it is a system of analogies erected on this unity of all created things at their divine source. From that source they all come; to it they all go back. This is as true of ideas as of fleshly things, of the world of the spirit as of the world of matter. All things, as a result, are related, at least by the analogy of being. When a poet chooses to make a flower stand for an idea, it is not simply because of an emblematic convention, but rather because there is a genuine correspondence between the two. Even the animals of fancy fit into the scheme, as the phoenix, for example, provides a bold image of the Resurrection. By their appeal to the sense of sight, such images make abstractions seem concrete and vivid, and hence easier to understand and more convincing. In this respect, the cosmology of the sixteenth century can be reduced to one primary function: to persuade.

Elizabethan rhetoric had a similar design: it was the translation into a verbal system of this system of values, step by step, using the memory and every logical device, using the shrewd and one hoped just disposition of parts, of voice and gesture and literary style, for one purpose—to persuade. In Shakespeare's time, the yield of the design was a galaxy of over three hundred figures of speech which gave to the work of even the least talented writer surfaces that sparkled, and to the work of the most gifted a depth properly suggestive of eternity.

Put Shakespeare into this context and one sees depth; one finds a multiplicity of meanings, as he and all his contemporaries clearly intended one should. Then bitterness, cynicism, degradation, and debauchery, even these, fall into place somewhere among the topics of invention, disposition and disputation. As the ugliness of hell fell into place in the ordered beauty of the universe for Dante, they fit in somewhere among the classifications of genus and species, definition, and division, consequents and antecedents, and become part of the extraordinary apparatus of investigation of Shakespeare, which is fitting not only for the sixteenth century or the Renaissance, but for all time.

All of this suggests a central part of Shakespeare's personality, his much heralded objectivity. He was able as a poet to proceed with something like the balance, the peace, and the serenity necessary to examine man in general and individual men and women as well, one at a time. He could assert that calm in the face of harrowing tragedy without which a universal viewpoint is impossible: thus the clarity and the control and the refusal to be overwhelmed by disaster; thus the refusal to yield to sentimental connivance with his characters on the one hand or annihilating judgments on the other.

Shakespeare saw much, and much of what he saw was not pretty: façades, disguises, every sort of dishonesty and deception. From the very beginning, he portrays a world of disguise in his plays. There are recognition scenes to strip the costumes and unmask the pretense, but only the first suggestion of true revelation. That comes much later with the mature Shakespeare, the Shakespeare of the problem plays and the great tragedies, the Shakespeare who seems savagely bitter and so much of the time without hope.

Man falls in love and fails in love. Man finds cures for the ills of society and finds his cures bring more ills—that is the fairly consistent program of Shakespeare's comedies and tragedies and histories. What is more, it is a pattern unrelieved by anything but a fairly cynical humor and a few moments of tenderness until the spleen seems to be nearly vented with the problem plays, *Troilus and Cressida, Measure for Measure, All's Well That Ends Well,* and *Hamlet.* How could there be any malice left after such a venting of venom?

What does love amount to, then, in the early plays? At the very least it is changeable and unreliable, as the name of that ungentlemanly gentleman of Verona, Proteus, indicates. At the worst, in the history plays, it is cruel and spotted by a venality that suggests every sort of human failure: there is no relationship that deserves the name of love in the three parts of *Henry VI, Richard III,* or *King John.* In-between, what is there? There is the fat body of a kitchen wench, "spherical, like a globe," which Antipholus and Dromio describe, country by country, in *The Comedy of Errors.* There is the rough and tumble dialogue of *Love's Labour's Lost* and *The Taming of the Shrew,* the somewhat more subdued exchanges of *The Merchant of Venice* and *As You Like It,* and there is the bludgeoning sexuality of the Falstaff plays—*1 and 2 Henry IV, Henry V,* and *The Merry Wives of Windsor*—and *Much Ado About Nothing* in which Shakespeare constructs a physiology of love altogether without equal for candor and coarseness in the literature of the West.

Love falls somewhere between dalliance and debauchery in these plays. When it is neither of these, but a kind of innocuous sport, as in *Midsummer Night's Dream* or *Twelfth Night,* it is very hard to take love seriously, for the lovers are merely stock figures. But Shakespeare's low estimate of man is not lost as a result: we know it well in the anti-sentimental strains of the *Dream*—the rifts in fairyland and the parody of Pyramus and Thisbe—and in the attack on the Puritans in the person of Malvolio in *Twelfth Night.* In *Romeo and Juliet,* we must take love seriously, for this is indeed a tragedy, a tragedy of the fleshly appetites, like Shakespeare's early long poems, *Venus and Adonis,* and *The Rape of Lucrece.* In the play of the star-crossed lovers, everything proclaims the ascendancy of the flesh—from the opening lines of the play, as bawdy a curtain-rising as is to be found in any drama, through every passage in which Mercutio or the Nurse participates. When Romeo's early affairs are discussed, the tone is venereal. When Romeo and Juliet meet, they talk in sonnets: a meretricious attraction is expressed artifically. Friar Laurence forgets his priestly duties; marries the lovers hastily, without significant inquiry; and worse, stoops to love potions in his eagerness to circumvent the prince's edict and to unite the feuding families, an eagerness, it is all too evident, motivated by personal ambition. There is still in Shakespeare's version of the much-told story, however muted, the atmosphere of its principal source, Arthur Brooke's *The Tragicall Historye of Romeus and Juliet:*

As eche flower yeldeth hony to the bee: so every exaumple ministreth good lessons, to the well disposed mynde. The glorious triumphe of the continent man upon the lustes of wanton fleshe, incourageth men to honest restraynt of wyld affections, the shamefull and wretched endes of such, as have yelded their libertie thrall to fowle desires, teache men to witholde them selves from the hedlong fall of loose dishonestie. So, to lyke effect, by sundry meanes, the good mans exaumple byddeth men to be good, and the evill mans mischefe, warneth men not to be evyll. To this good ende, serve all ill endes, of yll begynnynges. And to this ende (good Reader) is this tragicall matter written, to describe unto thee a coople of unfortunate lovers, thralling themselves to unhonest desire, neglecting the authoritie of parents and frendes, conferring their principall counsels with dronken gossypps, and superstitious friers (the naturally fitte instrumentes of unchastitie) attempting all adventures of peryll, for thattaynyng of their wishes lust, usyng auriculer confession (the kay of whoredome, and treason) for furtheraunce of theyr purpose, abusyng the honorable name of lawefull mariage, the cloke the shame of stolne contracts, finallye, by all meanes of unhonest lyfe, hastyng to most unhappye deaths.

Do the affairs of state run more smoothly? They do, finally, in *Henry V*, after a throne has been usurped (*Richard II*) and a prince has been educated by thieves and liars and drunkards (Falstaff and Bardolph, Pistol and Poins in *1 and 2 Henry IV*), entertaining, affable fellows all, but clearly based on medieval figures of vice and not meant to be emulated or imitated or even approved. Nothing runs smoothly in the other history plays—nothing but "Commodity, this bawd, this broker, this all-changing word," that is, expediency and self-interest, the trader and traitor, buyer and seller of everything in this world. "Mad world! mad kings! mad composition!"

the Bastard exclaims in *King John*. The world of Shakespeare's kings is mad; it is a world in which

> that same purpose-changer, that sly devil,
> That broker that still breaks the pate of faith,
> That daily break-vow, he that wins of all,
> Of kings, of beggars, old men, young men, maids,
> Who, having no external thing to lose
> But the word "maid," cheats the poor maid of that—
> That smooth-fac'd gentleman, tickling Commodity,
> Commodity, the bias of the world—
> The world, who of itself is peised well,
> Made to run even upon even ground
> Till this advantage, this vile drawing bias,
> This sway of motion, this Commodity,
> Makes it take head from all indifferency,
> From all direction, purpose, course, intent . . .
> (II, i, 561)

There is some honesty in this mad world, but it is a cynical honesty and even a bitter one. The Bastard, the play's hero and after a twisted fashion Shakespeare's as well, makes that clear:

> And why rail I on this Commodity?
> But for because he hath not woo'd me yet:
> Not that I have the power to clutch my hand
> When his fair angels would salute my palm,
> But for my hand, as unattempted yet,
> Like a poor beggar, raileth on the rich.
> Well, whiles I am a beggar, I will rail
> And say there is no sin but to be rich;
> And being rich, my virtue then shall be
> To say there is no vice but beggary.
> Since kings break faith upon commodity,
> Gain, be my lord, for I will worship thee!
> (II, i, 587)

The tone of the problem plays is anticipated by *The Merchant of Venice.* Here is a sweet exercise in tolerance, in mercy and justice. In it, after all of Shylock's injustices and Portia's high-sounding rhetoric about the quality of mercy, the Jew's baptism is forced on him, while one of the good Christians explains the sacrament to him:

> In christening thou shalt have two godfathers;
> Had I been judge, thou shouldst have had ten more,
> To bring thee to the gallows, not the font.
>
> (IV, i, 398)

All the Christians leave the stage chuckling merrily about their bawdy deceptions, and the same good man whose theology includes baptism by the gallows shows in the last lines of the play how superficial his values really are, by promising that

> while I live I'll fear no other thing
> So sore as keeping safe Nerissa's ring.
>
> (V, i, 306)

The point of the play is the point of all of Shakespeare's early texts: disguise—which is to say, hypocrisy—cloaks men's actions, deception rules, and vice parades as virtue. Bassanio says just that at the crossroads where so much is said in Shakespeare's plays, in the middle of the middle act:

> So may the outward shows be least themselves;
> The world is still deceiv'd with ornament.
> In law, what plea so tainted and corrupt
> But, being season'd with a gracious voice,
> Obscures the show of evil? In religion,
> What damned error but some sober brow
> Will bless it, and approve it with a text,
> Hiding the grossness with fair ornament?

> There is no vice so simple but assumes
> Some mark of virtue on his outward parts.
> (III, ii, 73)

Merely human love, love of the flesh, is the great deceiver in almost all of Shakespeare's plays, as it is in the narrative poems and many of the sonnets: "Past reason hunted, and no sooner had, Past reason hated . . ." Sonnet 129 is Shakespeare's succinct summary of "lust in action":

> Th' expense of spirit in a waste of shame
> Is lust in action; and till action, lust
> Is perjur'd, murd'rous, bloody, full of blame,
> Savage, extreme, rude, cruel, not to trust;
> Enjoy'd no sooner but despised straight;
> Past reason hunted, and no sooner had,
> Past reason hated, as a swallowed bait
> On purpose laid to make the taker mad;
> Mad in pursuit, and in possession so;
> Had, having, and in quest to have, extreme;
> A bliss in proof–and prov'd, a very woe;
> Before, a joy propos'd; behind, a dream.
> All this the world well knows; yet none knows well
> To shun the heaven that leads men to this hell.

Who are thus deceived? Troilus by Cressida, Ophelia by Hamlet, Desdemona by Othello and Othello by his own imagination, Antony and Cleopatra by each other and the Roman world by both: "Mad in pursuit, and in possession. . . . Had, having. . . . Before, a joy proposed; behind, a dream."

Shakespeare never tires of making his point, a large one, much larger than the mere deceptions and dissimulations of the flesh. It is a point sustained by rhetoric and explained by analogy. In the cosmology of correspondences, no more obvious set exists than that which compares marriage to the state and both to the planets. Disorder in any one of these may not only reflect but enjoin disorder in the others. The principle is established in Ulysses' great speech, delivered in *Troilus and Cressida* to the leaders of the Greeks, on the failure of those in his camp to maintain order. Degree is not observed, proportion has been upset. The parallels are many, the implications broad. It is an argument by analogy:

> The heavens themselves, the planets, and this centre
> Observe degree, priority, and place,
> Insisture, course, proportion, season, form,
> Office, and custom, in all line of order;
> And therefore is the glorious planet Sol
> In noble eminence enthron'd and spher'd
> Amidst the other, whose med'cinable eye
> Corrects the ill aspects of planets evil
> And posts, like the commandment of a king,
> Sans check, to good and bad. But when the planets
> In evil mixture to disorder wander,
> What plagues and what portents, what mutiny,
> What raging of the sea, shaking of earth,
> Commotion in the winds! Frights, changes, horrors
> Divert and crack, rend and deracinate
> The unity and married calm of states
> Quite from their fixure! O, when degree is shak'd,
> Which is the ladder to all high designs,
> Then enterprise is sick! How could communities,
> Degrees in schools and brotherhoods in cities,
> Peaceful commerce from dividable shores,
> The primogenity and due of birth,
> Prerogative of age, crowns, sceptres, laurels,
> But by degree, stand in authentic place?
> Take but degree away, untune that string,
> And hark what discord follows! Each thing meets
> In mere oppugnancy. The bounded waters
> Should lift their bosoms higher than the shores
> And make a sop of all this solid globe;

Strength should be lord of imbecility,
And the rude son should strike his father dead;
Force should be right; or rather, right and wrong
(Between whose endless jar justice resides)
Should lose their names, and so should justice too.
Then everything includes itself in power,
Power into will, will into appetite;
And appetite, an universal wolf,
So doubly seconded with will and power,
Must make perforce an universal prey,
And last eat up himself.

(I, iii, 85)

When Kate, in the last scene of *The Taming of the Shrew*, scolds her sister and an attendant widow for their stubborn refusal to acknowledge their wifely duties, she composes a gloss on marriage as a state and the husband as king and governor:

Thy husband is thy lord, thy life, thy keeper,
Thy head, thy sovereign; one that cares for thee
And for thy maintenance; commits his body
To painful labour both by sea and land,
To watch the night in storms, the day in cold,
Whilst thou li'st warm at home, secure and safe;
And craves no other tribute at thy hands
But love, fair looks, and true obedience–
Too little payment for so great a debt.
Such duty as the subject owes the prince,
Even such a woman oweth to her husband;
And when she is froward, peevish, sullen, sour,
And not obedient to his honest will,
What is she but a foul contending rebel
And graceless traitor to her loving lord?
I am asham'd that women are so simple
To offer war where they should kneel for peace;

Or seek for rule, supremacy, and sway
When they are bound to serve, love, and obey.
(V, ii, 146)

It is, the former shrew reminds her listeners, a proper distribution of responsibilities: women are fitted by nature for their roles; to think otherwise is to be deceived:

Why are our bodies soft and weak and smooth,
Unapt to toil and trouble in the world,
But that our soft conditions and our hearts
Should well agree with our external parts?
Come, come, you froward and unable worms!
My mind hath been as big as one of yours,
My heart as great, my reason haply more,
To bandy word for word and frown for frown;
But now I see our lances are but straws,
Our strength as weak, our weakness past compare.
That seeming to be most which we indeed least are.
(165)

When Duke Vincentio names Angelo to replace him as Lord of Vienna in *Measure for Measure*, he has, he says of his deputy,

Lent him our terror, dress'd him with our love,
And given his deputation all the organs
Of our own power.
(I, i, 20)

Angelo is no longer an ordinary man; he now has the strength of a giant, the authority of a Lord, of a Jove. But he abuses his authority and metes out justice without mercy. Isabella, Shakespeare's—and mercy's and justice's—spokesman in the play, protests:

Could great men thunder
As Jove himself does, Jove would ne'er be quiet,
For every pelting petty officer

Would use his heaven for thunder—nothing but thunder!
Merciful heaven,
Thou rather with thy sharp and sulphurous bolt
Split'st the unwedgeable and gnarled oak
Than the soft myrtle. But man, proud man,
Drest in a little brief authority,
Most ignorant of what he's most assur'd
(His glassy essence), like an angry ape,
Plays such fantastic tricks before high heaven
As make the angels weep; who, with our spleens,
Would all themselves laugh mortal.

(II, ii, 110)

Angelo's glassy essence cracks. He is sorely tempted by Isabella—a gross temptation indeed, for she is a novice of "The votarists of Saint Clare." He recognizes his own guilt, and translates it rhetorically from a figure of sexual transgression to one of sacrilege:

What's this? what's this? Is this her fault, or mine?
The tempter, or the tempted, who sins most, ha?
Not she. Nor doth she tempt. But it is I
That, lying by the violet in the sun,
Do as the carrion does, not as the flow'r,
Corrupt with virtuous season. Can it be
That modesty may more betray our sense
Than woman's lightness? Having waste ground enough,
Shall we desire to raze the sanctuary,
And pitch our evils there?

(163)

But, pompous man and Puritan that he is, the image he retains of himself is still that of a saint!

O cunning enemy, that, to catch a saint
With saints dost bait thy hook! Most dangerous
Is that temptation that doth goad us on
To sin in loving virtue. Never could the strumpet,

With all her double vigour—art and nature—
Once stir my temper; but this virtuous maid
Subdues me quiet. Ever till now,
When men were fond, I smil'd, and wond'red how.
(180)

Angelo falls. He tries to seduce Isabella, the crime for which he has sentenced her brother to death, promising her, if she yields, her brother's freedom. Now not only mercy has departed from Vienna, but justice as well, not to return until both can come back to the city with the Duke. When there is corruption—disorder—deception—at the center, then they must be general; society must be corrupt, disordered, and crowded with deceivers.

And so the corruption spreads, through Hamlet's Denmark and the France and Italy of that perfect inversion of the noble courtier, the very model of indecency, Bertram in *All's Well That Ends Well*. It gets worse. At the personal level it makes Desdemona easy prey for Othello's tall tales, recited first to please her father and then to woo her:

Her father lov'd me, oft invited me;
Still question'd me the story of my life
From year to year—the battles, sieges, fortunes
That I have pass'd.
I ran it through, even from my boyish days
To th' very moment that he bade me tell it.
Wherein I spake of most disastrous chances,
Of moving accidents by flood and field;
Of hairbreadth scapes i' th' imminent deadly breach;
Of being taken by the insolent foe
And sold to slavery; of my redemption thence
And portance in my travel's history;
Wherein of anters vast and deserts idle,
Rough quarries, rocks, and hills whose heads touch heaven,
It was my hint to speak—such was the process,

And of the Cannibals that each other eat,
The Antropophagi, and men whose heads
Do grow beneath their shoulders. This to hear
Would Desdemona seriously incline . . .

(I, iii, 128)

It turns Macbeth loose for damnation, along with Lear's daughters Regan and Goneril, with Iago, with Hamlet's uncle —all those whose appetite for power is insatiable and who go to their deaths unsated and unrepentant. It is the devil's appetite:

Then everything includes itself in power
Power into will, will into appetite;
And appetite, an universal wolf,
So doubly seconded with will and power,
Must make perforce an universal prey,
And last eat up himself.

The stench of corruption is almost unbearable in the brothel scene in *Pericles* (IV, i) in which a pimp boasts to a procuress, who has dispatched him on the town to cry the qualities of the play's heroine:

I warrant you, mistress, thunder shall not so awake the beds of eels as my giving out her beauty stirs up the lewdly inclined. I'll bring home some tonight.

The smell is as brackish in Shakespeare's masterpiece of misanthropy, *Timon of Athens*. Timon's prayer invokes hatred as a Christian's does love:

Matrons, turn incontinent!
Obedience fail in children! Slaves and fools
Pluck the grave wrinkled Senate from the bench
And minister in their steads! To general filths
Convert o' th' instant, green virginity!
Do't in your parents' eyes! Bankrupts, hold fast!
Rather than render back, out with your knives

And cut your trusters' throats! Bound servants, steal!
Large-handed robbers your grave masters are
And pill by law. Maid, to thy master's bed!
Thy mistress is o' th' brothel. Son of sixteen,
Pluck the lin'd crutch from thy old limping sire;
With it beat out his brains! Piety and fear,
Religion to the gods, peace, justice, truth,
Domestic awe, night-rest and neighborhood,
Instruction, manners, mysteries and trades,
Degrees, observances, customs and laws,
Decline to your confounding contraries
And let confusion live! Plagues incident to men,
Your potent and infectious fevers heap
On Athens, ripe for stroke! Thou cold sciatica,
Cripple our senators, that their limbs may halt
As lamely as their manners! Lust and liberty
Creep in the minds and marrows of our youth,
That 'gainst the stream of virtue they may strive
And drown themselves in riot! Itches, blains,
Sow all th' Athenian bosoms, and their crop
Be general leprosy! Breath infect breath,
That their society (as their friendship) may
Be merely poison! Nothing I'll bear from thee
But nakedness, thou detestable town!
Take thou that too, with multiplying bans!
Timon will to the woods, where he shall find
Th' unkindest beast more kinder than mankind.
The gods confound (hear me, you good gods all)
Th' Athenians both within and out that wall!
And grant, as Timon grows, his hate may grow
To the whole race of mankind, high and low!
Amen.

(IV, i, 3)

But Timon does not stop at man. The disorder he sees infects all; the very planets are corrupt and justify, by a special kind of logic, man's corruption:

I'll example you with thievery.
The sun's a thief, and with his great attraction
Robs the vast sea. The moon's an arrant thief,
And her pale fire she snatches from the sun.
The sea's a thief, whose liquid surge resolves
The moon into salt tears. The earth's a thief,
That feeds and breeds by a composture stol'n
From gen'ral excrement. Each thing's a thief.
The laws, your curb and whip, in their rough power
Have uncheck'd theft. Love not yourselves; away,
Rob one another. There's more gold. Cut throats,
All that you meet are thieves. To Athens go,
Break open shops; nothing can you steal
But thieves do lose it. Steal no less for this
I give you; and gold confound you howso'er!
Amen.

(IV, iii, 438)

The odor is not much fresher in *Henry VIII*, but it is perfumed with humor and that makes it endurable. Separately, but close enough in the play's action to make comparison inevitable, two of Henry's Queens are presented to us by Shakespeare, the outgoing Katherine of Aragon and the incoming Anne Bullen (Boleyn). These are Katherine's last lines, typical of the character given her in this play:

Remember me
In all humility unto his Highness.
Say his long trouble now is passing
Out of this world. Tell him in death I bless'd him,
For so I will. Mine eyes grow dim. Farewell,
My lord. Griffith, farewell. Nay, Patience,
You must not leave me yet. I must to bed;
Call in more women. When I am dead, good wench,
Let me be us'd with honour. Strew me over
With maiden flowers, that all the world may know
I was a chaste wife to my grave. Embalm me,

Then lay me forth. Although unqueen'd, yet like
A queen, and daughter to a king, inter me.
(IV, ii, 160)

This, in contrast, is the way we get to know Anne, in the only extensive presentation of her character in the play: She is Katherine's Maid of Honour and sits in the Queen's apartments bewailing Katherine's fate:

O, now, after
So many courses of the sun enthroned,
Still growing in a majesty and pomp, the which
To leave a thousandfold more bitter than
'Tis sweet at first t' acquire—after this process
To give her the avaunt, it is a pity
Would move a monster.
(II, iii, 5)

No, she says, summing up her reaction to such treatment with carefully calculated Shakespearean irony, no she would not have such a fate:

By my troth and maidenhead, I would not be a queen.

The Old Lady who is partner and comic conscience to this dialogue takes exception:

Old L. Beshrew me, I would,
And venture maidenhead for't! and so would you,
For all this spice of your hypocrisy.
You that have so fair parts of woman on you
Have, too, a woman's heart, which ever yet
Affected eminence, wealth, sovereignty;
Which, to say sooth, are blessings, and which gifts
(Saving your mincing) the capacity
Of your soft chiverel conscience would receive,
If you might please to stretch it.
Anne. Nay, good troth!

Old L. Yes, troth, and troth! You would not
be a queen?
Anne. No, not for all the riches under heaven.
Old L. 'Tis strange! A threepence bow'd
would hire me,
Old as I am, to queen it. But I pray you,
What think you of a duchess? Have you limbs
To bear that load of title?
Anne. No, in truth.
Old L. Then you are weakly made. Pluck off
a little.
I would not be a young count in your way
For more than blushing comes to. If your back
Cannot vouchsafe this burthen, 'tis too weak
Ever to get a boy.
Anne. How you do talk!
I swear again, I would not be a queen
For all the world.

(24)

The Old Lady's sense of humor is not delicate—nor is Shakespeare's. She insists that in return "for little England" Anne would gladly be seduced. At that moment the Lord Chamberlain enters with the good news that Anne has just been honored by the king with the title of Marchioness of Pembroke—and an added thousand pounds a year. Anne is not quite speechless:

I do not know
What kind of my obedience I should tender.
More than my all is nothing . . .

The Old Lady is not without words either:

Why, this it is! See, see!
I have been begging sixteen years in court
(Am yet a courtier beggarly) nor could
Come pat betwixt too early and too late

For any suit of pounds; and you (O fate!),
A very fresh fish here—fie, fie, fie upon
This compell'd fortune!—have your mouth
  fill'd up
Before you open it.

(81)

It is hard not to find an intended irony in the Chamberlain's breathless interjection in this scene with Anne—

and who knows yet
But from this lady may proceed a gem
To lighten all this isle?

—and again in the tribute paid by Thomas Cranmer in the last scene of the play to the "gem," Anne's daughter. Queen Elizabeth had been dead ten years when this play was first performed in 1613, and so the tribute is a kind of eulogy, but not a kind one; Cranmer's is too much a set speech for that, and his opening demurrer—"the words I utter Let none think flattery . . ."—not exactly convincing in a work by this playwright, even his last one.

Henry VIII is, like so many of Shakespeare's histories, a play about the rise and fall of famous men and women. In this, it exhibits a preoccupation not merely of Shakespeare's, but of the Renaissance mind. Katherine falls; Anne rises. The Duke of Buckingham and Cardinal Wolsey make spectacular descents, and Cranmer leaps from disgrace to the highest dignity, but as everybody in Shakespeare's audience knew, Cranmer was to fall again under Queen Mary, and to be burned at the stake. The pattern is clear and so is the parable it only half conceals: society is full of disorder, of sudden changes: even without any conspicuous display of pride, but especially with it, people in high places can look forward only to low ones.

The difference between the handling of this theme in the

early and the late plays is the difference between disillusionment and high hope. Even as late as the problem plays, Shakespeare is essentially an earth-centered man and contemptuous of his center of interest. But in the masterpieces of meditation which almost all his last works are, Shakespeare's focus has changed. The burden of his plays is now equally divided between the process of repentance and the spiritual illness that makes it necessary. There is still contempt for the world in *Lear* and *Coriolanus*, in *Cymbeline*, *The Winter's Tale*, and *The Tempest;* but now it is the quiet contempt of St. John of the Cross rather than the wild indignation of Bernard of Cluny. There is no longer any need to sicken over the suffering to which so many condemn themselves. Like Dante contemplating his submerged souls, Shakespeare can accept with equanimity the perdition of Lear's hellions, and of Macbeth and Iago; they have earned it. Like St. John, he can accept suffering and privation and renunciation elected, as Prospero chooses them, as the necessary means of advancing in the wisdom of God.

It would be little more than wishful thinking and very doubtful scholarship to posit any direct influence of St. John of the Cross upon Shakespeare. But the years of Shakespeare's lifetime, and those just before and after, were not only years of violent change and disorder, but also the time of Spanish mysticism, a spiritual outburst of such proportions that it produced several thousand works of a genuinely mystical kind. The influence on Shakespeare's circle of Francisco de Osuna, of St. Peter of Alcantara, of Juan of Avila and St. Teresa of the same remarkable place, of Luis de Granada and Luis de Leon, of Juan de Los Angeles and St. John of the Cross would have been indirect. But influence of some kind there must have been. St. Ignatius of Loyola, the most immediately influential of the sixteenth-century Spanish mystics, had more than one distinguished representative in Elizabethan and Jacobean England. Spanish was much read and much translated by Shakespeare's contemporaries; chiefly, it is true, the Spanish of novellas and dramas, but just a few years later in Richard Crashaw's time there was nothing obscure about any of the major Spanish mystics. However separated the Spanish mystics may have been from them, however indirect their influence, the Elizabethans would have understood them and would have enjoyed them. Men like St. John of the Cross suited the temper of the times.

Suffering gave John's life all its dimensions, even its narrowest, when from December 4, 1577 to August 15, 1578 he was imprisoned in a cell in Toledo exactly six feet wide and ten feet long. John not only suffered, he suffered at the hands of good men: it was his Calced Carmelite brethren who put the shoeless, the Discalced Carmelite, saint in jail. In that little place, he "expanded." He had "need of expansion," he said; and so, reduced to the life of a dungeon and the food that accompanied it, one small piece of bread and one sardine each day, he produced twenty or thirty of the forty stanzas of his *Spiritual Canticle*. In such confinement, his soul leaped through the dialogues of purgation and illumination.

John's life was not all so barren of human comfort. But apart from his friendship with St. Teresa, he found few consolations on earth. The point of his poetry and of his extensive commentaries on it is that there are not many comforts here below. John knew by experience the eviscerating mortifications that could be asked by God of man. He translated his experience into doctrine and devotion and a systematic procedure for stripping the soul of every impediment that might hinder its ascent of the mystic Mount Carmel.

Though he was well educated by the Jesuits at Medina del Campo and had a full year of theology at the University of Salamanca, John does not write as a theologian, even when composing his exalted glosses. He is a poet, and there is no understanding anything he says unless one brings to it the imaginative breadth and the willingness to expand that great poetry demands. For John speaks in metaphors, or rather in tropes, for he speaks to instruct, and he speaks to the imagination: no matter how much he himself demands the denuding of the intelligence and the renunciation of the imagination, there is no understanding him without the employment of both. John is a subtle poet, however, and a wise psychologist. What he really demands of his intelligent and imaginative readers is a mortified intelligence and a purified imagination. Following John closely, one gives up any appetite for imaginative experience; one ceases to prod the memory into active excitements, even of the least specious and most reliable and revealing kind. The will acts only to restrict and eventually to destroy action. In time, the active understanding will be replaced by faith, the active memory by hope, the active will by love. Free of all the insubstantial representations and confusing cognitions of this world, we will in effect extinguish our natural light and live in darkness, seeking an illumination that does not come through the senses. Free of illusion, we will also be free of disillusion.

Shakespeare's dark night was not altogether different from John's. Though he came to it more slowly, his progress was no less painful. More than John, he concentrated on the body. The mortification of his senses was apparently involuntary and their accompanying passions occupied him for years; he kicked bitterly at each ugly experience along the way, which taught him the inadequacy of merely human enjoyment and the degradation of those who bent their bodies to it alone. In time he too seemed to move out of time, renouncing or resigning to their proper places the senses, the imagination, the understanding, the memory, the will. When he came to his last works, he gave up almost completely any inclination to cling to worldly or even to human consolations. And what is more significant, perhaps, he did not feel abandoned. In these plays, he no longer leaves his reader with the feeling of abandonment. Every humiliation now is a preface to exaltation; and every shame, chagrin, or obstacle has, or at least may have, purpose.

Coriolanus, a noble man, is brought to ruin. He need not have been. He could have been saved by the mass of Romans, had they not pawned their collective honor to the worst kind of self-seeking rabble-rousers. The sickness of the Roman people is demonstrated logically and rhetorically in the opening scene of *Coriolanus*. Never has the body politic been so ingeniously dramatized. The point of the patrician Menenius, speaking to a group of rebellious citizens, is the low estate of authority in a land and civilization originally founded upon it:

> There was a time when all the body's
>   members
> Rebell'd against the belly; thus accus'd it:
> That only like a gulf it did remain
> I' th' midst o' th' body, idle and unactive,
> Still cupboarding the viand, never bearing
> Like labour with the rest; where th' other
>   instruments
> Did see and hear, devise, instruct, walk, feel,
> And, mutually participate, did minister
> Unto the appetite and affection common
> Of the whole body. The belly answer'd . . .
>
> "True is it, my incorporate friends," quoth he,
> "That I receive the general food at first
> Which you do live upon; and fit it is,
> Because I am the storehouse and the shop
> Of the whole body. But, if you do remember,
> I send it through the rivers of your blood
> Even to the court, the heart, to th' seat o' th'
>   brain,

And, through the cranks and offices of man,
The strongest nerves and small inferior veins
From me receive that natural competency
Whereby they live . . .

"Though all at once cannot
See what I do deliver out to each,
Yet I can make my audit up, that all
From me do back receive the flour of all
And leave me but the bran."

The senators of Rome are this good belly,
And you the mutinous members. For, examine
Their counsels and their cares, digest things
rightly,
Touching the weal o' th' common, you shall find
No public benefit which you receive
But it proceeds or comes from them to you,
And no way from yourselves.

(I, i, 99)

The citizens are not moved, except to revolt.

Coriolanus, a great soldier but a poor politician, is persuaded against his own judgment to stand for consul. He must make what are to him terrible concessions to the people; he must bare his head, point to his wounds and act the part of one who loves plebeians. For him, this is betrayal: it unmans him:

Well, I must do't.
Away, my disposition, and possess me
Some harlot's spirit! My throat of war
turn'd,
Which quier'd with my drum, into a pipe
Small as an eunuch or the virgin voice
That babies lulls asleep! The smiles of knaves
Tent in my cheeks, and schoolboys' tears take
up
The glasses of my sight! A beggar's tongue

Make motion through my lips, and my arm'd
knees,
Who bow'd but in my stirrup, bend like his
That hath receiv'd an alms!
(III, ii, 110)

He turns from it again, in repugnance, but yields at last to his mother's pleas:

Pray be content,
Mother, I am going to the market place.
Chide me no more. I'll mountebank their loves,
Cog their hearts from them, and come home
belov'd
Of all the trades in Rome. Look, I am going.
Commend me to my wife. I'll return consul,
Or never trust to what my tongue can do
I' th' way of flattery further.
(130)

But he cannot "mountebank their loves." Goaded by the rabble and their rousers, he is left finally with nothing but the truth and exile:

You common cry of curs, whose breath I hate
As reek o' th' rotten fens, whose loves I prize
As the dead carcasses of unburied men
That do corrupt my air, I banish you!
And here remain with your uncertainty.
Let every feeble rumour shake your hearts!
Your enemies with nodding of their plumes
Fan you into despair! Have the power still
To banish your defenders, till at length
Your ignorance (which finds not till it feels,
Making not reservation of yourselves,
Still your own foes) deliver you, as most
Abated captives, to some nation

That won you without blows! Despising
For you the city, thus I turn my back.
There is a world elsewhere.
(III, iii, 120)

"Now," says his mother of those to whom her son was to become beloved, "the red pestilence strike all trades in Rome, and occupations perish!"

Coriolanus is left with himself alone, with pride and with hatred. He turns against Rome and with the Volscians, Rome's enemies whom he had once defeated, attacks the city. In so doing he attacks everything he has been; he attacks his family and himself. He rejects Menenius's appeal for mercy:

Wife, mother, child I know not. My affairs
Are servanted to others. Though I owe
My revenge properly, my remission lies
In Volscian breasts. That we have been familiar,
Ingrate forgetfulness shall poison rather
Than pity note how much. Therefore be gone.
Mine ears against your suits are stronger than
Your gates against my force.
(V, ii, 88)

Not until his mother pleads with him, at almost unendurable length, does he agree to "frame convenient peace." The Volscians are outraged; they had expected not only victory over Rome but great spoils. Their leader Aufidius sees a way to work himself "a former fortune" and to triumph over Coriolanus. He accuses Coriolanus of betraying his new allies. In the accusation are the seeds both of Coriolanus's destruction and of his salvation. Coriolanus, Aufidius says, having shown himself merciful to Rome, is

a man by his own alms empoison'd
And with his charity slain.
(V, vi, 10)

There has been, the Volsce general explains, an unaccountable and insupportable change in Coriolanus:

> I rais'd him, and I pawn'd
> Mine honour for his truth: who being so heighten'd
> He watered his new plants with dews of flattery,
> Seducing so my friends; and to this end
> He bow'd his nature, never known before
> But to be rough, unswayable, and free.
>
> (20)

For such betrayal, he must be killed:

> At a few drops of women's rheum, which are
> As cheap as lies, he sold the blood and labour
> Of our great action. Therefore shall he die,
> And I'll renew me in his fall.
>
> (45)

The irony, typical of the late Shakespeare, is that it is not Aufidius but Coriolanus who is renewed by the fall.

Coriolanus's tragedy is perhaps Shakespeare's tragedy: his renewal comes late. The Roman and the Elizabethan have been a long time learning that the soul itself may not be responsible for the horrors which afflict it. Every trial and every humiliation, St. John of the Cross reminds us,

> comes to pass in the soul passively, without its doing or undoing anything of itself with respect to it. But in this connection it must be known that, when the good angel permits the devil to gain this advantage of assailing the soul with this spiritual horror, he does it to purify the soul and to prepare it by means of this spiritual vigil for some great spiritual favor and festival which he desires to grant it, for he never mortifies save to give life, nor humbles save to exalt, which comes to pass shortly afterwards . . . the spirit has been greatly refined by the preceding horror of the evil spirit, in order that it may be able to receive this blessing; for these spiritual visions belong to the next life rather

than to this, and when one of them is seen this is a preparation for the next.[1]

Renewal can only come through constancy in the face of every trial, and even a welcoming gladness. Thus we may be able at last, like the purged Lear, to "take upon's the mystery of things," that is, to make some sense of them. It may be that, like Lear too, we end as a "ruined piece of nature," but not of supernature, not if our purgation and our renewal come, whether early or late. The purged Lear is an illumined Lear: he has achieved childlikeness, and it is altogether becoming to him. When, shortly before the end of the play, Cordelia proposes that he visit his other daughters with her, Lear will have none of it; his innocence could not bear the visit; he is for eternity and fully equipped for it.

> No, no, no, no! Come, let's away to prison.
> We two alone will sing like birds i' th' cage.
> When thou dost ask me blessing, I'll kneel down
> And ask of thee forgiveness. So we'll live,
> And pray, and sing, and tell old tales, and laugh
> At gilded butterflies, and hear poor rogues
> Talk of court news; and we'll talk with them too–
> Who loses and who wins; who's in, who's out–
> And take upon's the mystery of things,
> As if we were God's spies; and we'll wear out,
> In a wall'd prison, packs and sects of great ones
> That ebb and flow by th' moon.
>
> (V, iii, 8)

This is a significant speech for what it reveals of Cordelia as well as of Lear. To her, Lear kneels–at least verbally. With her, he will live and pray. And well he might, for this is she

> Who redeems nature from the general curse . . .
>
> (IV, vi, 210)

This is she

that art most rich, being poor;
Most choice, forsaken; and most lov'd despis'd!
(I, i, 253)

as France explains in taking her for queen, even dowerless. When she seeks a doctor's help in restoring her father's wits, she calls upon all of nature, upon Creation itself, and identifies herself with it:

All blest secrets,
All you unpublish'd virtues of the earth,
Spring with my tears! be aidant and remediate
In the good man's distress!
(IV, iv, 15)

The terms are those of supreme holiness. *Lear* is an allegorical drama and Cordelia is an analogue of Christ and of His mother. Her name undoubtedly was intended to suggest as much by Shakespeare and Spenser, from whose brief telling of the Lear story Shakespeare seems to have taken it (*Faerie Queene*, ii, 10, 27–32). "Cor" is, of course, Latin for "heart," and "delia" a familiar enough Renaissance anagram for "ideal"; this would make Cordelia the Ideal Heart, the faithful one she is in this play. Delia is also one of the names of Artemis or Diana in Greek mythology; regularly in Renaissance allegory, Diana, the virgin goddess, is cast as the analogue of the Virgin Mother. In any case, it is perfectly clear that Cordelia's role in this play is to proclaim the annealing virtues of suffering, to transform Lear and others into what she, in her father's words, is herself: "a soul in bliss." It is her direct function: she is at least the efficient cause of Lear's distress, for her honesty throws him upon the mercy of his other daughters, that is, upon no mercy. She, in effect, sends him to his purgatory, and calmly enough:

We are not the first
Who with best meaning have incurr'd the worst.
(V, iii, 3)

The implicit counsel is St. John's:

> It greatly behoves the soul, then, to have much patience and constancy in all the tribulations and trials which God sends it, whether they come from without or within, and are spiritual or corporeal, greater or lesser. It must take them all as from His hand for its healing and good, and not flee from them, since they are health to it, but follow the counsel of the Wise Man, who says: "If the spirit of him that has the power descend upon thee, abandon not thy place" (that is, the place and abode of thy probation, by which is meant that trial that He sends thee); for the healing, he says, will cause great sins to cease. That is, it will cut the roots of thy sins and imperfections, which are evil habits; for battling with trials, perils, and temptations quenches the evil and imperfect habits of the soul, and purifies and strengthens it. Wherefore the soul must count it a great favor when God sends it interior and exterior trials, realizing that there are very few who deserve to be perfected by suffering, and to suffer that they may come to this lofty state.[2]

The whole of *Lear* is an allegorical expansion of the meaning of these words.

Such perceptions are not given to Othello, Antony, or Cleopatra. Their souls are impatient, inconstant, and never joyous in suffering. They are tied to creatures forever and therefore remain unpurged. Furthermore, the Everlasting has not relaxed his canon against self-slaughter in their cases and conditions any more than in Hamlet's. Perhaps not purgatory but perdition is their fate. And yet there is an honesty in their tormented farewells that may be allegorical of salvation, and that appeals at least as much to mercy as to sentimentality. Othello looks to fair judgment:

I have done the state some service, and they know't—
No more of that. I pray you, in your letters,
When you shall these unlucky deeds relate,
Speak of me as I am. Nothing extenuate.
Nor set down aught in malice.

(V, ii, 339)

Before he goes, he speaks the point of this as of so many of Shakespeare's plays: "Why should honour outlive honesty?" Why should the mere display of dignity survive true goodness? If Desdemona has been killed, then Othello must be too: deception must be defeated; the destroyer of goodness, punished; the promoter of disorder, destroyed, that order may be restored.

Of Antony and Cleopatra, the best that can be said is that they inspire love and loyalty in others and passion in each other that makes them look forward to fleshly satisfaction forever, just as Paolo and Francesca did, and with, one would guess, the same likelihood of pleasure in the permanent embrace. But a fidelity of sorts is theirs, of the kind that Dante found admirable even in hell and Shakespeare finds attractive on earth. We seem to be summoned, like Dolabella by Caesar, to "see High order in this great solemnity."

There is no condoning of sin in these plays, but rather commendation of mercy. Shakespeare expresses a subtle moral theology here and expresses it with dramatic delicacy. He has progressed far beyond the simple-minded forbearance of Helena, in *All's Well That Ends Well*, that will accept a knave for a prince. He can no longer be content with the sweet forgiveness that Isabella in *Measure for Measure* extends to Angelo:

Look, if it please you, on this man condemn'd
As if my brother liv'd. I partly think
A due sincerity governed his deeds
Till he did look on me. Since it is so,

> Let him not die. My brother had but justice
> In that he did the thing for which he died.
> For Angelo,
> His act did not o'ertake his bad intent,
> And must be buried but as an intent
> That perish'd by the way. Thoughts are no subjects,
> Intents but merely thoughts.
>
> (V, i, 449)

Even such charity is not enough, for it escapes too easily the reality of suffering as a preparation for salvation. Shakespeare presents us then with Lear, a "ruined piece of nature" but a salvaged one, and Coriolanus, "by his own alms empoison'd and with his charity slain." It takes the absolute destruction of love in Timon to turn Alcibiades into a conscientious soldier and statesman at the end of Timon's play. It requires the near destruction of the love between husband and wife, between daughter and father, and between king and subjects before the Roman hierarchy can be restored, and with it peace, in the England of *Cymbeline*. In Shakespeare's late heroines, pardon does not emerge, as Isabella's does, from a simple goodness only lightly challenged, but from misery and degradation. Pardon comes through sorrow accepted, from sorrowful women sorely tried: Cordelia in *Lear*, Imogen in *Cymbeline*, Hermione in *The Winter's Tale*, Katherine of Aragon in *Henry VIII*. Each is an analogue of Mary, the woman of sorrow. And so too are Hermione's daughter Perdita and Pericles' daughter Marina and perhaps Marina's mother Thaisa as well. Each is a suffering woman taken up with tenderness by Shakespeare. Each is graced with that *gentillesse* which from the time of the troubadours has made, for some poets at least, the singing of a lady's praises an art of the highest moral order.

The transformation of the Shakespearean heroine from Portia, Helena, and Isabella to Cordelia and Imogen, Hermione and Katherine, is matched by the exchange of Hamlet for Prospero. There has been a growth in Shakespeare's philosopher-king too. Hamlet's disposition is right, no matter how "heavily" it goes with him. If the earth seems sterile to him, if man delights him not, "nor woman neither," he has cause enough. But he has not the equilibrium of the just man he should be to cope with the corruption and disorder which have made Denmark rotten. He is not the just man his beloved Horatio is:

> For thou hast been
> As one, in suff'ring all, that suffers nothing;
> A man that Fortune's buffets and rewards
> Hast ta'en with equal thanks; and blest are those
> Whose blood and judgment are so well commingled
> That they are not a pipe for Fortune's finger
> To sound what stop she please. Give me that man
> That is not passion's slave, and I will wear him
> In my heart's core, ay, in my heart of heart,
> As I do thee.
>
> (III, ii, 70)

St. John makes distinctions which show the difference between a Hamlet and a Horatio, between a Hamlet and a Prospero:

> virtue consists not in apprehensions and feelings concerning God, howsoever sublime they be, nor in anything of this kind that a man can feel within himself; but, on the contrary, in that which has nothing to do with feeling—namely, a great humility and contempt of oneself and of all that pertains to oneself, firmly rooted in the soul and keenly felt by it; and likewise in being glad that others feel in this very way concerning oneself and in not wishing to be of any account in the esteem of others.[3]

Hamlet's whole life in Shakespeare's play consists of "apprehensions and feelings concerning God" and everything else. He has contempt enough for himself at times, but one wonders how great his humility can be when he proclaims that

> heaven hath pleas'd it so,
> To punish me with this, and this with me,
> That I must be their scourge and minister.
> (III, iv, 173)

The role of avenging angel does not become him or any other man. He is, besides, more scourge than minister. He is too much concerned to set all right, too little concerned with right itself. He is too much occupied with phantoms of the senses, with "the image of a murther done" in Denmark, and with a ghost who may not be "honest." John of the Cross's warnings speak directly to Hamlet's condition:

> It remains, then, to be pointed out that the soul must not allow its eyes to rest upon that outer husk—namely, figures and objects set before it supernaturally. These may be presented to the exterior senses, as are locutions and words audible to the ear; or, to the eyes, visions of saints, and of beauteous radiance or perfumes to the sense of smell; or tastes and sweetnesses to the palate; or other delights to the touch, which are wont to proceed from the spirit, a thing that very commonly happens to spiritual persons. Or the soul may have to avert its eyes from visions of interior sense, such as imaginary visions, which it must renounce entirely. It must set its eyes only on the spiritual good which they produce, striving to preserve it in its works and to practise that which is for the due service of God, paying no heed to those representations nor desiring any pleasure of sense. And in this way, the soul takes from these things only that which God intends and wills—namely, the spirit of devotion . . .[4]

Prospero learns this lesson well, and all its many implications. Like Hamlet, he has tried to set all right, and with far more "potent art." But he has obeyed God who wills the conversion, not the death, of the sinner; he has made not corpses but penitents, for

> The rarer action is
> In virtue than in vengeance. They being penitent,
> The sole drift of my purpose doth extend
> Not a frown further.
>
> (V, i, 27)

Thus persuaded, he removes his magic robes and relinquishes his charms:

> this rough magic
> I here abjure; and when I have requir'd
> Some heavenly music (which even now I do)
> To work mine end upon their senses that
> This airy charm is for, I'll break my staff,
> Bury it certain fathoms in the earth,
> And deeper than did ever plummet sound
> I'll drown my book.
>
> (50)

Miranda, his daughter and Grace's, is now "by immortal Providence" tied to Ferdinand. Prospero is free to leave the world and retire to Milan, where he will meditate on eternity as he awaits it: "Every third thought shall be my grave."

It is not difficult to recognize the figure of Shakespeare in Prospero and to see the playwright's retirement to Stratford represented in the return to Milan, and few scholars have missed the point. But the identification extends beyond the drama into the epilogue, the last words spoken by Shakespeare's last great spokesman. When at the end Prospero has "pardon'd the deceiver," so has Shakespeare. When Prospero prays—

> Now I want
> Spirits to enforce, art to enchant;
> And my ending is despair

Unless I be reliev'd by prayer,
Which pierces so that it assaults
Mercy itself and frees all faults.
As you from crimes would pardon'd be,
Let your indulgence set me free.

—so does Shakespeare. The playwright begs his audience's indulgence, for many reasons. He has renounced imaginary visions entirely, he seems to be saying; but right up to the very end he has shown contempt for the world and a continuing interest in exposing the masks and robes with which worldly men disguise themselves. As despair may be relieved by prayer, however, so may contempt be lightened by hope and a good disguise replace a bad. The words are St. John's; at this point in Shakespeare's life, they could just as well be his:

For this green colour of living hope in God gives the soul such ardour and courage and aspiration to the things of eternal life that, by comparison with what it hopes for therein, all things of the world seem to it to be, as in truth they are, dry and faded and dead and nothing worth. The soul now divests and strips itself of all these worldly vestments and garments, setting its heart upon naught that is in the world and hoping for naught, whether of that which is or of that which is to be, but living clad only in the hope of eternal life. Wherefore, when the heart is thus lifted up above the world, not only can the world neither touch the heart nor lay hold on it, but it cannot even come within sight of it.

And thus, in this green livery and disguise, the soul journeys in complete security from this second enemy, which is the world.[5]

CHAPTER XI

Pascal: Fire and Fact

BLAISE PASCAL DIED AT HIS SISTER'S HOUSE ON AUGUST 19, 1662, three months to the day after his thirty-ninth birthday. When his belongings were examined shortly afterward, two copies of a document were found sewn in the lining of his doublet. One was a scribbled narrative on paper, the other a careful copy of the same words on parchment. Pascal called the account his *Mémorial.* What it records, in a short series of disjointed statements, is an unforgettable experience, a long one, a loving one, a full one, a fiery one:

Memorial

In the year of grace 1654
Monday 23 November, feast of St. Clement, Pope and Martyr, and others in the Martyrology.
Vigil of St. Chrysogonus, Martyr, and others.
From about half past ten in the evening until about half past twelve.

Fire

God of Abraham, God of Isaac, God of Jacob,
not of the philosophers and scholars.
Certitude, certitude; feeling, joy, peace.
God of Jesus Christ.
My God and Thy God.
Thy God shall be my God.
Forgetfulness of the world and of all save God.
He is to be found only by the means taught in the Gospel.
Greatness of the human soul.
Righteous Father, the world hath not known Thee, but
I have known Thee.
Joy, joy, joy, tears of joy.
I have separated myself from him.

They have forsaken me, the fountain of living waters.
My God, wilt Thou leave me?
Let me not be separated from him forever.
This is eternal life, that they might know Thee, the only true
God and Him whom Thou hast sent, Jesus Christ.
Jesus Christ.
Jesus Christ.
I parted from Him; fled, denied, crucified Him.
Let me never be separated from Him.
We hold to him only by the means taught in the Gospel.
Renunciation, total and sweet.
Total submission to Jesus Christ and to my director.
Eternal joy for one day of labor on earth.
I will not forget Thy Commandments. Amen.

In the eighteenth of his *Provincial Letters*, on the authority of St. Augustine and St. Thomas Aquinas, Pascal defines three principles of knowledge, the senses, reason, and faith, each with its own distinct sphere, its own object, its own mode of certainty:

And as God has seen fit to make use of the senses as the medium of faith—*fides ex auditu*—so far is faith from destroying the certainty of the senses, that it would be destructive to faith to call in question the fidelity of the senses. St. Thomas, therefore, expressly says, that God has appointed sensible accidents to subsist in the Eucharist, that the senses, which judge only from these accidents, might not be deceived—*ut sensus a deceptione reddantur immunes.*

We may hence infer, that whatever proposition is presented for our examination, it is necessary, in the first place, to ascertain the nature of it, to know to which of these three principles we must have recourse. If the question refer to anything supernatural, we must neither judge of it by the senses nor by reason, but by Scripture and the decisions of the Church: if it be an unrevealed proposition, and within the sphere of our natural sense, that must be the judge; but if it relate to a point of fact, we must believe our senses, to whose cognizance it naturally belongs.

If Scripture itself contains a passage with a literal meaning clearly contrary to the certainties of the senses and reason, we must not force reason and the senses to conform to Scripture but find another possible meaning for the holy text which agrees with the findings of the senses and reason—if, that is, they are operating within their proper spheres. This is, he says, an essential procedure:

> Were we to do otherwise, we should not render the Scripture venerable, but expose it to the contempt of infidels; "because," as St. Augustine remarks, "should it be said that we believe in things contained in Scripture, which they know to be false, they would ridicule our credulity in other things more concealed from human discernment, such as the resurrection of the dead, and eternal life": "and thus," adds St. Thomas, "our religion would be rendered contemptible, and their conversion to it utterly prevented."

The principle is simple:

> Matters of fact can only be proved by the senses. If what you maintain be true, show it; if not, pray desist from soliciting anyone to believe it, for this is perfectly useless. All the powers of the world cannot, by their utmost authority, persuade a person of a point of fact, any more than they can alter it; for nothing can make that which is, not to be.

Illustrations abound, and they are simple too. He explains that Pope Leo IX, for example, could not convincingly maintain that the body of St. Denis had been taken from France to the monastery of Ratisbon. For the French who opened the shrine of the saint found intact the relics it was supposed to contain. They could not confess that they no longer had these relics, as the pope required; they "knew that this was not the fact, from the evidence of their own eyes." Similarly, it is worthless to condemn Galileo's "opinion respecting the motion of the earth. This will never prove that it stands still; and if it have been ascertained, from careful observations, that it turns, all mankind together cannot prevent its turning, nor prevent their being carried round with it."

The fire of faith and matters of fact ascertained through the senses alone—between these two poles Pascal's soul raced and his personality took shape. The means of motion were always the same: experimentation. Whether constructing his calculating machine or laying the foundations of calculus, founding what may have been the first omnibus company or finding certitude and joy in a mystical transport, Pascal based all his conclusions on personal experience. Data of the senses or data of the spirit, he himself collected them, collated them, and came to conclusions about them. He held himself rigorously responsible for his least speculation; he expected others to be equally reliable and trustworthy.

The inductive mind of the seventeenth century has no better representative than Pascal, none that covers a wider field or does more with its experimental findings. One may doubt the validity of some of the findings. Questions could be and should be asked about the examples of casuistry with which Pascal arraigns the Jesuits in *The Provincial Letters*. One may have reservations about the accuracy of his reading of Augustine on the nature of grace. One must challenge the interpretation he presents of the doctrine of grace of the Spanish Jesuit Luis Molina and his followers, and particularly his lumping together of Molinists and Calvinists as equally deranged theologically. But to do Pascal and the facts justice these questions must be raised on an experimental basis. For by the soundness of his science and the devotion of his faith he has removed himself and his works from the nagging criticism of mere opinion.

In the map of ideas Pascal has so long been located just this side of Jansenism, if not right at Port-Royal, that he has been caught again and again in controversies. He proves so many things for so many eager to find champions for their side that what he really did prove is almost entirely obscured in senseless argument. In spite of a good death and the clearest devotion to the Catholic Church as an institution, Pascal was not a perfectly orthodox thinker, and nothing will make him one. But at the same time, in spite of his attachment to Port-Royal, one of whose community of solitaries his sister Jacqueline was, and his close friendship with the defenders and disciples of Jansenius, he was not an enemy of Rome, and nothing will make him one. He tried very hard to be a good Augustinian; most of the time he succeeded. Always, whether trying or not, he was a successful propagandist, one of the most persuasive writers of Christian apologetics of the modern era. And here too the method was experimental, the ground Pascal's personal experience.

Sometime after the evening of fire in 1654, Pascal began to organize a monumental Apology for Christianity. It was to be a *summa contra gentiles*, an answer to free-thinkers of the kind Pascal had known so long and so well, and had just narrowly—by the breadth of a vision—missed becoming. He never finished the work; it never got beyond a bundle of oddly fitted and unfitted papers enclosing equally disconnected and fragmentary notations. These are Pascal's *Pensées*, his great cullings of personal experience, thought by thought.

There is in his *Thoughts* some apparent order. More coherence and organization can be found by imposing on the *Pensées* the plan of the Apology preserved at some length by Filleau de la Chaise, a friend of Pascal's dear friend the Duc de Roannez, and abbreviated by Pascal's nephew Etienne Périer. But still puzzles remain; there are lacunae. No scholar has been able to reconstruct in detail or with any great amount of security Pascal's own conception of the Apology. And that is just as it should be. For Pascal's triumph is in his very failure to present a cohesive work, with an unmistakable ground-plan and a chapter-by-chapter structure that follows it. The *Pensées*, in any edition, however organized or disorganized, have about them the irresistible appeal that Dom Butler finds in the Memorial:

> Of all the attempts to describe such experiences these barely articulate, incoherent exclamations of Pascal—the intellectual, the philosopher, the master of language and style—are, for me, beyond all compare the most eloquent and the most realistic.[1]

In the *Pensées* Pascal cannot be described as "barely articulate" or "incoherent." But his work is hardly consistent or well integrated. It is often eccentric in its organization, as it jumps from epigram to *obiter dictum*, from short dissertation to ejaculation, prophecy, and prediction. Side by side with elegantly ordered and eloquently articulated reflections there are jottings that are little more than notes to be consulted at some future time, accepted or rejected, expanded or contracted. But it all holds together remarkably well, and skillfully and persuasively reflects Augustinian teaching.

With the exception of the turbulent problem of grace, there are no great difficulties in the *Pensées* for anyone at all familiar with Augustinian thinking. There is in Pascal, as in his master, the "know thyself" theme, with the dramatic accent provided by a late Renaissance emphasis on man's conspicuous weaknesses: his concupiscences and the many disguises with which he deceives not only others but himself. There is also the raging heart of Pascal, again so much like Augustine's, in its tossing, tumbling, tearing efforts to find rest in God. These are the low and the high tides of Pascal's sea of thoughts. In their ebb and flow a great human spirit is revealed.

Pascal was well aware of what he was doing and much of the time of how he was doing it. He worked by a literary as well as theological plan. In a brief paper on *The Art of Persuasion,* he outlines his rhetorical principles, excepting from these orderings only the "divine verities, which I should by no means associate with the art of persuasion, for they have their place infinitely above nature. God alone can place them in the soul and do this in a manner pleasing to Him." To be pleasing to both God and man is Pascal's aim. He recognizes that "the art of persuasion is just as much the art of being ingratiating as of being convincing; for men are governed so much more by caprice than by reason." But the principles of pleasure are almost hopelessly unstable:

> They differ in all men, they vary so greatly in all individuals that no man differs more from another than he does from himself at various times. A man's pleasures are not like a woman's; a rich man and a poor man have different pleasures; a prince, a soldier, a merchant, a bourgeois, a peasant, the old, the young, the healthy, and the sick all differ, and the slightest happenings change them.

There are ways of reaching people, however: through the definition of terms, the promulgation of principles or self-evident axioms, and the demonstration of obscure propositions by axioms or propositions on which agreement has already been reached.

While he does not always stick to the methods he has outlined, this is a rhetoric Pascal knew well, the art, quite obviously, of a geometrician. It is a method stressing clarity and simplicity, not only for purposes of persuasion, but because "good things" are common and thoroughly accessible:

> Nothing is more common than good things; it is only a matter of discerning them, and it is certain that they are all natural and within our reach, and even known to everyone. But people do not know how to distinguish them. This is universal. Excellence of any kind is not to be found in extraordinary and bizarre things. We climb to reach it, and we merely become farther removed from it; most often we need to bend down, instead. The

best books are those which their readers believe they could have written. Nature, which alone is good, is quite familiar and common. Hence I do not doubt at all that these rules, being true, must be simple, naive, and natural as they are . . . It is not necessary to strain the mind; strained and labored manners fill it with silly presumption through queer affectation and vain, ridiculous inflation instead of with solid, vigorous nourishment.

One of the principal reasons why those who enter the realm of knowledge are carried so far from the true course they should follow is their first notion that good things are inaccessible. That is why they call them grand, high, elevated, sublime. This undoes everything. I should like to call them low, common, familiar; these suit them better; I hate swollen words . . . [sentence incomplete].[2]

Thus he ends the discourse and prepares himself and his readers for the *Pensées*. It is important to bear in mind the rhetorical advice of this physician of souls while reading his thoughts: avoid strain. Do not labor after meanings. The Apology may be truncated; it is not abstruse.

Pascal reveals himself again and again in simple phrases:

Men despise Religion, they hate it and fear to find it true. To cure this, I must begin by showing that Religion is not contrary to reason—is venerable—inspire respect for it; next, render it attractive; make good men wish it were true, and then show that it *is* true. Venerable, because it really knows man; attractive, because it promises the true good.

He notes a possible organization for the Apology and then immediately rescinds it, not by disputing the wisdom of the projected program but by showing the higher order that follows no surface plan at all, that digresses constantly and holds only to the central point, man's supernatural end:

Part I: Man's misery without God.
Part II: Man's happiness with God.

Alternatively:

Part I: Nature is corrupt, proved by nature.

Part II: There is a Redeemer, proved by Scripture.

Order: against the objection that Scripture lacks order. The heart has its order, the mind has its order by premiss and proof; the heart has another. We do not prove that we should be loved, by setting forth in order the causes of love; that would be too foolish.

Jesus Christ, St. Paul, follow the order not of the mind but of charity, for they meant not to teach but to inflame. Similarly, St. Augustine. The essence of that order is digression at every point, with constant reference to the main end, never losing sight of that.

That is the kind of order made commendable in the *Pensées*. That is the kind of insight one gathers from the book, whether one reads right through the work or examines just one thought at a time, whether one skips back and forth, looking for connected points, or is content with a passing sentence, a phrase or a word or two.

A fitful and uncertain approach to the *Pensées* is inescapable; it is Pascal's own approach and, by implication at least, has his sanction. In the midst of one of his masterful long speculations, on disproportion in man, he describes the pattern:

We sail over a vast expanse, ever uncertain, ever adrift, carried to and fro. To whatever point we think to fix and fasten ourselves it shifts and leaves us; and if we pursue it it escapes our grasp, slips away, fleeing in eternal flight. Nothing stays for us. That is our condition, natural, yet most contrary to our inclination; we have a burning desire to find a sure resting place and a final fixed basis whereon to build a tower rising to the Infinite; but our whole foundation cracks, and the earth yawns to the abyss. Let us then cease to look for security and stability. Our reason is ever cheated by misleading appearances: nothing can fix the finite between the two Infinites which enclose it and fly from it.

Nothing stays for us, not even the passage. Pascal is aware of it. At the end of this extended *Pensée* come three short snorts directed at himself, at his readers, and at man:

> Two infinites, the mean: Reading too fast or too gently you are unintelligible.
>
> Too much and too little wine: give him none, he cannot find truth; similarly if you give him too much.
>
> Feed the body little by little. Too much food produces little substance.

But this mood too will go. For whatever man's weaknesses, what greatness and dignity he has in his ability to think! The subject of thought elicits perhaps the most famous of all of Pascal's *Thoughts:*

> Man is but a reed, the weakest thing in nature; but a thinking reed. It does not need the whole universe to take up arms to crush him: a vapor, a drop of water, is enough to kill him. But, though the universe should crush him, man would still be nobler than his destroyer, because he knows that he is dying, and knows that the universe has got the better of him; the universe knows nothing of that.
>
> All our dignity then consists in thought. We must look to that in order to rise aloft and not to space or time which we can never fill. Let us strive then to think correctly: that is the first principle of the moral life.

The starts and stops, the incomplete sentences, the terse condensations of folklore and proverb, the apparent reversals of positions, the paradoxes, the antinomies, the multiplicity of methods of presenting his perceptions—all are indispensable and yet none is essential. For this is a work of contradictions based on the contradictory nature of man, and its form partakes of its content. Man is a mass of miseries; man alone of earth's inhabitants is miserable. But the very misery is proof of man's greatness, for he knows he is miserable and finds his misery along with his greatness only in knowing it. A tree does not know that it is miserable. Man seeks truth and finds only uncertainty, looks for happiness and finds only misery and death. By his nature man is both credulous and incredulous, bold and timid. Man is neither an angel nor a beast; unfortunately, when he tries to act an angel he becomes a beast. Within him there is a continual warfare between reason and the passions. If only he had reason without passions or passions without reason. But having both, he must be at war, divided, self-contradictory.

In speculating on the two natures of man, Pascal once more uses Augustine as his guide. The motions of the soul toward self or toward God as Augustine has defined them preoccupy Pascal and impose a firm structure on even his most rambling discourse. He hates concupiscence as he finds it dominating men, and wants men to come to hate all the foolish efforts to gratify themselves which cripple their wills and blind them to eternity.

Yet this eternity abides, and death, which is its portal and which momentarily threatens them, must without fail very soon lay them under the terrible necessity of eternal annihilation or eternal misery, without their knowing which of these eternities is for ever in store for them.

This is a dilemma of terrible import. They are threatened with eternal misery; and in addition, as if it were not worth the trouble, they refuse to examine whether this be one of those opinions which the credulous multitude swallow too easily, or one of those which, essentially obscure, have a solid though hidden foundation. Thus they know not whether there be truth or falsehood here, nor whether the proofs be strong or weak. They have them before their eyes; they refuse to look at them, and, in their ignorance, they decide to do their best to fall into this state of misery if it exists, to put off making trial of it till the moment of death, yet to be quite content with it, to make profession of it, yea to boast of it. Can we think seriously of this important matter and not be shocked at conduct so extravagant?

He is appalled that men can say "*Je ne scay*," and then attack what they do not know, that they can accept the possibility of a void after death or an angry God with indifference. How can the same man who worries over the slightest trifle, who passes "whole nights and days in rage and despair over loss of office or some imaginary affront to his honor" be insensible to the possible loss of being or an eternity of misery? For atheists' arguments he has St. Gregory's answers:

What right have they to say that one cannot rise again? Which is the more difficult, birth or resurrection; that what has never been should be, or that what has once been should recur? Is it more difficult to come into existence than to return to it? Habit makes the one seem easy for us, want of habit makes the other seem impossible; popular reasoning!

Why cannot a virgin bear a child? Does not a hen lay eggs without a cock? What distinguishes them outwardly from the others? And who has ever said that the hen cannot form the germ as well as the cock?

What have they to say against the Resurrection and the Virgin Birth? Which is more difficult, to produce a man or an animal, or to reproduce one? And if they had never seen a certain species of animal, could they guess whether they were produced without collaboration?

But these are not all the questions; Christians can explain only so much. We cannot even give adequate reasons for our belief, for while we know that there is an infinite, we do not know its nature. Here, we know by faith that God exists; in glory, we shall know Him as He really is. But a purely natural explanation cannot account for an infinitely incomprehensible God, "since, having neither parts nor limits, He has no relation to us. We are therefore incapable of knowing what He is, or whether He is." How then does one solve the problem if one has no faith? Pascal's answer is well known: by making a wager: "Let us weigh gain and loss in calling heads that God is. Reckon these two chances: if you win, you win all; if you lose, you lose naught. Then do not hesitate, wager that He is." How can anyone hesitate? The possible gain: infinite happiness. The possible loss: nothingness, the void. Pascal concludes the passage with a pair of delicate ironies. He imagines the polished response of a socially alert freethinker in formulas of delight, and his own reply, with the unexpected truth, the truth of charity:

"Oh, your words transport me, charm me, etc."

If they please you and seem cogent, know that they are the utterance of a man who has been on his knees before and after, beseeching that Being, infinite and without parts, to whom he submits all his being, that He may likewise bring into submission all your being for your good and for His glory; that so strength may come to the help of weakness.

The terms of the wager are fair ones for understanding the color and texture of Pascal's mind. It is the mind of a geometrician who recognizes the existence of many self-evident truths and many which are elusive, who knows that not all words can be defined and that definition is an arbitrary art, though a perfectly defensible one as long as we do not fall into the "vicious habit" of "giving the same name to two different things." But larger than definitions and even self-evident truths are the truths experience teaches. That is how Pascal learned about justice:

I passed much of my life believing in the existence of justice; and I was not mistaken; for it does exist in the measure in which God has vouchsafed to reveal it. But that is not how I took it, and here I was mistaken; for I thought that our justice was essentially just, and that I possessed the means to know it and weigh it. But I have found myself so often wanting in right judgment that at last I have come to mistrust myself, and then to mistrust others. I have seen men in process of change in all countries; and so, after many variations of opinion concerning true justice, I recognized that our nature was a perpetual changing, and I have not changed since; if I came to change it would confirm my opinion.

Upon such experience, Pascal rests much. He distrusts human reason; it is corrupt, untrustworthy, buried in paradox:

> Know then, proud man, your own paradox. Down, helpless reason! Silence, futile nature! Learn that man is infinitely beyond the reach of man, and hear from your Master what is your true condition, so far unknown to you. Hearken to God!
>
> For, in a word, if man had never been corrupted he would in his innocence enjoy truth and happiness with confidence, and if he had never been other than corrupt he would have no notion of either truth nor happiness. But, poor wretches that we are, and all the more so than if there were no greatness in us, we have a notion of happiness, and cannot reach it; we are conscious of an image of the truth, and only hold a lie; incapable of entire ignorance and of certain knowledge, so obvious is it that we stood once at a point of perfection from which we have unfortunately fallen.

There is only one way out—experience teaches this too: "*Escoutez Dieu!*" "Listen to God!" It is true that man is unworthy of God, but he can be made worthy. He must start by learning who he is and what, and then Who God is and What. Nature reveals everywhere the evidence of a God who has been lost. But no less than all things hide Him do they all act as signs that show Him forth: "He both hides Himself from them that defy Him and reveals Himself to them that seek Him, because men are at once unworthy of God and capable of Him. . . ." In Scripture, man can find both himself and God revealed, but the revelation is by type and symbol. To read Scripture accurately is always to look beyond the letter to the spirit, beyond disagreement to harmony, not for "the meat that perishes, but that which perishes not." The Bible presents the truth, but in cipher:

> A cipher has two meanings. When you come upon a letter which has a clear meaning, of which it is nevertheless affirmed that the meaning is veiled and dark, that it is so hidden that one may see the letter without seeing it, and hear it without understanding it, what must we think but that it is a cipher with a double meaning, and all the more because we discover obvious contradiction in the literal meaning? The prophets have clearly stated that Israel would always be beloved of God, and that the law would be eternal, and they have said that their meaning would not be understood, and that it was veiled.

The Apostles broke the seal of scriptural figure; Jesus rent the veil and exposed the spirit. Why? To teach us that "the enemies of man are his passions; that the Redeemer would be spiritual and His reign spiritual; that there would be two Advents, one in misery to abase the proud, the other in glory to exalt the humble; that Jesus Christ would be God and man." All the exegesis in the *Pensées* is directed toward these revelations: they sit well with the image of man, half-angel and half-beast, with which Pascal was engrossed, an image much like Hamlet's, in words much like Hamlet's:

> What a monster then is man! What a novelty, what a portent, what a chaos, what a contradiction, what a prodigy! Universal judge and helpless worm; trustee of truth, and sink of uncertainty and error; glory and off-scouring of the universe.

Like Pico, Pascal was fascinated by rabbinical commentaries, by Cabalist readings, by every possible approach to the mysteries of Scripture. Montaigne, about whom Pascal had passionately mixed feelings, presented him with some insights; Hugo Grotius's *De Veritate Religionis Christianae, On the Truth of the Christian Religion*, offered more. He used many different translations of the Bible and as much of Augustine and Bernard as he could get his hands on. He read the Fathers and was persuaded by them. Like Augustine, like Boethius, like Gregory and Bernard, he stresses the God of those prophets who say about Him and to Him: "*Vere tu es Deus absconditus*," "Truly, thou art a hidden God." (Is 45:15) There must be obscurity, then, but there must be light, too:

> If there were no obscurity, man would not feel his corruption; if there were no light, man would not hope for relief. Thus it is not only right, but to our good, that God should be partly hidden and partly manifest, since to know God without knowing his own misery, and to know his misery without knowing God, are equal dangers for man.

Pascal delights in the obscurities and in the light. In the figurative writing of the Old Testament he finds signs of joy to come; in the New Testament, means to reach it. The figures are of happiness, the means are of penitence, the link is Christ. The "two oldest books in the world," those of Moses and Job, reveal as much. Both point to Jesus as "their common center and object," Moses in his prophecies and in recording God's promises to Abraham and Jacob, Job in reporting "I know that my Redeemer liveth." But not everybody who reads Scripture can see this. And that makes sense too, for God's will is to blind some and enlighten others. Christians not only accept this fact; they glory in it:

> What say the prophets concerning Jesus Christ? That He will be God openly? Nay, but that He is a truly hidden God; that He will be misunderstood, that none will think that it is He, that He will be a stone of stumbling for many, etc. Cease then to cast up against us want of clearness, for of that we make our boast.
>
> But, say they, "the obscurities!" Yet without them Jesus Christ would not be a stumbling block, and that He is this is a formal pronouncement of the prophets. "*Blind them.*" (Is 6:10)

In most of his exegetical writing, Pascal tries to hold to fact, at least wherever fact can be found. He revolts against the extremes, against taking everything as either exclusively literal or spiritual. He cautions himself "To speak against exaggerated figurative language" and shows his good sense as a Scripture scholar in a note on charity:

> Charity is not a figurative precept. To say that Jesus Christ, who came to replace type by reality, came only to establish the figure of Charity and remove existing reality, is shocking. "If the light be darkness, what will darkness be?"

But when he comes to deal with Christ, neither fact nor figure is enough. The facts are impressive enough:

> All that Jesus Christ did was to teach men that they were selfish, slaves, blind, sick, unhappy, sinners; that He must deliver, enlighten, bless and cure them; that this would come about by hating self, and following Him through woe and crucifixion.
>
> Without Jesus Christ, man must abide in vice and misery; with Jesus Christ, man is delivered from vice and misery. In Him lies all our virtue and felicity. Apart from Him is naught but vice, misery, error, darkness, despair.

The figures of speech that describe Jesus are striking too: "Saviour, father, sacrificial priest, victim, food, king, sage, lawgiver, afflicted, poor man . . ." But as fact or figure Jesus Christ is both transcendent and immanent and requires all at once an eye that leaps beyond earthly limitations and yet sees Him in everything. That is Pascal's vision:

> I contemplate Jesus Christ in all individuals and in ourselves: Jesus Christ as father in His Father, Jesus Christ as brother in His brethren, Jesus Christ as poor in the poor, Jesus Christ as rich in the rich, Jesus Christ as doctor and priest in the priests, Jesus Christ as sovereign in princes . . .

Pascal's pages on Jesus, in the *Pensées* and elsewhere, together form a meditative work quite worthy of a place beside *The Imitation of Christ.* The substance of them is contained in two *aperçus:* "Jesus Christ," Pascal says in the *Pensées,* "is a God to whom we draw near without pride, and before whom we bow low without despair." In his meditation on the agony of Christ, which he calls "The Mystery of Jesus," Pascal echoes the words St. Bernard put in Jesus's mouth: "Take comfort. Thou wouldst not be seeking Me, hadst thou not found Me."

But everybody has not found Him: some because of hardness of heart, some because of concupiscence, some for want of grace, some for fear of grace, some because they have surrendered everything to reason, some because they have yielded nothing to reason—and all because they have not trusted the urgings of their own hearts:

> We know Truth not only through reason, but also by the heart; it is in this way that we have knowledge of first principles, and it is in vain that Reason, which has no share in them, tries to dispute them . . . We know we do not dream; however helpless we are to prove it by reason, our impotence merely demonstrates the weakness of our reason, not the uncertainty of all our knowledge . . . For knowledge of first principles, such as the existence of space, time, motion, numbers, is as sound as any knowledge furnished by our reasoning. And it is on the knowledge supplied by the heart and intuition that reason rests, founding thereon all its utterances . . . And it is as useless and absurd for reason to ask the heart to prove its first principles before agreeing to them, as it would be for the heart to ask reason to feel all the propositions it demonstrates, before accepting them.[3]

The testimony is particularly impressive because it comes from such a master of fact and lover of reason. But the greatest of all the facts in Pascal's life was that in the year of grace 1654, Monday 23 November, feast of St. Clement . . . Vigil of St. Chrysogonus. . . . From about half past ten in the evening until about half past twelve,

Fire.

CHAPTER XII

Sterne and Fielding: The Allegory of Irony

MIDWAY IN THE COURSE OF HIS FIRST SERMON, AN "INquiry After Happiness," Laurence Sterne invites his reader to look with him "into the disappointments of human happiness, on some of the most received plans on which 'tis generally sought for and expected by the bulk of mankind." What follows is by no means an exhaustive inquiry into human happiness. It is certainly not distinguished by any startling insights into the vanity of human wishes, which is really Sterne's theme. It does, however, offer some more than casual guidance in the reading of Sterne's book, *A Sentimental Journey Through France and Italy*, and in so doing poses some questions about Sterne's imagination, the reader's, and that of his central character, Yorick, which are entirely relevant to an examination of the celebrated eighteenth-century voyage across the English channel and the mind responsible for it.

The "insufficiency of our enjoyments," Sterne says in his sermon, is a vexing subject; none has been more examined, discussed, argued over, or declaimed about than this one. Many "good things have been said" on the subject, but "they have generally had the fate to be considered either as the overflowings of disgust from sated appetites . . . or, as the declamatory opinions of recluse and splenetic men, who had never tasted them at all, and, consequently, were thought no judges of the matter." Rather than trust to second-hand information, Sterne wants to look at the facts.

All through the life of man, Sterne says, he hurries himself along; rushing from one engagement to another, always disappointed in his expectations, never finding rest. So too with Yorick as he moves from Calais to Montriul, from Montriul to Nampont, from Nampont to Amiens, from Amiens to Paris, and from Paris to Versailles and Moulines. His is not a leisurely journey; he never finds rest; his expectations and the reader's are continually frustrated. Through four of the terse, ejaculatory chapters which make up the *Sentimental Journey*, Yorick sits in a coach in Calais with the hand of a lady in his and with "their faces both turned closer to the door of the remise than what was absolutely necessary." Before taking his leave, he has managed to squeeze her hand (but only with "some slight efforts toward a closer compression") and has finally been "suffered . . . to kiss her hand twice." In spite of "every dirty passion and bad propensity" in his nature taking "the alarm" as he proposes to share his chaise with the lady, he has achieved nothing more than the bland physical exchanges noted above and a certain amount of heated conversation, "of making love by *sentiments!*" as he calls it. Yorick dismisses the idea of such love-making contemptuously:

> I should as soon think of making a genteel suit out of remnants; and to do it, pop, at first sight, by declaration, is submitting the offer, and themselves with it, to be sifted with all their *pours* and *contres*, by an unheated mind.

But this is just what he and the lady have been doing and what she means when she "solemnly" declares that "you have been making love to me all this while." The arrival of her brother is fatal to a proposal that Yorick was about to make to her. You need not tell it to me, she replies: "A man . . . has seldom an offer of kindness to make to a woman, but she has a presentiment of it some moments before." Looking right at him, she says boldly, "I had no evil to apprehend; and, to deal frankly with you, had determined to accept" the proposal. If there had been anything to fear, she concludes, "I believe your good-will would have drawn a story from me, which would have made pity the only dangerous thing in the journey." And so it is with the rest of the voyage which draws so heavily upon the reader's imagination for its variously sentimental and sensual inflections: the plans never evolve as they seem inevitably about to do; the heat rests uncomfortably in the imagination as Yorick moves restlessly from place to place.

Yorick's thoughts are, as Sterne says in his first sermon on a young man who has just been graduated from the care of tutors, "generally full of the mighty happiness which he is going to enter upon." Every thing, every person provokes a heated response in the youth of Sterne's sermon, just as it does in the Yorick of the *Journey:*

> take notice how his imagination is caught by every glittering appearance that flatters this expectation. Observe what impressions are made upon his senses, by diversions, music, dress, and beauty, and how his spirits are upon the wing, flying in pursuit of them, that you would think he could never have enough.

Just before leaving Calais, Yorick recollects that he has been there only a few moments longer than an hour. But how much has occurred! The speculation is stirring:

> What a large volume of adventures may be grasped within this little span of life, by him who interests his heart in every thing, and who, having eyes to see what time and chance are perpetually holding out to him as he journeyeth on his way, misses nothing he can *fairly* lay his hands on!
>
> If this won't turn out something, another will; no matter, 'tis an essay upon human nature; I get my labor for my pains, 'tis enough; the pleasure of the experiment has kept my senses and the best part of my blood awake, and laid the gross to sleep.

It is at this point that the two speculations upon human nature —book and sermon—dovetail. The rest of *A Sentimental Journey* is devoted to demonstrations of the alarms that awaken

Yorick's senses and "the best part" of his blood. His imagination is so stirred by an "apostrophe" to a dead ass, and he interests his heart so deeply in the beast's inconsolable owner that the result is a general lamentation: "Shame on the world! said I to myself. Did we but love each other as this poor soul loved his ass, 'twould be something." He is still "making love by *sentiments*"; dead ass or live woman, the response is out of all proportion to the stimulus.

Everything in Yorick's journey is sentimental and therefore exaggerated. A *grisette*—a working girl—gives him street directions: "If *tones and manners* have a meaning, which certainly they have, unless to hearts which shut them out, she seemed really interested that I should not lose myself." He is much obliged to the girl and repeats his thanks to her over and over again. But before he has taken more than a few steps, he discovers he has completely forgotten the directions. He returns to the shop and arranges to be led along his way by a messenger-boy, but not until—

> "He will be ready, Monsieur," said she, "in a moment." "And in that moment," replied I, "most willingly would I say something very civil to you for all these courtesies. Any one may do a casual act of good-nature, but a continuation of them shows it is a part of the temperature; and, certainly," added I, "if it is the same blood which comes from the heart which descends to the extremes (touching her wrist) I am sure you must have one of the best pulses of any woman in the world." "Feel it," said she, holding out her arm. So laying down my hat, I took hold of her fingers in one hand, and applied the two fore-fingers of my other to the artery.
>
> Would to Heaven! my dear Eugenius, thou hadst passed by, and beheld me sitting in my black coat, and in my lack-a-day-sical manner, counting the throbs of it, one by one, with as much true devotion as if I had been watching the critical ebb or flow of her fever! How wouldst thou have laughed and moralized upon my new profession! and thou shouldst have laughed and

moralized on. Trust me, my dear Eugenius, I should have said "there are worse occupations in this world than *feeling a woman's pulse.*" But a *grisette's!* thou wouldst have said, and in an open shop, Yorick! So much the better: for when my views are direct, Eugenius, I care not if all the world saw me feel it.

I had counted twenty pulsations, and was going on fast towards the fortieth, when her husband coming unexpected from a back-parlor into the shop, put me a little out in my reckoning. 'Twas nobody but her husband, she said—so I began a fresh score. "Monsieur is so good," quoth she, as he passed by us, "as to give himself the trouble of feeling my pulse." The husband took off his hat, and making me a bow, said, I did him too much honor; and having said that, he put on his hat and walked out.

Good God! said I to myself, as he went out, and can this man be the husband of this woman!

The journey continues by the same paths: "I think there is a fatality in it; I seldom go to the place I set out for." There is a pretense at a narrative: Yorick is in need of a passport and must seek the intervention of the noble and highly placed to secure one. But the book is a series of digressions; it must be, for Yorick's mode of travel is to feel his way along. He is at last equipped with a passport, made out in the name of "Mr. Yorick, the King's jester." Nothing he can say will convince the Count de B**** that he is not Hamlet Senior's jester, "dead and buried eight hundred years ago," but only an eighteenth-century writer of sermons. " 'Twas all one, he replied." Monsieur is Yorick? the Count cries. Yes, Yorick must reply. "*Mon Dieu!* said he, embracing me, *Vous êtes Yorick!*" Yorick explains the mistake and corrects the Count's knowledge of England at the same time:

"We have no jester at court, Mons. le Count," said I; "the last we had was in the licentious reign of Charles II; since which time, our manners have been so gradually refining, that our court at present is so full of patriots, who wish for *nothing* but the honors and wealth of our country; and our ladies are all so chaste, so spotless, so good, so devout, there is nothing for a jester to make a jest of."

"*Voilà un persiflage!*" cried the Count.

The Count is not the only one to fail to recognize in Yorick a writer of sermons. Most of those who read the story of his travels are amused but still taken in by it. They miss the ironies, the exquisitely curled inventions of one of the most detached writers the world has ever known. They miss the sermon underneath and catch only the teasing on the surface. Not that the teasing is not worth catching and holding on to —anyone who turns too quickly from it loses the point of Sterne's sermon as well, for as with the earlier allegorists, every level, starting with the literal, signifies. The veil that cannot be seen cannot be rent. One must pause, then, not exactly reverently, but with at least some literary solemnity, before the elaborate hand-play between Yorick and almost every woman he meets in France and Italy, encounters which set their pulses and his and the reader's fluttering. The hand-play means nothing in itself. It leads nowhere, like the story within a story within a story contained on a piece of scrap paper wrapped around a currant-leaf which encloses a pat of butter: the hand-play and the story and the *Journey* itself come to nothing but innuendo, innuendo which the reader snatches at too eagerly. And that leads to more hand-play, for now Sterne slaps the reader's hand. How? By not completing any of the affairs that begin so auspiciously in the dark entries in which the writer finds his material:

The man who either disdains or fears to walk up a dark entry, may be an excellent good man, and fit for a hundred things; but he will not do to make a good Sentimental Traveller. I count little of the many things I see pass at broad noon-day, in large and open streets. Nature is shy, and hates to act before spectators; but in such an unobserved corner you sometimes see a single short scene of hers, worth all the sentiments of a dozen French plays compounded together, and yet they are *absolutely* fine; and whenever I have a more brilliant affair upon my hands than common, as they suit a preacher just as well as a hero, I generally make my sermon out of 'em. . . .

The book ends upon such a dark entry. Yorick is in Italy, forced by a break in the road and a storm to put up at a roadside inn. At the inn, he must share the one bedchamber with a lady and her maidservant. The three beds are apportioned, the only one with curtains going to the lady. Monsieur not being possessed of a *robe de chambre*, it is agreed that he should sleep in his black silk breeches. A further proviso, the third article in the treaty between Monsieur and Madame, enjoins any conversation at all after the candle and fire are put out, except for Monsieur's prayers. Finding it hard to sleep, Yorick twists and turns in his bed and at last cries out, "O my God!" The lady's response is immediate:

"You have broke the treaty, Monsieur," said the lady, who had no more sleep than myself. I begg'd a thousand pardons; but insisted it was no more than an ejaculation. She maintain'd it was an entire infraction of the treaty; I maintained it was provided for in the clause of the third article.

The lady would by no means give up the point, though she weaken'd her barrier by it; for, in the warmth of the dispute, I could hear two or three cork-pins fall out of the curtain to the ground.

"Upon my word and honor, Madame," said I, stretching my arm out of bed by way of asseveration,

(I was going to have added, that I would not have trespass'd against the remotest idea of decorum for the world)—

But the *fille de chambre* hearing there were words between us, and fearing that hostilities would ensue in course, had crept silently out of her closet; and it being totally dark, had stolen so close to our beds, that she had got herself into the narrow passage which separated them, and had advanced so far up as to be in a line betwixt her mistress and me;

So that when I stretch'd out my hand, I caught hold of the *fille de chambre's*—

Thus the journey ends, with a long dash, which is just as heated or as unheated as the reader's imagination makes it. "If it is not thought a chaste book," Sterne himself wrote during the composition of *A Sentimental Journey*, "mercy on them that read it, for they must have warm imaginations indeed!" Sterne's purpose in writing the book, he told good friends, "was to teach us to love the world and our fellow-creatures better than we do: so it runs most upon those gentler passions and affections, which aid so much to it." But the book does its running and makes its points not on its feet as the world normally does, but upside down, on its head. The wise reader will be happy to turn a few somersaults with Sterne. If he does so, he will find a wise book, perhaps not so full of surface wit as Sterne's *Tristram Shandy*, but dedicated to the same needling of the reader into a state of painful self-awareness, the necessary prelude to recollection and recovery.

"Nothing so powerfully calls home the mind as distress!" Sterne writes in a sermon on the prodigal son; "the tense fibre then relaxes, the soul retires to itself, sits pensive and susceptible of right impressions . . ." This is Pascalian paradox translated into eighteenth-century English:

Man surely is a compound of riddles and contradictions: by the law of his nature he avoids pain, and yet, "unless he suffers in the flesh, he will not cease from sin," though it is sure to bring pain and misery upon his head for ever.

Whilst all went pleasurably on with the prodigal, we hear not one word concerning his father; no pang of remorse for the sufferings in which he had left him, or resolution of returning, to make up the account of his folly: his first hour of distress seemed to be his first hour of wisdom.

Sterne makes no direct allusion to the prodigal son in his *Sentimental Journey*. He does not at any point spell out the purpose of the novel. But his meaning is clear enough to those who are not tone-deaf. For those who are unwilling to look below or above the surface, there are always the sermons. They are ingeniously contrived too and brilliantly worked with a subtle, if not devious rhetoric. In them the texts are exposed and the glosses open. In the sermon on the prodigal son, for example, he underlines his point:

> The intention of this parable is so clear, from the occasion of it, that it will not be necessary to perplex it with any tedious explanation: it was designed by way of indirect remonstrance to the Scribes and Pharisees, who animadverted upon our Saviour's conduct, for entering so freely into conferences with sinners, in order to reclaim them. To that end, he proposes the parable of the shepherd, who left his ninety-and-nine sheep that were safe in the fold, to go and seek for one sheep that was gone astray—telling them, in other places, they who were whole wanted not a physician—but they who were sick: and here, to carry on the same lesson, and to prove how acceptable such a recovery was to God, he relates this account of the prodigal son and his welcome reception.

As a matter of fact, Sterne explains, so much good use has been made of the prodigal son in sermons that he will concentrate on "that fatal passion which led him—and so many thousands after the example, 'to gather all he had together, and take his journey into a far country.' " The rest of the sermon is a chart of eager expectations and meager results.

The prodigal son in modern life expects to "learn the languages, the laws and customs, and understand the government and interest, of other nations—to acquire an urbanity and confidence of behavior . . ." He is fortunate, Sterne says, "if he returns to his country only as naked" as he left it: he leaves home at much too tender an age to learn anything. Some parents are prepared for this: they "send an able pilot," a scholar, along with their son. The result? The "unhappy youth will have the tutor to carry, and not the tutor to carry him," for the scholar has only read about the world and not experienced it. Other parents attempt to "avoid this extreme; he shall be escorted by one who knows the world not merely from books —but from his own experience; a man who has been employed on such services, and thrice made the tour of Europe with success." The result of this expediency? "If he is such as my eyes have seen! some broken *Swiss valet de chambre*—some general undertaker, who will perform the journey in so many months, *if God permit*, much knowledge will not accrue; some profit at least—he will learn the amount, to a halfpenny, of every stage from Calais to Rome; he will be carried to the best inns, instructed where there is the best wine, and sup a livre cheaper than if the youth had been left to make the tour and the bargain himself."

Such poor prodigals are Yorick and all his sentimental breed. All go forth with the same sort of anticipation. All feel their way as they go, literally or figuratively or both. All are badly advised. Few, if any, are capable of the sort of searching self-examination that is necessary to avoid the plight, often entertaining but more frequently pathetic, of the poor prodigal.

The same rhetorical devices that expose the fatal passion for voyaging abroad of the sentimentalist reveal the shabbiness of his self-examination. Sterne—who shows himself as convinced of the value of self-knowledge as Augustine, Boethius, and Bernard—lists five "false measures" usually taken by those who only pretend to examine themselves:

1. Setting about the examination of our works before we are

prepared with honest dispositions to amend them: this is beginning the work at the wrong end.

2. When a man is going to enter upon this work of self-examination, there is nothing so common as to see him look *round* him, instead of looking *within* him.

3. We leave out of the calculation the only material parts of them; I mean, the motives and first principles whence they proceeded.

4. Committing the task to others.

5. The last mistake which I shall have time to mention is that which the Methodists have revived. . . . I mean that extraordinary impulse and intercourse with the Spirit of God which they pretend to, and whose operations (if you trust them) are so sensibly felt in their hearts and souls as to render at once all other proofs of their works needless to themselves. This, I own, is one of the most summary ways of proceeding in this duty of self-examination; and, as it proves a man's works in the gross, it saves him a world of sober thought and inquiry after many vexatious particulars.

If man knows himself so little, is so easily deceived, is concupiscent by conviction as well as nature, can one reach him at all? Yes, says Sterne, one can: by a rhetoric of inversion. If you want to be understood by pigs, you must grunt, he explains in a sermon on a text from Philippians (3:20): "For our conversation is in heaven."

Preach to a voluptuous epicure, who knows of no other happiness in this world but what rises from good eating and drinking; such a one, in the Apostle's language, whose God was his belly; preach to him of the abstraction of his soul, tell of its flights and brisker motion in the pure regions of immensity; represent to him that saints and angels eat not—but that the spirit of a man lives for ever upon wisdom and holiness, and heavenly contemplations: why, the only effect would be, that the fat glutton would stare awhile upon the preacher, and in a few minutes fall fast asleep. No; if you would catch his attention, and make him take in your discourse greedily—you must preach to him out of the Alcoran—talk of the raptures of sensual enjoyments, and the pleasures of the perpetual feasting which Mahomet has described; there you touch upon a note which awakens and sinks into the inmost recesses of his soul; without which, discourse as wisely and abstractedly as you will of heaven, your representations of it, however glorious and exalted, will pass like the songs of melody over an ear incapable of discerning the distinction of sounds.

Laurence Sterne's ironic defense of obliquity is at the same time a design for an allegory of irony. He has no high hopes of heaven for the unvirtuous:

> Can it enter into our hearts even to hope that those hands can ever receive the reward of righteousness that are full of blood, laden with the wages of iniquity, of theft, rapine, violence, extortion, or other unlawful gain? or that those feet shall ever be beautiful upon the mountains of light and joy that were never shod for the preparation of the gospel—that have run quite out of the way of God's word, and made haste only to do evil? No, surely. In this sense, he that is unjust, let him be unjust still, and he which is filthy, let him be filthy still.

But the world's filth should not win a victory over us by causing us to despair; detachment is always possible. We can turn our thoughts from this world to the next and, "by so having our conversation in heaven whilst we are here, we may be thought fit inhabitants for it hereafter. . ." However little or much Sterne succeeds in turning his readers to that conversation, he himself prepared well for it; as a writer, at least, he was detached. He had to be. The ironic method he practised so skillfully demands detachment.

Henry Fielding does not maintain the same imperial attitude to his characters as Sterne does to his. He is warmly, even sentimentally attached to Squire Western and Parson Abraham Adams, whose name gives away his identity as Everyman. He takes sides in his stories with every clear expectation of seeing good triumph over evil and villains punished. He presides with joy, like the good representative of justice he is, over the unions of his heroes and heroines, and tucks his favorites in bed with a positive benignity, even if it is the bed of a whore. For if a whore shares her counterpane with one of Fielding's elect, she will turn out to be a whore with a heart of gold. But every time there is danger of Fielding falling prey to the wiles of guilelessness, he takes himself firmly in hand. He speculates on his art. He meditates on his religion. He reads himself a severe lesson on the perils of credulity. Best of all, he shares all—speculation, meditation, and lesson—with his readers. The liveliest, the most engrossing, and surely the most edifying pages of *Tom Jones* are the introductions to the eighteen books into which the novel is divided. More than introductions, they are interludes. And more than interludes, they are asides, soliloquies on the part of the writer—and really on his part, written in his defense. There is, for example, the beginning of Book VIII. The matter under discussion is "that species of writing which is called the marvellous":

> First, then, I think it may very reasonably be required of every writer, that he keeps within the bounds of possibility; and still remembers that what it is not possible for man to perform, it is scarce possible for man to believe he did perform. This conviction perhaps gave birth to many stories of the ancient heathen deities (for most of them are of poetical origin). The poet, being desirous to indulge a wanton and extravagant imagination, took refuge in that power, of the extent of which his readers were no judges, or rather which they imagined to be infinite, and consequently they could not be shocked at any prodigies related of it . . .
>
> But I have rested too long on a doctrine which can be of no

use to a Christian writer; for as he cannot introduce into his works any of that heavenly host which make a part of his creed, so it is horrid puerility to search the heathen theology for any of those deities who have been long since dethroned from their immortality . . .

The only supernatural agents which can in any manner be allowed to us moderns, are ghosts; but of these I would advise an author to be extremely sparing. These are indeed, like arsenic, and other dangerous drugs in physic, to be used with the utmost caution; nor would I advise the introduction of them at all in those works, or by those authors, to which, or to whom, a horse-laugh in the reader would be any great prejudice or mortification . . .

. . . We who deal in private character, who search into the most retired recesses, and draw forth examples of virtue and vice from holes and corners of the world, are in a . . . dangerous situation. As we have no public notoriety, no concurrent testimony, no records to support and corroborate what we deliver, it becomes us to keep within the limits not only of possibility, but of probability too; and this more especially in painting what is greatly good and amiable. Knavery and folly, though never so exorbitant, will more easily meet with assent; for ill-nature adds great support and strength to faith.

Probity, then, and accurate observation, are required of the writer. But modern critics, Fielding has been informed, have "begun to assert that all kind of learning is entirely useless to a writer"; it only restrains his imagination. Fielding is moved to protest, once more with irony in the fire:

This doctrine, I am afraid, is at present carried much too far; for why should writing differ so much from all other arts? The nimbleness of a dancing-master is not at all prejudiced by being taught to move; nor doth any mechanic, I believe, exercise his tools the worse by having learnt to use them. For my own part, I cannot conceive that Homer or Virgil would have writ with more fire, if, instead of being masters of all the learning of their times, they had been as ignorant as most of the authors of the present age . . .

I would not here be understood to insist on the same fund of learning in any of my brethren as Cicero persuades us is necessary to the composition of an orator. On the contrary, very little reading is, I conceive, necessary to the poet, less to the critic, and the least of all to the politician . . .

. . . one reason why many English writers have totally failed in describing the manners of upper life, may possibly be that in reality they know nothing of it . . .

Hence those strange monsters in lace and embroidery, in silks and brocades, with vast wigs and hoops; which, under the name of lords and ladies, strut the stage, to the great delight of attorneys and their clerks in the pit, and of the citizens and their apprentices in the galleries; and which are no more to be found in real life than the centaur, the chimera, or any other creature of mere fiction . . .

For Tom Jones and Squire Western and his daughter Sophia, Fielding preserves the amenities of the author-character relationship: many times he protests his love for those he writes about. With Abraham Adams, that much bedeviled angelic parson, and Partridge, who plays Sancho Panza to Tom Jones's Don Quixote, Fielding acts the part of a doting father: his paternity oozes in beatific syntax. But Fielding is not always so kind. He knows too the noble measures of detachment and does not always confine those measures to brief interludes.

In *The History of the Life of the Late Mr. Jonathan Wild the Great*, Fielding steps far outside the action. His function is to maintain an impeccably ironic tone as a pedal point throughout the novel. He does so, sounding his pedal quickly to make an essential distinction:

But before we enter on this great work we must endeavour to remove some errors of opinion which mankind have, by the disingenuity of writers, contracted: for these, from their fear of contradicting the obsolete and absurd doctrines of a set of simple fellows, called, in derision, sages or philosophers, have endeavoured, as much as possible, to confound the ideas of greatness and goodness; whereas no two things can possibly be more distinct from each other, for greatness consists in bringing all manner of mischief on mankind, and goodness in removing it from them. It seems, therefore, very unlikely that the same person should possess them both; and yet nothing is more usual with writers, who find many instances of greatness in their favourite hero, than to make him a compliment of goodness into the bargain; and this, without considering that by such means they destroy the great perfection called uniformity of character. In the histories of Alexander and Caesar we are frequently, and indeed impertinently, reminded of their benevolence and generosity, of their clemency and kindness. When the former had with fire and sword overrun a vast empire, had destroyed the lives of an immense number of innocent wretches, had scattered ruin and desolation like a whirlwind, we are told, as an example of his clemency, that he did not cut the throat of an old woman, and ravish her daughters, but was content with only undoing them. And when the mighty Caesar, with wonderful greatness of mind, had destroyed the liberties of his country, and with all the means of fraud and force had placed himself at the head of his equals, had corrupted and enslaved the greatest people whom the sun ever saw, we are reminded, as an evidence of his generosity, of his largeness to his followers and tools, by whose means he had accomplished his purpose, and by whose assistance he was to establish it.

Now, who doth not see that such sneaking qualities as these are rather to be bewailed as imperfections than admired as ornaments in these great men; rather obscuring their glory, and holding them back in their race to greatness, indeed unworthy the end for which they seem to have come into the world, viz., of perpetrating vast and mighty mischief?

No such imperfections mar the uniform character of Jonathan Wild. He is descended from a line of great men, such as the Wild of the time of Henry III, "surnamed Langfanger, or Longfinger," who "could, without the knowledge of the proprietor, with great ease and dexterity, draw forth a man's purse from any part of his garment where it was deposited . . ." Master Wild shows early that he is "to be bribed to anything, which made many say he was certainly born to be a great man." As a schoolboy, he is much moved by "that passage in the eleventh Iliad where Achilles is said to have bound two sons of Priam upon a mountain, and afterwards to have released them for a sum of money." His favorite book is *The Spanish Rogue*, his favorite play *The Cheats of Scapin.* Boy or man, he is consistent. His character, like his conscience, is pure. When he is out in the world, he steals from friends as equably as from strangers, but never allows his difficult, nay harsh, professional duties to interfere with his friendships:

He was none of those half-bred fellows who are ashamed to see their friends when they have plundered and betrayed them; from which base and pitiful temper many monstrous cruelties have been transacted by men, who have sometimes carried their modesty so far as to the murder or utter ruin of those against whom their consciences have suggested to them that they have committed some small trespass, either by the debauching a friend's wife or daughter, belying or betraying the friend himself, or some other such trifling instance. In our hero there was nothing not truly great: he could, without the least abashment, drink a bottle with the man who knew he had the moment before picked his pocket; and, when he had stripped him of everything he had, never desired to do him any further mischief; for he carried good-nature to that wonderful and uncommon height that he never did a single injury to man or woman by which he himself did not expect to reap some advantage.

Wild's greatness is subjected to many attacks and temptations before his history comes to an end, but none so abrasive as those which grow out of his encounters with an old schoolfellow, Mr. Thomas Heartfree. Heartfree is not endowed with greatness. Neither is his wife. On the contrary:

He was possessed of several great weaknesses of mind, being good-natured, friendly, and generous to a great excess. He had, indeed, too little regard to common justice, for he had forgiven some debts to his acquaintance only because they could not pay him, and had entrusted a bankrupt, on his setting up a second time, from having been convinced that he had dealt in his bankruptcy with a fair and honest heart, and that he had broke through misfortune only, and not from neglect or imposture. He was withal so silly a fellow that he never took the least advantage of the ignorance of his customers, and contented himself with very moderate gains on his goods; which he was the better enabled to do, notwithstanding his generosity, because his life was extremely temperate, his expenses being solely confined to the cheerful entertainment of his friends at home, and now and then a moderate glass of wine, in which he indulged himself in the company of his wife, who, with an agreeable person, was a mean-spirited, poor, domestic, low-bred animal, who confined herself mostly to the care of her family, placed her happiness in her husband and her children, followed no expensive fashions or diversions, and indeed rarely went abroad, unless to return the visits of a few plain neighbours, and twice a year afforded herself in company with her husband, the diversion of a play, where she never sat in a higher place than the pit.

As a result of schemes too ingenious to be reduced to brief description, our great man succeeds in sending Mr. Heartfree to Newgate prison, Mrs. Heartfree to sea, and himself after her. Wild has great designs for Heartfree's lady, but as with all the ladies in this history, she does not measure up to greatness. Neither, for that matter, do the members of Wild's gang. Because of their failures, the great man is himself conveyed to Newgate, there to await death by hanging. Once again, however, he shows his true stature: he attains to "place and power" in the prison.

With the "ordinary" of the establishment, the minister who is delegated to prepare his soul for eternity, Wild exchanges sentiments worthy both of greatness and of the cloth. The conversation is preserved in a transcription that is not altogether legible. But even an elliptic version of worthy sentiments deserves close inspection:

Jonathan. . . . I assure you, doctor, I had much rather be happy than miserable. But * * * * * * * * * * * * *

Ordinary. Nothing can be plainer. St. * * * * * * * * * * *

Jonathan. * * * * * If once convinced * * * * * * * no man * lives of * * * * * * * * * whereas sure the clergy * opportunity * * better informed * * * * all manner of vice * * * * * * *

Ordinary. * are * atheist. * deist * ari * * cinian * hanged ** burnt ** oiled * oasted. *** dev ** his an *** ell fire ** ternal da***tion.

Jonathan. You *** to frighten me out of my wits. But the good *** is, I doubt not, more merciful than his wicked ** If I should believe all you say, I am sure I should die in inexpressible horror.

A great man cannot be left in such theological straits for long. Jonathan reproves the ordinary for trying to send him to perdition. But then he remembers who he is. He commiserates with the cleric as a man of "vast learning and abilities obliged to exert them in so low a sphere, when so many of your inferiors wallow in wealth in preferment." He is saved. The ordinary bids him not to despair: "I have known many a man reprieved who had less reason to expect it." But what if hope is unfulfilled, Jonathan asks; "What then would become of my soul?" The ordinary's response is comforting: "Pugh! Never mind your soul—leave that to me, I will render a good account of it, I warrant you. I have a sermon in my pocket which may be of some use to you to hear. . . . His text is "—To the Greeks FOOLISHNESS." Upon it the clergyman composes a masterful commentary:

> What was their great master Plato, or their other great light Aristotle? Both fools, mere quibblers and sophists, idly and vainly attached to certain ridiculous notions of their own, founded neither on truth nor on reason. Their whole works are a strange medley of the greatest falsehoods, scarce covered over with the colour of truth: their precepts are neither borrowed from nature nor guided by reason; mere fictions, serving only to evince the dreadful height of human pride; in one word, FOOLISHNESS. It may be perhaps expected of me that I should give some instances from their works to prove this charge; but, as to transcribe every passage to my purpose would be to transcribe their whole works, and as in such a plentiful crop it is difficult to choose; instead of trespassing on your patience, I shall conclude this first head with asserting what I have so fully proved, and what may indeed be inferred from the text, that the philosophy of the Greeks was FOOLISHNESS.

And so with high-sounding phrases in his ear, Jonathan Wild the Great prepares for death—by falling asleep.

The death of the great man is "as glorious as his life had been." He makes one last show of his professional integrity by removing from the ordinary's pocket a bottlescrew, which he then takes with him on his last journey. He swears vigorously at the crowd, which earns him "universal applause." To that happy sound, "our hero swung out of this world."

Before the end of the book, Fielding offers the reader what might be called a prig's-eye view of the world—*prig* being the criminal's word for thief. This consists of fifteen rules of conduct for all who would attain greatness. Several of the precepts are succinct treatises in themselves on the art and theology of *priggism:*

Never to do more mischief to another than was necessary to the effecting his purpose; for that mischief was too precious a thing to be thrown away.
Not to trust him who hath deceived you, nor who knows he hath been deceived by you.
Never to reward any one equal to his merit; but always to insinuate that the reward was above it.
That virtues, like precious stones, were easily counterfeited; that the counterfeits in both cases adorned the wearer equally, and that very few had knowledge or discernment sufficient to distinguish the counterfeit jewel from the real.
That men proclaim their own virtues, as shopkeepers expose their goods, in order to profit by them.
That the heart was the proper seat of hatred, and the countenance of affection and friendship.

The greatness in Wild leaves his chronicler in awe at the end. For his character is not marred by any blemishes at all, except those few defects which show him human. He is never really guilty of compassion, though he does weaken for a moment when it looks as if Heartfree is going to precede him to the gallows. The tribute carved by Fielding is deserved:

Indeed, while greatness consists in power, pride, insolence, and doing mischief to mankind—to speak out—while a great man and great rogue are synonymous terms, so long shall Wild stand unrivalled on the pinnacle of GREATNESS. Nor must we omit here, as the finishing of his character, what indeed ought to be remembered on his tomb or his statue, the conformity above mentioned on his death to his life; and that Jonathan Wild the Great, after all his mighty exploits, was, what so few GREAT men can accomplish—hanged by the neck till he was dead.

Fielding treats his reader's emotions with an ascetical detachment right to the very end of his book. Only the most abandoned indulger in vicarious experience could or would project himself into the character of Wild or one of the near-great who are his colleagues. This is a work to be read with the same sort of coolness and detachment that *A Sentimental Journey* invites. But underlying its detachment is a deep strain of moral indignation. Fielding's design in it, like Sterne's in his book, clearly is "to teach us to love the world and our fellow-creatures better than we do." And equally clearly, "If it is not thought a chaste book, mercy on them that read it, for they must have warm imaginations indeed!"

CHAPTER XIII

Newman and Dostoevsky: The Politics of Salvation

ONLY VERY CLOSE TO DESPAIR CAN WE DEVELOP THE highest hopes. That is the paradoxical meaning of all of the poems of Gerard Manley Hopkins' "winter world"; that is the substance of the terrible tuneful despair of "The Leaden Echo" and the discordant comfort of "The Golden Echo":

O then, weary then why should we tread? Oh why are we so
 haggard at the heart, so care-coiled, care-killed, so fagged,
 so fashed, so cogged, so cumbered,
When the thing we freely forfeit is kept with fonder a care,
Fonder a care kept than we could have kept it, kept
Far with fonder a care (and we, we should have lost it) finer,
 fonder
A care kept.—Where kept? Do but tell us where kept, where.—
Yonder.—What high as that! We follow, now we follow.—Yon-
 der, yes yonder, yonder,
Yonder.

And that is the significance too of those words of John Henry Newman written in his journal "under the image of the Patriarch Job, without intending to liken myself to him":

I have so depressing a feeling that I have done nothing through my long life—and especially that now I am doing nothing at all. Anglicans indeed rather think more of what I have written than they did, if I may judge from letters I receive—but, as to Catholics, they would not deny that I have done some good service towards bringing Anglicans into the Church, nay am perhaps doing so still; but, as to the great controversies of the day, about the divinity of Christianity &c, they think I am passé—at least this, (perhaps rather,) that I have taken a wrong line in respect to them . . .

But then I think—what is this to me? God will provide—He knows what is best. Is He less careful for the Church, less able to defend it than I am? Why need I fash myself about it? What am I? my time is out. I am passé—I may have done something in my day—but I can do nothing now. It is the turn of others. And if things seem done clumsily, my business is, not to criticize, but to have faith in God. . . . It is enough for me to prepare for death—for, as it would appear, nothing else awaits me—there is nothing else to do.

And He Who has been with me so marvellously all through my life, will not fail me now, I know—though I have no claim upon Him, . . .[1]

The key word in both plaints is "fash" or "fashed," meaning "weary" or "wearied," "troubled" or "worried," meaning any one or all of these things. How these men did weary themselves in God's cause! How they worried themselves! Disappointment seemed the only wages of their weariness. But they went on; Hopkins briefly enough—he lasted less than forty-five years; Newman much longer, nearly twice as long. But long or short, fagged or fashed, cogged or cumbered, they fought the terrible tiredness faithfully and with equal devotion planned and plotted their attacks on the doubts of others.

It finally came to that: doubt or faith. Hope grew out of despair, faith out of doubt. What made for anguish was the constancy of the temptations to despair and doubt. What made for torture was that no sooner was the despair conquered than doubt took its place. What made for sanity—and sanctity—and literature—was the equally invariable dedication to hope and faith which assured both men of never being "passé," not in their own lifetimes or ours or any others to come. But assurance was not for them, only theirs to give.

Newman in particular devoted himself to bringing faith and hope wherever he could, however he could, to whomever he could. The paradox he saw so well in the life of St. Alphonsus Liguori—"he who has the repute of being so lax a moralist had one of the most scrupulous and anxious of consciences himself"—was his. He who had the repute of being so persuasive an apologist had one of the most scrupulous and anxious of consciences himself.

Conscience finds its special spokesman and practical prophet in Newman. Weighed down as few men by its burdens, he knew as well its tenderness, its illuminations, its soft and simple strength:

> Conscience is a personal guide, and I use it because I must use myself; I am as little able to think by any mind but my own as to breathe with another's lungs. Conscience is nearer to me than any other means of knowledge. And as it is given to me, so also is it given to others; and being carried about by every individual in his own breast, and requiring nothing besides itself, it is thus adapted for the communication to each separately of that knowledge which is most momentous to him individually,—adapted for the use of all classes and conditions of men, for high and low, young and old, men and women, independently of books, of educated reasoning, of physical knowledge, or of philosophy. Conscience, too, teaches us, not only that God is, but what He is; it provides for the mind a real image of Him, as a medium of worship; it gives us a rule of right and wrong, as being His rule, and a code of moral duties. Moreover, it is so constituted that, if obeyed, it becomes clearer in its injunctions, and wider in their range, and corrects and completes the accidental feebleness of its initial teachings. Conscience, then, considered as our guide, is fully furnished for its office.

From conscience we learn Who is our Master, our Judge, our Provider. The intimations of conscience yield man his natural religion: severe, it is true; painful; aching with the awareness of God's "absence (if I may so speak) from His own world." But that same religion, on the same natural level, is full of promptings that "bring home to our experience the fact of a Good God, in spite of the tumult and confusion of the world." Why? The answer is of a piece with the *De Ordine*. It shares Augustine's confident faith and the rich rhetoric which expresses it:

It is possible to give an interpretation to the course of things, by which every event or occurrence in its order becomes providential: and though that interpretation does not hold good unless the world is contemplated from a particular point of view, in one given aspect, and with certain inward experiences, and personal first principles and judgments, yet these may be fairly pronounced to be common conditions of human thought, that is, till they are wilfully or accidentally lost; and they issue in fact, in leading the great majority of men to recognize the Hand of unseen power, directing in mercy or in judgment the physical and moral system. In the prominent events of the world, past and contemporary, the fate, evil or happy, of great men, the rise and fall of states, popular revolutions, decisive battles, the migration of races, the replenishing of the earth, earthquakes and pestilences, critical discoveries and inventions, the history of philosophy, the advancement of knowledge, in these the spontaneous piety of the human mind discerns a Divine Supervision. Nay, there is a general feeling, originating directly in the workings of conscience, that a similar governance is extended over the persons of individuals, who thereby both fulfill the purposes and receive the just recompenses of an Omnipotent Providence. Good to the good, and evil to the evil, is instinctively felt to be, even from what we see, amid whatever obscurity and confusion, the universal rule of God's dealings with us. Hence come the great proverbs, indigenous in both Christian and heathen nations, that punishment is sure, though slow, that murder will out, that treason never prospers, that pride will have a fall, that honesty is the best policy, and that curses fall on the heads of those who utter them. To the unsophisticated apprehension of the many, the successive passages of life, social, or political, are so many miracles, if that is to be accounted miraculous which brings before them the immediate Divine Presence; and should it be objected that this is an illogical exercise of reason, I answer, that since it actually brings them to a right conclusion, and was intended to bring them to it, if logic finds fault with it, so much the worse for logic.

Newman stands, not untouched by logic, but refusing to be too much touched by it. Its arbitrary dispositions have no significant place in his grammar of assent. As he explains in *The Tamworth Reading Room*, "Logic makes but a sorry rhetoric with the multitude; first shout round corners, and you may not despair of converting by a syllogism." Furthermore, "Logicians are more set upon concluding rightly than on right conclusions. They cannot see the end for the process." Newman's grammar, then, is no science, but the far more defensible construction of an artist. He is "suspicious," he says, "of scientific demonstrations in a question of concrete fact, in a discussion between fallible men." Let those demonstrate who can: "For me, it is more congenial to my own judgment to attempt to prove Christianity in the same informal way in which I can prove for certain that I have been born into this world, and that I shall die out of it." Another such certainty is the sense of sin, which we experience as acutely as we do bodily pain. This sense of sin makes itself felt in three ways, each a challenge to the God Whose presence we know so well:

He Himself is Sanctity, Truth, and Love; and the three offenses against His Majesty are impurity, inveracity, and cruelty. All men are not distressed at these offenses alike; but the piercing pain and sharp remorse which one or other inflicts upon the mind, till habituated to them, brings home to it the notion of what sin is, and is the vivid type and representative of its intrinsic hatefulness.

Newman could work only in this way, with what he found in himself. To others he commended only this way. With a psychological exactness matched only by his syntactical precision, he reminds us of where we are, of what we are, and of what we may become. Where are we?

> We are in a world of facts, and we use them; for there is nothing else to use. We do not quarrel with them, but we take them as they are, and avail ourselves of what they can do for us. It would be out of place to demand of fire, water, earth, and air their credentials, so to say, for acting upon us, or ministering to us. We call them elements, and turn them to account, and make the most of them. We speculate on them at our leisure . . . We are conscious of the objects of external nature, and we reflect and act upon them, and this consciousness, reflection, and action we call our own rationality.

What are we?

> I am what I am, or I am nothing. I cannot think, reflect, or judge about my being, without starting from the very point which I aim at concluding. My ideas are all assumptions, and I am ever moving in a circle. I cannot avoid being sufficient for myself, for I cannot make myself any thing else, and to change me is to destroy me. If I do not use myself, I have no other self to use. My only business is to ascertain what I am, in order to put it to use. It is enough for the proof of the value and authority of any function which I possess, to be able to pronounce that it is natural. What I have to ascertain is the laws under which I live. My first elementary lesson of duty is that of resignation to the laws of my nature, whatever they are; my first disobedience is to be impatient at what I am, and to indulge an ambitious aspiration after what I cannot be, to cherish a distrust of my powers, and to desire to change laws which are identical with myself.

What may we become?

> though man cannot change what he is born with, he is a being

of progress with relation to his perfection and characteristic good. Other beings are complete from their first existence, in that line of excellence which is allotted to them; but man begins with nothing realized . . . and he has to make capital for himself by the exercise of those faculties which are his natural inheritance. Thus he gradually advances to the fulness of his original destiny. Nor is this progress mechanical, nor is it of necessity; it is committed to the personal efforts of each individual of the species; each of us has the prerogative of completing his inchoate and rudimental nature, and of developing his own perfection out of the living elements with which his mind began to be. It is his gift to be the creator of his own sufficiency; and to be emphatically self-made. This is the law of his being, which he cannot escape; and whatever is involved in that law he is bound, or rather he is carried on, to fulfil.[2]

The inheritance of Christianity from the past is large and valuable, but not shackling: "It is no dreary matter of antiquarianism; we do not contemplate it in conclusions drawn from dumb documents and dead events, but by faith exercised in everliving objects, and by the appropriation and use of ever-recurring gifts." Furthermore, the sense of reality in Christianity is not diminished, but increased by its mysteries. Transcending time and place, the mysteries insistently return us to persons, divine and human. For Christianity "speaks to us one by one, and it is received by us one by one, as the counterpart, so to say, of ourselves, and is real as we are real."

The Church makes its way into the world according to the same method, speaking to us all, one by one, and being received or rejected, one by one. The politics of belief is directed to a private voting-booth. With a wide franchise, man there elects faith or doubt or prejudice, to name the principal parties to whose representatives Newman directs his appeals. Not the least pertinent and enjoyable of those appeals is the one to the party of prejudice. Here Newman admits himself concerned "not with Protestants quiescent and peaceable, but with Protestants malevolent, belligerent, busy, and zealous in an aggression upon our character and conduct." He cannot help himself. They make up the party of prejudice. His only answer to them is a systematic examination of their position.

For the purposes of analysis, Newman personifies "that narrow, ungenerous spirit which energizes and operates so widely and so unweariedly in the Protestant community—the Prejudiced man . . ." To begin with, there are his first principles. The Prejudiced Man "takes it for granted . . . not only that he himself is in possession of divine truth . . . but that we, who differ from him, are universally impostors, tyrants, hypocrites, cowards, and slaves." For him there are no authorities, no answers from fact, no facts indeed but his own convictions, no corrections to calumnies but more slander. However, says Newman, for purposes literary, polemical, and psychological, let us for the moment pretend that he is well disposed:

> you set about undeceiving him on some point on which he misstates the Catholic faith. He is determined to be candor and fairness itself, and to do full justice to your argument. So you begin your explanation;—you assure him he misconceives your doctrines; he has got a wrong view of facts. You appeal to original authorities, and show him how shamefully they have been misquoted; you appeal to history and prove it has been garbled. Nothing is wanted to your representation; it is triumphant. He is silent for a moment, then he begins with a sentiment. "What clever fellows these Catholics are!" he says, "I defy you to catch them tripping; they have a way out of everything. I thought we had you, but I fairly own I am beaten. This is how the Jesuits got on; always educated, subtle, well up in their books; a Protestant has no chance with them."[3]

Nothing bothers the Prejudiced Man as much as the success

of "Popery." To nothing does he respond with greater variety or virtuosity of imagination. He does his dance of prejudice in nine nimble steps:

First, he denies that there are any conversions or converts at all. This is a bold game, and will not succeed in England, though I have been told that in Ireland it has been strenuously maintained. However, let him grant the fact, that converts there are, and he has a second ground to fall back upon: the converts are weak and foolish persons,–notoriously so; all their friends think so; there is not a man of any strength of character or force of intellect among them . . . Thirdly, in corroboration:–they went over, he says, on such exceedingly wrong motives . . . it was love of notoriety, it was restlessness, it was resentment, it was lightness of mind, it was self-will . . . They went too soon, or they ought to have gone sooner . . . In short, they did not become Catholics at the right moment; so that, however numerous they may be, no weight whatever attaches to their conversion . . . His fourth remark is of this sort: they are sure to come back. He prophesies that by this time next year, not one of them will be a Catholic. His fifth is as bold as the first;–they *have* come back . . . directly a new Catholic is safely lodged two or three thousand miles away, out comes the confident news that he has returned to Protestantism; when no friend has the means to refute it. When this argument fails, as fail it must, by the time a letter can be answered, our Prejudiced Man falls back on his sixth common-place, which is to the effect that the converts are very unhappy. He knows this on the first authority; he has seen letters declaring or showing it. They are quite altered men, very much disappointed with Catholicism, restless, and desirous to come back except from false shame. Seventhly, they are altogether deteriorated in character; they have become harsh, or overbearing, or conceited, or vulgar. They speak with extreme bitterness against Protestantism, have cast off their late friends, or seem to forget that they ever were Protestants themselves. Eighthly, they have become infidels;–alas! heedless of false witness, the Prej-

> udiced Man spreads the news about, right and left, in a tone of great concern and distress; he considers it very awful.
>
> Lastly, when every resource has failed, and in spite of all that can be said, and surmised, and expressed, and hoped, about the persons in question, Catholics they have become, and Catholics they remain, the Prejudiced Man has a last resource, he simply forgets that Protestants they ever were. They cease to have antecedents; they cease to have any character, any history to which they may appeal: they merge in the great fog, in which to his eyes everything Catholic is enveloped: they are dwellers in the land of romance and fable; and, if he dimly contemplates them plunging and floundering amid the gloom, it is as griffins, wiverns, salamanders, the spawn of Popery, such as are said to sport in the depths of the sea, or to range amid the central sands of Africa. He forgets he ever heard of them; he has no duties to their names, he is released from all anxiety about them; they die to him.

Newman spoke from personal experience. When he became a Catholic, "grave persons" reported that he was either mad or in "imminent danger" of insanity. Then they "put about" that he had had the strongest differences, first with Cardinal Wiseman and then with authorities in Rome, and finally that not only had he privately repudiated Catholic doctrines but that he had "given up Revealed Religion altogether." He knew the temper of the times so well because he was so much of them, because those of the time were so much concerned with him, and because he was so much concerned with them. When he wrote about the Prejudiced Man, though he did it with high good humor and seemed at times to be just this side of hyperbole, he wrote with accuracy: "Our Prejudiced Man of course sees Catholics and Jesuits in everything, in every failure of the potato crop, every strike of the operatives, and every mercantile stoppage. . . . A Catholic Priest cannot be grave or gay, silent or talkative, without giving matter of offence or suspicion. There is peril in his frown, there is greater peril in his smile." The Prejudiced Man journeys abroad: "There are no private homes, as in England, families live on staircases; see what it is to belong to a Popish country. Why do the Roman labourers wheel their barrows so slow on the Forum? why do the Lazzaroni of Naples lie so listlessly on the beach? why, but because they are under the *malaria* of a false religion. . . . Bloodletting is as frequent and as much a matter of course in the South, as hair-cutting in England; it is a trick borrowed from the convents, when they wish to tame down refractory spirits . . . what is this? the figure of a woman: who can it be? His Protestant cicerone at his elbow, who perhaps has been chosen by his good father or guardian to protect him on his travels from a Catholic taint, whispers that it is Pope Joan and he notes it down in his pocket-book accordingly."

Newman laughs, but prejudice is no laughing matter. For prejudice corrupts the soul as much as the pride in which it has its source: "It argues so astonishing a want of mere natural charity or love of our kind. It is piercing enough to think what little faith there is in the country; but it is quite heart-rending to witness so utter a deficiency in a mere natural virtue." He was haunted by the horror—and to him horror it was—

Oh, is it possible, that so many, many men, and women too, good and kind otherwise, should take such delight in being quite sure that millions of men have the sign and seal of the Evil One upon them! . . . They delight to look at us, and to believe that we are the veriest reptiles and vermin which belied the human form divine . . . They are tenacious of what they believe, they are impatient of being argued with, they are angry at being contradicted, they are disappointed when a point is cleared up; they had rather that *we* should be guilty than *they* mistaken; they have no wish at all we should not be blaspheming hypocrites, stupid idolaters, loathsome profligates, unprincipled rogues and bloodthirsty demons. They are kinder even to their dogs and their cats than to us.

Just how serious is this prejudice? How intense? How threatening? Newman's answer is blunt: "Calm as may be the sky, and gentle the breeze, we cannot trust the morning: at any moment a furious tempest may be raised against us, and scatter calamity through our quiet homes. . . . We never are secure against the access of madness in that people, whose name and blood we share." Anything—a papal document, a scandal among religious, a foolish or false statement—anything "may raise all England against us."

That was 1851. Twenty-two years later, preaching at the opening of a seminary, Newman suggested that there was still worse to fear, "The Infidelity of the Future." He knew "that all times are perilous, and that in every time serious and anxious minds, alive to the honour of God and the needs of man, are apt to consider no time so perilous as their own." But the future is faced with a plague:

that plague of infidelity, that the Apostles and our Lord Himself have predicted as the worst calamity of the last times of the Church. And at least a shadow, a typical image of the last times is coming over the world. I do not mean to presume to say that this is the last time, but that it has had the evil prerogative of being like that more terrible season, when it is said that the elect themselves will be in danger of falling away.

The signs were clear. First, there was the fact that the large number of different sects, once of such "great service to us in shielding and sheltering us from the assaults of those who believed less than themselves or nothing at all," had become bold in their opposition to Catholics and weak in their support of their own beliefs. Secondly, the very success of the Church presaged difficulties, invited prejudice and fear. Catholics could in the future look forward to being grouped together in people's minds as members of an international conspiracy against civil liberties and progress: "In this way we may suffer disadvantages which have not weighed against the Catholic Church since the age of Constantine." Thirdly, with the growth of literacy and newspapers, the slightest failure would immediately be served to the appetite of the masses: "If there ever was a time when one priest will be a spectacle to men and angels it is in the age now opening upon us."

In that age—in which we are now living—the popular appeal to reason can only in part be gratified by the Church, since "the true religion must be full of mysteries." Therefore to the populace at every level it must seem that the Church suffocates reason and that her educated men, her priests, do not really believe what cannot really be believed, what is patently contrary to reason; and that therefore they "must be hypocrites, professing what in their hearts they reject." The result is likely to be arguments poor in their effect because necessarily incomplete, because words can only go so far with mysteries, can only signify them but not explain them away. Catholics may be disheartened and depressed, because they live in a world which does not acknowledge any ground for their faith, an experience new to Christianity. For now there can be no appeal, like that of St. Paul among the Athenian doubters, to the Unknown God; now, no sharing of faith in some supernatural government, as with the barbarians of the North; now, no common belief in the moral law, not even the most rudimentary belief.

My Brethren, you are coming into a world, if present appearances do not deceive, such as priests never came into before, that is, so far forth as you do go into it, so far as you go beyond your flocks, and so far as those flocks may be in great danger as under the influence of the prevailing epidemic.[4]

The only weapons that avail under such circumstances are those of the seminary and the educated spirit steeped in Catholic theology. Once again, "as in the revolted kingdom of Israel, there will be a remnant." It must be a remnant notable for its seriousness, its recollection, its prudence, its wisdom, its closeness to God. "And thus an elevation of mind will be created, which is the true weapon . . . against the infidelity of the world." Infidelity is the position of the enemy, of Liberalism. Liberals, as Newman defines them in a note to the *Apologia Pro Vita Sua*, advocate "false liberty of thought," that is, "the exercise of thought upon matters, in which, from the constitution of the human mind, thought cannot be brought to any successful issue, and therefore is out of place." Liberals make the fundamental "mistake of submitting to human judgment those revealed doctrines which are in their nature beyond and independent of it, and of claiming to determine on intrinsic grounds the truth and value of propositions which rest for their reception simply on the external authority of the Divine Word."

The more he aged, the more Newman was haunted by the spectre of Liberalism. On the bright day of May in 1879 when he received his Cardinal's hat in Rome, he felt impelled, there on home ground, to alarm and thus to arm Holy Church. His agony, he explained, had been long-lived: "For 30, 40, 50 years I have resisted to the best of my powers the spirit of liberalism in religion." Once more he will speak. Once more he will protest "this great *apostasia*" which has made of religion "a private luxury" and of the religious the helpless victims of noble principles—"the precepts of justice, truthfulness, sobriety, self-command, benevolence"—drawn from their own creeds but now craftily turned against them.

> It is not till we find that this array of principles is intended to supersede, to block out, religion, that we pronounce it to be evil.

There never was a device of the enemy, so cleverly framed, and with such promise of success. And already it has answered to the expectations which have been formed of it. It is sweeping into its own ranks great numbers of able, earnest, virtuous men, elderly men of approved antecedents, young men with a career before them.

Newman never ceased to remind the remnant of the faithful, or those who would instruct it in the faith, of the terrors that lay ahead. Whenever possible, he showed them the ugly signs already apparent in his own day. It was a long day he lived but not a bright one. The darkness was lowering steadily, stonily, scarily. "In this day," he warned in 1854 in *The Idea of a University*, "Truth and Error lie over against each other with a valley between them, and David goes forward in the sight of all men . . . to engage with the Philistine." He looked over into the enemy's camp and tried "to trace the outlines of the hostile movements and the preparations for assault which are there in agitation against us." What he saw was a great blur, the blur of those themselves insensible to the truths of revelation and determined to make them meaningless to others. They had an argument which Newman, as an honest adversary, understood and presented candidly; putting himself in the Liberal's place, he explained:

"without denying that in the matter of religion some things are true and some things false, still we certainly are not in a position to determine the one or the other. And, as it would be absurd to dogmatize about the weather, and say that 1860 will be a wet season or a dry season, a time of peace or war, so it is absurd for men in our present state to teach anything positively about the next world, that there is a heaven, or a hell, or a last judgment, or that the soul is immortal, or that there is a God. It is not that you have not a right to your own opinion, as you have a right to place implicit trust in your own banker, or in your own physician; but undeniably such persuasions are not knowledge, they are not scientific, they cannot become public property, they are consistent with your allowing your friend to entertain the opposite opinion; and, if you are tempted to be violent in the defence of your own view of the case in this matter of religion, then it is well to lay seriously to heart whether sensitiveness on the subject of your banker or your doctor, when he is handled sceptically by another, would not be taken to argue a secret misgiving in your mind about him, in spite of your confident profession, an absence of clear, unruffled certainty in his honesty or in his skill."

The full force of this dogmatic attack on dogma and revelation was not realized by many in Newman's time, though he made tireless efforts to explain the attack and to instruct the attacked. See, he told Catholics, see what the tactics are of this new school of philosophers:

Knowing little, and caring less for the depth and largeness of that heavenly Wisdom, on which the Apostle delights to expatiate, or the variety of those sciences, dogmatic or ethical, mystical or hagiological, historical or exegetical, which Revelation has created, these philosophers know perfectly well that, in matter of fact, to beings, constituted as we are, sciences which concern this world and this state of existence are worth far more, are more arresting and attractive, than those which relate to a system of things which they do not see and cannot master by their natural powers. Sciences which deal with tangible facts, practical results, ever-growing discoveries, and perpetual novelties, which feed curiosity, sustain attention, and stimulate expectation, require, they consider, but a fair stage and no favour to distance that Ancient Truth, which never changes and but cautiously advances, in the race for popularity and power. And therefore they look out for the day when they shall have put down Religion, not by shutting its schools, but by emptying them, not by disputing its tenets, but by the superior worth and persuasiveness of their own.[5]

Is there a better, a more succinct, summary of the procedures of positivism in our day, "logical" or "therapeutic" or whatever kind? There is some comfort, perhaps, in the twentieth century in the realization that these procedures have resulted in no progress at all for philosophy, however much they may have restricted and enfeebled theology. But that is carrion comfort, if it is any comfort at all. For the decay of philosophy, for which philosophers themselves must be held responsible, represents the collapse of one more bulwark against infidelity. As Newman explained in a letter describing the possible effects of the fall of the Establishment in England: "Infidelity would take possession of the bulk of the men, and the women, so they had something to worship, would not care whether it was an unknown tongue, or a book of Mormon, or a pudding sleeve gown. Infidel literature would be the fashion, and there would be a sort of fanatical contempt and hatred of all profession of belief in a definite revelation."

Much of Newman's analysis is of this sort, is what may be called "destructive." He is a prophet, and his tone is prophetic: the dominant note is sorrowful; the predictions are made with a heavy heart; the future is bleak. Learning will disappear when revelation is no longer trusted, and wisdom will not be far behind. Quick defenses will have to be thrown up all over the place, as in fact Newman was having to do already, assigned, officially or unofficially, to do the dirty work and consequently much dirtied himself. One never knew what would have to be defended, or how the need would arise. The Vatican Council asserted as a dogma of divine revelation the infallibility of the pope, when he speaks *ex cathedra*, defining a doctrine of faith or morals; and Newman anguished—not for himself, but for others. He thought the promulgation of the doctrine at that time a tactical error that to those outside would make the Church seem less acceptable than ever. But he decided against making his feelings public: "all I do is to pray those great early Doctors of the Church whose intercession would decide the matter–Augustine and the rest–to avert so great a calamity." Of course, the trials came, something less than a calamity as it turned out. But how often, how nearly calamitously, Newman had to repeat to the newspapers, to friends, to enemies, in public statement and private, in refutations of the many misinterpretations of the dogma: "No Pope can make evil good. No Pope has any power over those moral principles which God has imprinted on our hearts and consciences. If any Pope has, with his eyes open, approved treachery or cruelty, let those defend that Pope who can." Again and again and again: "Infallibility is not impeccability." Finally, and inevitably, there were the personal attacks upon him, which unaccountably made his private correspondence public, and distorted it. His doubts about the expediency of the promulgation of the dogma were turned into questionings of the doctrine itself and into evasions which in effect made him a hypocrite and a liar.

To personal attacks, Newman could rejoin with documentary evidence: passages in quantity attested to his own long sustained belief in the newly proclaimed but long-held doctrine of papal infallibility. But against general attacks on the Faith no such strategy was sufficient. Only faith itself would do. And so, to begin with, he asserted his own faith, clearly and simply and often, as, for example, in a letter to a newspaper in 1862:

> I have not had one moment's wavering of trust in the Catholic Church ever since I was received into her fold. I hold, and ever have held, that her Sovereign Pontiff is the centre of unity and the Vicar of Christ; and I ever have had, and have still, an unclouded faith in her creed in all its articles; a supreme satisfaction in her worship, discipline, and teaching; and an eager longing and a hope against hope that the many dear friends whom I have left in Protestantism may be partakers of my happiness.

This being my state of mind, to add, as I hereby go on to do, that I have no intention, and never had any intention, of leaving the Catholic Church and becoming a Protestant again, would be superfluous, except that Protestants are always on the look-out for some loophole or evasion in a Catholic's statement of fact. Therefore, in order to give them full satisfaction, if I can, I do hereby profess *ex animo*, with an absolute internal assent and consent, that Protestantism is the dreariest of possible religions; that the thought of the Anglican service makes me shiver, and the thought of the Thirty-nine Articles makes me shudder. Return to the Church of England! No! "The net is broken, and we are delivered." I should be a consummate fool (to use a mild term) if in my old age I left "the land flowing with milk and honey" for the city of confusion and the house of bondage.[6]

He made equally clear, whenever possible, his strong conviction, based on history, of the ultimate powerlessness of the parties of hate and hollowness and the "new philosophy." However much they may dream and hope, theirs is "hatred of a Power which Julian and Frederic, Shaftesbury and Voltaire, and a thousand other great sovereigns and subtle thinkers, have assailed in vain."

The lasting program of action in defense of faith is an old one in Newman's life. It reaches back in time to the *Lectures on the Doctrine of Justification* which he delivered as an Anglican in 1838 and, with very few emendations, was pleased as a Catholic to reprint in 1874. The Apostles have the last word, as they had the first, in the campaign to make men believe:

they did not rest their cause on argument; they did not rely on eloquence, wisdom, or reputation; nay, nor did they make miracles necessary to the enforcement of their claims. They did not resolve faith into sight or reason; they contrasted it with both, and bade their hearers believe, sometimes in spite, sometimes in default, sometimes in aid, of sight and reason . . . for faith, as a principle of knowledge, cannot be exactly analyzed or made intelligible to man, but is the secret, inexplicable, spontaneous movement of the mind (however arising) towards the external word,—a movement not to the exclusion of sight and reason, for the miracles appeal to both, nor of experience, for all who venture for Christ receive daily returns of good in confirmation of their choice, but independent of sight or reason before, or of experience after. The Apostles appealed to men's hearts, and, according to their hearts, so they answered them.

The appeal to men's hearts is an appeal to the loving contemplation of their Creator, an invitation to become not "their own historians and panegyrists" but God's:

where the thought of self obscures the thought of God, prayer and praise languish, and only preaching flourishes. Divine worship is simply contemplating our Maker, Redeemer, Sanctifier, and Judge; but discoursing, conversing, making speeches, arguing, reading, and writing about religion, tend to make us forget Him in ourselves. The Ancients worshipped; they went out of their own minds into the Infinite Temple which was around them. They saw Christ in the Gospels, in the Creed, in the Sacraments and other Rites; in the visible structure and ornaments of His House, in the Altar, and in the Cross; and, not content with giving the service of their eyes, they gave Him their voices, their bodies, and their time, gave up their rest by night and their leisure by day, all that could evidence the offering of their hearts to Him. Theirs was not a service once a week, or some one day, now and then, painfully, as if ambitiously and lavishly given to thanksgiving or humiliation; not some extraordinary address to the throne of grace, offered by one for many, when friends met, with much point and impressiveness, and as much like an exhortation, and as little like a prayer, as might be; but every day and every portion of the day was begun and sanctified with devotion.[7]

This way lies perfection—in the fullness and the frequency of our recollection of God. This is Newman's "Short Road to Perfection":

It does not mean any extraordinary service, anything out of the way, or especially heroic–not all have the opportunity of heroic acts, of sufferings–but it means what the word perfection ordinarily means. By perfect we mean that which has no flaw in it, that which is complete, that which is consistent, that which is sound–we mean the opposite to imperfect. As we know well what *im*perfection in religious service means, we know by the contrast what is meant by perfection.

He, then, is perfect who does the work of the day perfectly, and we need not go beyond this to seek for perfection. You need not go out of the *round* of the day.

I insist on this because I think it will simplify our views, and fix our exertions on a definite aim. If you ask me what you are to do in order to be perfect, I say, first–Do not lie in bed beyond the due time of rising; give your first thoughts to God; make a good visit to the Blessed Sacrament; say the Angelus devoutly; eat and drink to God's glory; say the Rosary well; be recollected; keep out bad thoughts; make your evening meditation well; examine yourself daily; go to bed in good time, and you are already perfect.

The prescription is simple but thorough. It answers to the terrible times. It rests on Newman's absolute conviction: the necessity to live by faith. No prayer sums up his life, his learning, his most passionate desire so briefly or so well as this one: "If I am tempted to leave *Thee*, do not Thou, O my God, leave *me!*" Perhaps, he thinks, he is not worthy "to ask to be allowed to make reparation to Thee for all the unbelief of the world, and all the insults offered to Thy Name, Thy Church, and the Sacrament of Love." But this at least he can pray:

O accept my homage, my praise, my adoration!–let me at least not be found wanting. I cannot help the sins of others–but one at least of those whom Thou hast redeemed shall turn round and with a loud voice glorify God. The more men scoff, the more will I believe in Thee, the good God, the good Jesus, the hidden Lord of life, who hast done me nothing else but good from the very first moment that I began to live.[8]

Typically, his own faith and the unbelief of others were on his mind when on Passion Sunday in 1864, thinking himself about to die, he wrote some words "in prospect of death." Characteristically, the concluding prayer was for others: "After the pattern of Him, who seeks so diligently for those who are astray, I would ask Him especially to have mercy on those who are external to the True Fold, and to bring them into it before they die."

The monster that leaps over Dostoevsky's horizon is the same one that haunted Newman: the future. Like Newman, he witnessed its encroachments on the present, saw it growing bigger and more monstrous, and nothing rising to stop it. He saw the secularism of the future already pushing underground men of good will, in the process turning good will into bad or making goodness so eccentric in the new society that it was rapidly becoming the preserve of freaks and the policy of madmen.

Like Newman, too, Dostoevsky began his maneuvers against the infidelity of the future with a simple trust in organizations and movements. For the young Newman it was the reform of Christianity that he hoped would spread through the Established Church and ultimately all of England from Oxford beginnings, assured of success by the inspired tracts of the reformers. For the young Dostoevsky it was the reform of society that he hoped would spread through Russia, inspired by the collectivist doctrines of Fourier and assured of success by monastic Socialist communities consisting of such devoted men as himself. Newman's faith in reform through tract was shattered by his conversion to a deeper and more realistic faith. Dostoevsky's break with secularist nostrum and social panacea came during ten years of disillusioning exile in the country of the dead in Siberia. But it began before a firing squad to which he was condemned in 1849 for his political activities. At the last minute a courier arrived with a reprieve and a commutation of his sentence to hard labor and army service in Siberia. The reprieve was not from death alone; it was release as well from the oppression of a five-minute life, of a farewell to this world without clarity and order. Myshkin, in *The Idiot*, describes those last moments, disguised as the experience of "another man." The man, of course, was Dostoevsky:

"He had only five minutes more to live. He told me that those five minutes seemed to him an infinite time, a vast wealth; he felt that he had so many lives left in those five minutes that there was no need yet to think of the last moment, so much so that he divided his time up. He set aside time to take leave of his comrades, two minutes for that; then he kept another two minutes to think for the last time; and then a minute to look about him for the last time. He remembered very well having divided his time like that. He was dying at twenty-seven, strong and healthy. As he took leave of his comrades, he remembered asking one of them a somewhat irrelevant question and being particularly interested in the answer. Then when he had said good-bye, the two minutes came that he had set apart for *thinking* to himself. He knew beforehand what he would think about. He wanted to realise as quickly and clearly as possible how it could be that now he existed and was living and in three minutes he would be *something*—some one or something. But what? Where? He meant to decide all that in those two minutes! Not far off there was a church, and the gilt roof was glittering in the bright sunshine. He remembered that he stared very persistently at that roof and the light flashing from it; he could not tear himself away from the light. It seemed to him that those rays were his new nature and that in three minutes he would somehow melt into them. . . . The uncertainty and feeling of aversion for that new thing which would be and was just coming was awful. But he said that nothing was so dreadful at that time as the continual thought, 'What if I were not to die! What if I could go back to life—what eternity! And it would all be mine! I would turn every minute into an age; I would lose nothing. I would count every minute as it passed, I would not waste one!' He said that this idea turned to such a fury at last that he longed to be shot quickly."

Dostoevsky came back from the dead full of the mystery of life. He dutifully wrote his memoirs of Siberia, *The House of the Dead;* and then began his massive journal of notes for the living, notes dictated *iz podpolya,* "from the underground." The short novel *Notes from the Underground* is the first part of the long chronicle which ends with the incomplete *Brothers Karamazov.* It is a biting parable of the hell of modern society delivered by a bitter man, a sinful man, but an honest one. He lives underground—or at least those are the terms of Dostoevsky's allegory. He lives somewhere in the darkness between the house of man and its foundation, spilling his hate and his honesty through the crevices and cracks, tunnels and spaces that zig-zag through rotting planks and crumbling concrete. There a spiteful man lives. There, sinking into his mud, dying of a diseased liver, a truthful man speaks—there, not elsewhere. For there humiliation is complete and yet is strangely enjoyable:

I got to the point of feeling a sort of secret abnormal, despicable enjoyment in returning home to my corner on some disgusting Petersburg night, acutely conscious that that day I had committed a loathsome action again, that what was done could never be undone, and secretly, inwardly gnawing, gnawing at myself for it, tearing and consuming myself till at last the bitterness turned into a sort of shameful accursed sweetness, and at last—

into positive real enjoyment! Yes, into enjoyment, into enjoyment! I insist upon that. I have spoken of this because I keep wanting to know for a fact whether other people feel such enjoyment. I will explain: the enjoyment was just from the too intense consciousness of one's own degradation; it was from feeling oneself that one had reached the last barrier, that it was horrible, but that it could not be otherwise; that there was no escape for you; that you never could become a different man; that even if time and faith were still left you to change into something different you would most likely not wish to change; or if you did wish to, even then you would do nothing; because perhaps in reality there was nothing for you to change into.

Change seems to be impossible for such a man. He envies the "normal" man who is also, he thinks scornfully, a stupid man, dulled and unconscious; for in his stupid way, unaware of his limitations, the normal man is self-confident. The underground man enjoys his own perversity and his failures. What sort of enjoyment is this? The enjoyment of consciousness, of existence, of intensely vivid experience, even of a toothache. It is the enjoyment of aimless pain; it is the satisfaction man can take in experience, even when he finds it meaningless:

it is just in that cold, abominable half despair, half belief, in that conscious burying oneself alive for grief in the underworld for forty years, in that acutely recognized and yet partly doubtful hopelessness of one's position, in that hell of unsatisfied desires turned inward, in that fever of oscillations, of resolutions determined for ever and repented of again a minute later—that the savour of that strange enjoyment of which I have spoken lies. It is so subtle, so difficult of analysis, that persons who are a little limited, or even simply persons of strong nerves, will not understand a single atom of it.

It is not exactly a glorification of the uncertain and the irrational to which the Underground Man gives himself. No one who takes such pride in his consciousness could altogether reject reason. But a truly conscious man must recognize the existence of the irrational, the complex, the compulsive, and the disordered elements in life. And if he finds glory where he logically should, in his consciousness, he must at the same time take pleasure in these other stray elements, see in them some of the mystery of man, the dignity of man, the intellectual and spiritual depth of man. Thus, without becoming a thoroughgoing irrationalist, the Underground Man declares himself an implacable anti-rationalist, no matter what the consequences, no matter how difficult he finds it to convince anyone else:

> "Upon my word," they will shout at you, "it is no use protesting: it is a case of twice two makes four! Nature does not ask your permission, she has nothing to do with your wishes, and whether you like her laws or dislike them, you are bound to accept her as she is, and consequently all her conclusions. A wall, you see, is a wall . . . and so on, and so on."
>
> Merciful heavens! but what do I care for the laws of nature and arithmetic, when, for some reason, I dislike those laws and the fact that twice two makes four? Of course I cannot break through the wall by battering my head against it if I really have not the strength to knock it down, but I am not going to be reconciled to it simply because it is a stone wall and I have not the strength.
>
> As though such a stone wall really were a consolation, and really did contain some word of conciliation, simply because it is as true as twice two makes four. Oh, absurdity of absurdities! How much better it is to understand it all, to recognize it all, all the impossibilities and the stone wall; not to be reconciled to one of those impossibilities and stone walls if it disgusts you to be reconciled to it . . .

There is a plot in *Notes from the Underground.* There are other people in it besides the Underground Man. But it is the fulmination against the restrictions of a doctrinaire rationalism that controls everything and everybody in this book; and it is the accompanying apotheosis of freedom of the will that gives point to the fulmination, transforming every splenetic outburst into a vigorous, if inverted, confession of faith. For example, the "best definition of man," he says, is "the ungrateful biped," but his very ingratitude—by which the Underground Man really means perversity—gives man moral stature and establishes his freedom:

> Shower upon him every earthly blessing, drown him in a sea of happiness, so that nothing but bubbles of bliss can be seen on the surface; give him economic prosperity, such that he should have nothing else to do but sleep, eat cakes and busy himself with the continuation of his species, and even then out of sheer ingratitude, sheer spite, man would play you some nasty trick. He would even risk his cakes and would deliberately desire the most fatal rubbish, the most uneconomical absurdity, simply to introduce into all this positive good sense his fatal fantastic element. It is just his fantastic dreams, his vulgar folly, that he will desire to retain, simply in order to prove to himself—as though that were so necessary—that men still are men and not the keys of a piano, which the laws of nature threaten to control so completely that soon one will be able to desire nothing but by the calendar. And that is not all: even if man really were nothing but a piano-key, even if this were proved to him by natural science and mathematics, even then he would not become reasonable, but would purposely do something perverse out of simple ingratitude, simply to gain his point. And if he does not find means he will contrive destruction and chaos, will contrive sufferings of all sorts, only to gain his point! He will launch a curse upon the world, and as only man can curse (it is his privilege, the primary distinction between him and other animals) it may be by his curse alone he will attain his object—that is, convince himself that he is a man and not a piano-key! If you say that all this, too, can be calculated and tabulated—chaos and darkness and

curses, so that the mere possibility of calculating it all beforehand would stop it all, and reason would reassert itself—then man would purposely go mad in order to be rid of reason and gain his point! I believe in it, I answer for it, for the whole work of man really seems to consist in nothing but proving to himself every minute that he is a man and not a piano-key! It may be at the cost of his skin, it may be by cannibalism! And this being so, can one help being tempted to rejoice that it has not yet come off, and that desire still depends on something we don't know?

The Underground Man drives his argument up the moral scale, note by note. "Does not man, perhaps, love something besides well-being?" he asks. "Perhaps he is just as fond of suffering? Perhaps suffering is just as great a benefit to him as well-being? Man is sometimes extraordinarily, passionately, in love with suffering, and that is a fact." That fact is the axis of Dostoevsky's spiritual world, nowhere better revealed than in these *Notes*. The logic is Aristotelian and thus straightforward enough, though it is disguised by more than one paradox and antinomy:

man will never renounce real suffering, that is, destruction and chaos. Why, suffering is the sole origin of consciousness. Though I did lay it down at the beginning that consciousness is the greatest misfortune for man, yet I know man prizes it and would not give it up for any satisfaction. Consciousness, for instance, is infinitely superior to twice two makes four. Once you have mathematical certainty there is nothing left to do or to understand. There will be nothing left but to bottle up your five senses and plunge into contemplation. While if you stick to consciousness, even though the same result is attained, you can at least flog yourself at times, and that will, at any rate, liven you up. Reactionary as it is, corporal punishment is better than nothing.

Where does one go, then? What does one do? One goes nowhere. One does nothing. "The long and short of it is, gentlemen, that it is better to do nothing! Better conscious inertia! And so hurrah for underground!"

The jubilant "hurrah" is echoed once again in Dostoevsky. At the end of *The Brothers Karamazov*, at Ilyusha's funeral, young Kolya ecstatically shouts "Hurrah for Karamazov!" He is cheering Alyosha Karamazov for his own ecstatic shouting, for his own soft hurrahs, addressed to Kolya and Ilyusha's other young friends:

"My little doves—let me call you so, for you are very like them, those pretty blue birds, at this minute as I look at your good dear faces. My dear children, perhaps you won't understand what I am saying to you, because I often speak very unintelligibly, but you'll remember it all the same and will agree with my words sometime. You must know that there is nothing higher and stronger and more wholesome and good for life in the future than some good memory, especially a memory of childhood, of home. People talk to you a great deal about your education, but some good, sacred memory, preserved from childhood, is perhaps the best education. If a man carries many such memories with him into life, he is safe to the end of his days, and if one has only one good memory left in one's heart, even that may sometime be the means of saving us. Perhaps we may even grow wicked later on, may be unable to refrain from a bad action, may laugh at men's tears and at those people who say as Kolya did just now, 'I want to suffer for all men,' and may even jeer spitefully at such people. But however bad we may become—which God forbid—yet, when we recall how we buried Ilyusha, how we loved him in his last days, and how we have been talking like friends all together, at this stone, the cruellest and most mocking of us—if we do become so—will not dare to laugh inwardly at having been kind and good at this moment! What's more, perhaps, that one memory may keep him from great evil and he will reflect and say, 'Yes, I was good and brave and honest then!' Let him laugh to himself, that's no matter, a man often laughs at what's good and kind. That's only from thought-

lessness. But I assure you, boys, that as he laughs he will say at once in his heart, 'No, I do wrong to laugh, for that's not a thing to laugh at.' "

The Underground Man has different memories. He has been afraid to face them; but now, welcoming suffering and humiliation, he can shout his "hurrah" too and recall the underground sources of his joyful joylessness. He has spent his life in an atmosphere of abasement, his own and others'. He has looked for kicks and shoves and every sort of humiliation —and has always found them—in a tavern and on the Nevsky Prospect; in his government bureau, at the hands of his colleagues; at home, in the treatment he receives from his lisping servant with sarcastic stare. He has tried to give others kicks and shoves and every sort of humiliation, and once or twice at least has succeeded. The first time was in school:

I attempted to get on friendly terms with some of my schoolfellows; but somehow or other my intimacy with them was always strained and soon ended of itself. Once, indeed, I did have a friend. But I was already a tyrant at heart; I wanted to exercise unbounded sway over him; I tried to instil into him a contempt for his surroundings; I required of him a disdainful and complete break with those surroundings. I frightened him with my passionate affection; I reduced him to tears, to hysterics. He was a simple and devoted soul; but when he devoted himself to me entirely I began to hate him immediately and repulsed him—as though all I needed him for was to win a victory over him, to subjugate him and nothing else.

The second time is in the last pages of the novel. The pattern is the same. The episode begins in the daytime hatshop and nighttime bordello where he meets the prostitute Liza. Now he has found a proper "object" to torture, a simple and devoted soul to subjugate:

Something suddenly flared up in me. An object had appeared before me.

". . . I may degrade and defile myself, but I am not any one's slave. I come and go, and that's an end of it. I shake it off, and I am a different man. But you are a slave from the start. Yes, a slave! You give up everything, your whole freedom. If you want to break your chains afterwards, you won't be able to: you will be more and more fast in the snares. It is an accursed bondage. I know it. I won't speak of anything else, maybe you won't understand, but tell me: no doubt you are in debt to your madam? There, you see," I added, though she made no answer, but only listened in silence, entirely absorbed, "that's a bondage for you! You will never buy your freedom. They will see to that. It's like selling your soul to the Devil . . . And besides . . . perhaps I, too, am just as unlucky—how do you know—and wallow in the mud on purpose, out of misery? You know, men take to drink from grief; well, maybe I am here from grief. Come, tell me, what is there good here? Here you and I . . . came together . . . just now and did not say one word to one another all the time, and it was only afterwards you began staring at me like a wild creature, and I at you. Is that loving? Is that how one human being should meet another? It's hideous, that's what it is!"

"Yes!" she assented sharply and hurriedly.

I was positively astounded by the promptitude of this "Yes." So the same thought may have been straying through her mind when she was staring at me just before. So she, too, was capable of certain thoughts? "Damn it all, this was interesting, this was a point of likeness!" I thought, almost rubbing my hands. And indeed it's easy to turn a young soul like that!

It was the exercise of my power that attracted me most.

The Underground Man recognizes in Liza a modest and chaste girl, attached to dreams of respectable love, with a letter from a medical student to give sanction to the dreams. She imagines that the Underground Man can "save" her, can rescue her from her "millinery establishment." He throws her dreams, all of them, in her face, firing away at her sensibilities

as he runs up and down his room. But they are not only her dreams that he destroys; they are his too, he confesses:

"Save you from what? But perhaps I am worse than you myself. Why didn't you throw it in my teeth when I was giving you that sermon: 'But what did you come here yourself for? Was it to read us a sermon?' Power, power was what I wanted then, sport was what I wanted, I wanted to wring out your tears, your humiliation, your hysteria—that was what I wanted then! Of course, I couldn't keep it up then, because I am a wretched creature, I was frightened, and, the devil knows why, gave you my address in my folly. Afterwards, before I got home, I was cursing and swearing at you because of that address, I hated you already because of the lies I had told you. Because I only like playing with words, only dreaming, but, do you know, what I really want is that you should all go to hell. That is what I want. I want peace; yes, I'd sell the whole world for a farthing, straight off, so long as I was left in peace. Is the world to go to pot, or am I to go without my tea? I say that the world may go to pot for me so long as I always get my tea."

He can never forgive Liza for finding him in his "wretched dressing-gown," cursing away at his valet. He will always hate her, he explains, for finding him out, for the impulse to speak the truth which she evoked in him: "How I hated her and how I was drawn to her at that minute! The one feeling intensified the other. It was almost like an act of vengeance. At first there was a look of amazement, even of terror, on her face, but only for one instant. She warmly and rapturously embraced me."

Liza understands at last. "She realized that my outburst of passion had been simply revenge, a fresh humiliation, and that to my earlier, almost causeless hatred was added now a *personal hatred*, born of envy. . . . Though I do not maintain that she understood all this distinctly; but she certainly did fully understand that I was a despicable man, and what was worse, incapable of loving her." She goes away, then, followed by a "spiteful grin, which was forced, however, to *keep up appearances . . .*" He runs after her, down into the snow, the wet snow which pursues him all through this tale. There he muses: "Should I not begin to hate her, perhaps even tomorrow, just because I had kissed her feet today? Should I give her happiness? Had I not recognized that day, for the hundredth time, what I was worth? Should I not torture her?"

He never meets Liza again. He is left now with "many evil memories," a self-styled "anti-hero," retreating into books, frightened by life. But so, he tells us, are we all. Freedom is too much for man:

Come, try, give any one of us, for instance, a little more independence, untie our hands, widen the spheres of our activity, relax the control and we . . . yes, I assure you . . . we should be begging to be under control again at once. I know that you will very likely be angry with me for that, and will begin shouting and stamping. Speak for yourself, you will say, and for your miseries in your underground holes, and don't dare to say all of us—excuse me, gentlemen, I am not justifying myself with that "all of us." As for what concerns me in particular I have only in my life carried to an extreme what you have not dared to carry halfway, and what's more, you have taken your cowardice for good sense, and have found comfort in deceiving yourselves. So that perhaps, after all, there is more life in me than in you. Look into it more carefully! Why, we don't even know what living means now, what it is, and what it is called! Leave us alone without books and we shall be lost and in confusion at once. We shall not know what to join on to, what to cling to, what to love and what to hate, what to respect and what to despise. We are oppressed at being men—men with a real individual body and blood, we are ashamed of it, we think it a disgrace and try to contrive to be some sort of impossible generalized man.

The Underground Man is obsessed with his antirationalism, determined to be free of systems, determined to be free of organizations, determined to be conscious at all times, and freely to accept what comes into his consciousness, and thus determined to be free. He asserts an independence of others that seems at times anti-human and certainly always, in the creedal sense of the term, altogether anti-humanist. But he is in fact neither anti-human nor anti-humanist. Like all the great venters of spleen, like Swift and Petrarch and Baudelaire, Dostoevsky speaking through the Underground Man is moved by a devotion to humanity, a devotion almost too intense to bear—to humanity disgraced, to humanity abased, to humanity humiliated. He is devoted to all his fellow-sufferers, and he understands his fellow-sufferers supremely well, for he stands before them, in his darkness, as tyrant and tyrannized, as bearer of all the marks of suffering, those made by others and those made by himself. He carries his stigmata into the light. But he cannot stop there. He cannot rest on the Cross. He must pull others up beside him. He must share the splendors of suffering. He is not only determined to be free himself—so determined that he enslaves himself to freedom—but he is equally determined to make others free in spite of themselves, to make others free as he is free. And thus he ends up trying to enslave everyone else. That is how he becomes—that is why he is—a spiteful man.

It is easy to be outraged by the Underground Man and thus to miss the power and the truth of his confession. For there is much that is challenging in his notes. They mock all who mistake passivity for passion and complacency for tranquillity. They show how dark is the light in which some people live and at the same time how full of shattering illumination the darkness can be.

Dostoevsky's humanism is of this kind: it is not simply a Christian humanism; it is the humanism of the Crucified; not love of mere man, but of suffering man. Apart from the Cross, Dostoevsky's allegorical apologetic says, there is nothing to assure us of our humanity. Apart from the Cross, there is only the belly-feeding, soul-destroying humanism of such pharisees as the freedom-hating Grand Inquisitor, a humanism that offers certainty, stability, and slavery, and rejects Christ to His face and on His Cross, because

> instead of giving a firm foundation for setting the conscience of man at rest for ever, Thou didst choose all that is exceptional, vague and enigmatic; Thou didst choose what was utterly beyond the strength of men, acting as though Thou didst not love them at all—Thou who didst come to give Thy life for them! Instead of taking possession of men's freedom, Thou didst increase it, and burdened the spiritual kingdom of mankind with its sufferings for ever. Thou didst desire man's free love, that he should follow Thee freely, enticed and taken captive by Thee. In place of the rigid ancient law, man must hereafter with free heart decide for himself what is good and what is evil, having only Thy image before him as his guide. But didst Thou not know he would at last reject even Thy image and Thy truth, if he is weighed down with the fearful burden of free choice? They will cry aloud at last that the truth is not in Thee, for they could not have been left in greater confusion and suffering than Thou hast caused, laying upon them so many cares and unanswerable problems.

The Cross does not merely ask things of man, it assumes them; it finds man free and leaves him more free and more loved, and if he responds in kind, more loving. But man may not always respond in kind—that is, freely and lovingly. He is equally free to refuse. He may respond as the Grand Inquisitor says his "weak and vile" nature requires—pridefully, in rebellion. And even a just rebellion directed against tyranny and oppression is as ineffective as a child's revolt, the rebels no more than "little children rioting and barring out the teacher at school." All rebellion is bound to end in misery and failure and frustration, because rebels hate their enemies and through their hatred come to imitate those they hate, treating all—not only their enemies—with rebellious cruelty instead of with redeeming love. The analysis of the Grand Inquisitor is scathing and scornful and precise:

They will cast down temples and drench the earth with blood. But they will see at last, the foolish children, that, though they are rebels, they are impotent rebels, unable to keep up their own rebellion. Bathed in their foolish tears, they will recognize at last that He who created them rebels must have meant to mock at them. They will say this in despair, and their utterance will be a blasphemy which will make them more unhappy still, for man's nature cannot bear blasphemy, and in the end always avenges it on itself. And so unrest, confusion and unhappiness—that is the present lot of man after Thou didst bear so much for their freedom!

Need one make the obvious application of this passage to the twentieth century, to Communism, to Soviet Russia? This is the great prophetic voice of Dostoevsky: man who revolts for the sake of revolting ceases to be man. Man who makes a god of freedom ceases to be free. When man seeks by himself to establish perfection on earth, by himself to disestablish suffering, himself to become the Creator, he not only achieves a greater imperfection than ever known before, a more ceaseless suffering, and a truncated Creation, he is actually no longer human, he has become a beast, the most savage of all the beasts. That is the answer to Ivan Karamazov's rebellion, made indirectly, by parable and prophecy and tortuous dialogue in *The Brothers Karamazov.* That is the end-result of the plotting of Nikolai Stavrogin and his "possessed" associates, the title characters of *The Devils,* who not only doom and dupe and destroy themselves, but bring Russia itself—and through Russia, one understands, the whole world—within sight of Armageddon, within sound of the last battle.

All the contempt that the Underground Man feels for rationalists and rationalism is poured on the diabolic plotters, whom Dostoevsky compares in his scriptural title to the Gadarene swine. No expression of that contempt is more complete than his description of the moment in which the system to end all systems is presented. The scene is a gathering of the "reddest" radicals in a small town in Russia in the early 1870's. The speaker is Dostoevsky's model rationalist, the social scientist Shigalyov:

"Dedicating my energies to the study of the social organisation which is in the future to replace the present condition of things, I've come to the conviction that all makers of social systems from ancient times up to the present year, 187-, have been dreamers, tellers of fairy-tales, fools who contradicted themselves, who understood nothing of natural science and the strange animal called man. Plato, Rousseau, Fourier, columns of aluminum, are only fit for sparrows and not for human society. But, now that we are all at last preparing to act, a new form of social organisation is essential. In order to avoid further uncertainty, I propose my own system of world-organisation. Here it is." He tapped the notebook. "I wanted to expound my views to the meeting in the most concise form possible, but I see that I should need to add a great many verbal explanations, and so the whole exposition would occupy at least ten evenings, one for each of my chapters." (There was the sound of laughter.) "I must add, besides, that my system is not yet complete." (Laughter again.) "I am perplexed by my own data and my conclusion is a direct contradiction of the original idea with which I start. Starting from unlimited freedom, I arrive at unlimited despotism. I will add, however, that there can be no solution of the social problem but mine."

Just as easily as the reader, the listeners in the book see the ridiculousness of Shigalyov's "irrefutable" argument. But their behavior is not changed as a result. Even when doubt begins to spread among the members of the terrorist band, nothing can stop the rot, certainly not murder or suicide, which only hasten its effects. The monstrous future has begun.

Against such horrors, what weapons will avail? Not the sociological weapons of Shigalyov and the rationalist planners. Not the revolutionary weapons of the plotters. Not the materialist weapons of the Grand Inquisitor. The weapons Dostoevsky offers are those of the spirit. They can be named. They can be found. They can be aimed. But ordinary men do not know them, cannot see them, will not use them. They are the weapons of those extraordinary men who reject the mathematics of rationalism, the materialism of the Inquisitor, and the simple solutions of the social sciences and elect the mysteries of the spirit. This is their strength, this is the true strength of the Russians, Dostoevsky told his beloved people. He told them as a Christian artist does, in figure. He told them with his inspired eccentrics, his holy epileptics, Kirilov in *The Devils* and Myshkin in *The Idiot.*

Kirilov insists upon the terrible freedom of belief in nothing. But nonetheless Kirilov finds joy: his epileptic fits reveal the presence of God to him—no less:

"There are seconds—they come five or six at a time—when you suddenly feel the presence of the eternal harmony perfectly attained. It's something not earthly—I don't mean in the sense that it's heavenly—but in that sense that man cannot endure it in his earthly aspect. He must be physically changed or die. This feeling is clear and unmistakable; it's as though you apprehend all nature and suddenly say, 'Yes, that's right.' God, when He created the world, said at the end of each day of creation, 'Yes, it's right, it's good.' It . . . it's not being deeply moved, but simply joy. You don't forgive anything because there is no more need of forgiveness. It's not that you love—oh, there's something in it higher than love—what's most awful is that it's terribly clear and such joy. If it lasted more than five seconds, the soul could not endure it and must perish. In those five seconds I live through a lifetime, and I'd give my whole life for them, because they are worth it."

That a nihilist should experience such supernatural ecstasy is no greater paradox than that the vision should be the direct consequence of epilepsy. But "what if it is disease?" Myshkin, who has had similar experiences, asks himself:

"What does it matter that it is an abnormal intensity, if the result, if the minute of sensation, remembered and analysed afterwards in health, turns out to be the acme of harmony and beauty, and gives a feeling, unknown and undivined till then, of completeness, of proportion, of reconciliation, and of ecstatic devotional merging in the highest synthesis of life?" These vague expressions seemed to him very comprehensible, though too weak. That it really was "beauty and worship," that it really was the "highest synthesis of life" he could not doubt, and could not admit the possibility of doubt. It was not as though he saw abnormal and unreal visions of some sort at that moment, as from hashish, opium, or wine, destroying the reason and distorting the soul. He was quite capable of judging of that when the attack was over. These moments were only an extraordinary quickening of self-consciousness—if the condition was to be expressed in one word—and at the same time of the direct sensation of existence in the most intense degree. Since at that second, that is at the very last conscious moment before the fit, he had time to say to himself clearly and consciously, "Yes, for this moment one might give one's whole life!" then without doubt that moment was really worth the whole of life.

A similar vision is granted Alyosha Karamazov—who is no epileptic—when he sits in vigil over the body of Father Zossima. The saintly monk seems to rise from the dead and take Alyosha by the hand. From the pages of the gospel narration of the first miracle of Jesus, the Wedding of Cana in Galilee, the monk draws the image of Dostoevsky's God:

"He is terrible in His greatness, awful in His sublimity, but infinitely merciful. He has made Himself like unto us from love and rejoices with us. He is changing the water into wine that the gladness of the guests may not be cut short. He is expecting new guests, He is calling new ones unceasingly for ever and ever. . . . There they are bringing new wine. Do you see they are bringing the vessels . . ."

Alyosha's very being bursts with the joy of this meeting with Zossima, with God, and with his interior self. Mysteries come together in a transcendent spiritual astronomy—earth and stars, man and God, the dead and the living. Like the good Russian he is, Alyosha embraces the earth, kisses it, waters it with his tears, and promises eternal fealty to it. "What was he weeping over?" Dostoevsky asks—and answers:

Oh! in his rapture he was weeping even over those stars, which were shining to him from the abyss of space, and "he was not ashamed of that ecstasy." There seemed to be threads from all those innumerable worlds of God, linking his soul to them, and it was trembling all over "in contact with other worlds." He longed to forgive every one and for everything, and to beg forgiveness. Oh, not for himself, but for all men, for all and for everything. "And others are praying for me too," echoed again in his soul. But with every instant he felt clearly and, as it were, tangibly, that something firm and unshakable as that vault of heaven had entered into his soul. It was as though some idea had seized the sovereignty of his mind—and it was for all his life and for ever and ever. He had fallen on the earth a weak boy, but he rose up a resolute champion, and he knew and felt it suddenly at the very moment of his ectasy. And never, never, all his life long, could Alyosha forget that minute.

Dostoevsky himself lived for such minutes as these, for the universal harmony thus unveiled, for the great promise they indicated. He himself held that promise out to the Russians, for he himself had seen it made to the Russians in his own moments of ecstasy. A year before his death, speaking to the Society of Lovers of Russian Literature on the prophetic character of Pushkin's poetry, he offered Pushkin's people and his, a hope for their future: "To become a genuine Russian means to seek finally to reconcile all European controversies, to show the solution of European anguish in our all-humanitarian and all-unifying Russian soul, to embrace in it with brotherly love all our brethren, and finally, perhaps, to utter the ultimate word of great universal harmony, of the brotherly accord of all nations abiding by the law of Christ's gospel." Why the Russians, of all peoples, victims of a poor land, a destitute one? Just because they were victims, because Christ, "in a serf's garb," had traveled back and forth across Russia. "Why shouldn't we embrace His ultimate word? Wasn't He born in a manger?"

To those who questioned his exultant dreams for the Russian people, who were "indignant at the idea that the Russian people possess truth of their own," Dostoevsky retorted with his own experience: "Don't tell me that I do not know the people! I know them: it was because of them that I again received into my soul Christ Who had been revealed to me in my parents' home and Whom I was about to lose when I became in my turn a 'European liberal.'" He is not upset because the Russians sin—"And in the West, is there less drunkenness and stealing?" The point is that "sin is stench, and stench is dispelled when the sun rises. Sin is a transient matter, whereas Christ is eternal. Daily the people sin and commit villainies; yet in their best moments, when they turn to Christ, they never err in truth. . . . And the people's ideal is—Christ." And if there are not many "true Christians," why worry about that? After all, "how do you know how many of them are needed to preserve the Christian ideal among the people—and with it the people's great hope?"

Like Newman, then, Dostoevsky saw hope in a faithful remnant, saw that even in the depths of the underground, where men are driven by society to faithlessness, hopelessness, and lovelessness, there was reason for hope, saw that faith and love assured hope regardless of what disasters the future might bring:

> For if I believe that truth is here, precisely in what I believe, what do I care if even the whole world should refuse to believe in my truth, should ridicule me and should choose a different road?—Therein is the strength of a great moral idea that it cements men into a most solid union; that it is not measured in terms of benefit but makes men aspire to the future, to eternal aims and absolute gladness.[9]

CHAPTER XIV

The Modern Assimilation

THE FATHERS EXAMINED THE WORLD BEFORE THE COMING of Christ with a mixture of respect and hostility. They usually admired pagan rhetoric; they often despised the purposes for which it was used. No matter how gleaming the surfaces of pagan speculation, there was decay beneath; and the Fathers worked with a dentist's skill to expose it. They would not lose such gold and silver as might be buried in the cavities; they carried off huge amounts of precious stuff from the Greeks and Romans. They carried off—they were not carried away. And thus a pattern was set which was held to, with few exceptions, until the Renaissance.

For the Renaissance the decay of the pagans was harder to discover. Renaissance poets and philosophers were not as interested in assaying the ruins as the Fathers were; they were content merely to recover from them anything of value that could be found, in any condition, as long as it was old. Corruption was often the companion of beauty and wisdom in antiquity, and just as frequently the collaborator of piety in the Renaissance; the world and all its contents were tarnished, had always been, and could always be expected to be. To avoid, or rather to elude, despair was not easy; but it was not impossible either. One could flee the world, run like Lot from Sodom; or one could make a troubled peace with the world, somehow finding the formulas of appeasement, both for the raging flesh and the rebelling spirit. Appeasement came through synthesis, through systematic reconciliation of Platonists and Aristotelians, of pagans and Christians, of this world and the next; or it came through a more subtle acceptance of the corruption of this world, as a necessary preparation for the contemplation of the next. Whichever way one chose, there was always room for pagan antiquity. But it was still, no matter how perilously, an antiquity assimilated, not a Christianity absorbed. And the mode of assimilation was still allegorical: mere literal acceptance was obviously too hasty, too shallow and unimaginative, and without grace.

Modern man, proud of his arrival at the top of the evolutionary compost heap, usually exhibits very little sense of the past. Without this sense, he works with blunted tools. Almost deliberately, he makes his sight astigmatic and dulls his hearing at the top and at the bottom. Without a sense of the past, he sacrifices dimension and thus gives up any clear understanding of the present moment as well. His future is perilous, an uncertainty erected upon uncertainty which can yield only more uncertainty.

When modern man does turn to the past, he usually looks at it with condescension or with contempt. He seeks guidance from it of a sort; he looks for fixed patterns, for cycles, and for mistakes. He seeks and finds evidence of his ancestors' agreement with him or of their inferiority. He looks not for revelation, but for confirmation of his own convictions. In earlier ages he finds reason as he understands it sweetly and ingeniously served or transgressed. What he discovers he accepts or rejects, quite literally.

For modern man the past is assimilable in its entirety or piecemeal. With less knowledge of it than most of the previous centuries possessed, the twentieth century thinks of history only as its servant. The peaks and valleys and plateaus of history have been explored tirelessly by many of our contemporaries—on maps and charts. Many visits have been made to the past by many different means of intellectual transportation. Many compliments have been paid the past, by devotees of the different civilizations. Every kind of command has been issued the past, by disciples of the various determinisms. On the basis of these explorations, these compliments and commands, civilization has been remade. And the measurers of past time, having found the dimensions of utopia, have been working zealously to force the present to conform to it.

The price of such certainties is too much certainty, as the twentieth century should have learned all too well by now. A measured civilization, based on blueprints captured from a past that never realized it had made any blueprints, is a totalitarian society. It must be; it always will be. For it substitutes for human freedom, inhuman predictability; for many levels of communication and performance, just one; for the indecisions of the allegorist, the precisions of the literalist.

The historical determinist, who since Hegel has dominated Western thought, calls himself a realist. But his systematic rearrangement of the past to fit what he imagines it to have been is based, like all vast creations of man, on myth. In his case it is the myth of human perfectibility on earth, probably the least realistic fancy ever to enter man's imagination. This is humanism without Christianity. This is paradise without Adam, humanity without Christ, redemption without a redeemer. This is man made into a god, a pitifully uninteresting one, with the intellectual depth of a Mars and the spiritual range of a Venus.

The imagination of the Christian humanist is not so narrow, not so naive, not so self-centered as this. It is a realistic imagination, based on solid evidence. It sees man as he is, as he always has been: imperfect here, perfectible elsewhere; the restless victim of his own cupidity, the tranquil master of his own charity; in himself, very little, a creature, but made in the image of a Supreme Creator. There is room in such an imagination for statistics, for all the findings of modern science, but in their place, a small one that is continually being emptied and refilled. In the realism of the Christian humanist a greater reliance must be placed upon man than upon his tools. For if man is not infallible, how much more unreliable must his creations be?

This is the only empiricism worthy of the name. It does not rearrange the past to conform to the present or the present to fit the past. It is not awed by history, nor does it expect from it any more than it can give: limited guidance on limited evidence. There is no room in this system of values for worship of anything or anybody merely human, although there is the profoundest respect for the potentialities of human beings. These, in fact, are conceived in far more awesome terms than those of the materialist, whose imagination ends with his senses.

To accommodate his vision, which ends not with man as God, but as purged by Him and illumined by Him and united with Him, the Christian humanist sees man as he is. That means steering an uneasy course between the poles of angelism and diabolism, but refusing to yield to either magnetic current. It means recognizing the authentic pictures of man drawn by the saints, the sages, the learned of all sorts, whose contributions have filled to overflowing the library of Christian humanism. But to recognize a truth—whether incarnated in an image, a book, or a man—one must confront it or be confronted by it. Is this self-evident? Not really. If it were, the encounters between Christians and their own saints and sages would be more frequent, and more upsetting. There would not be, in Christian society, such ignorance of the Christian humanist works of Augustine, Boethius, Gregory, Bernard, Thomas, and Dante, of Renaissance and eighteenth-century writers, or of those of less than a century ago. There would not be so cheerful a ceding of humanism to the non-Christian, so cheerless an acceptance of Christianity as anti- or non-human, and such complacency about both the concession and the acceptance.

There are few greater rewards for literacy than the library of Christian humanism and few more easily accessible, but how few have claimed it! In not claiming this inheritance, Christians have lost far more than a few books. They have come close to giving up the image of God in which they are made, with which they are stamped, and which gives them being. They have thus come very near to losing themselves. It is no exaggeration to say that at the very least they have "forgotten" themselves, lost hold of human nature in general and of their own nature in particular. That is the first thing that Christian humanists return to those who follow them in their reconstruction of history: understanding of their own nature: human nature. Acting as agents of grace and wisdom, the saints and sages of Christian humanism give back to man his sixth sense, his sense of dimension, which is as essential to his well-being as his sight or hearing or taste or touch or smell. With the past, present, and future seen as a whole, integrated and ordered and purposeful, comes a center, the central fact in human history, the Incarnation.

Everything we do, think, read–everything we are–must be conditioned by this fact. For fact it is. History changes with the Incarnation. Man changes with it. It is the center of all human events and gives new shape to human behavior. For with it the present is always redeemed, has been since the day in which, to quote Hopkins, Christ Eastered in us–and truly redeemed, not determined in some futile game of chance with loaded dice. The result is a future we need never fear. Some speculation about the world to come may be edifying, but sufficient unto the year and decade and century is the good thereof. Consider the Fathers of the Church; they boil not, neither do they tremble. They are much too sure that the Providence of God guides humanity, and they are too busy learning who and what humans are, reminding themselves and us of the dignity to which man holds title when he has hold of himself.

Thus it is that every pursuit, every perception, every undertaking of these men starts: with the intense self-examination that yields something like a proper knowledge of self. It is a relentless probing of self to which Augustine and Bernard and Pico and St. John of the Cross and Pascal and Newman summon us, to examples of which Boethius and Dante and Shakespeare and Sterne and Fielding and Dostoevsky lead us, to which all commit themselves. The investigation is thorough. It goes wherever man's interests go, through all the branches of speculative and practical philosophy, through every order of being, through every literary discipline accepted in the past or projected into the future. It did not wait for the theories of the biological behaviorists to examine the place of fear, hunger, and love in the economy of salvation or the roles of need and greed in the economy of survival. Long before the social scientists began to codify and categorize, the rites of society and the dynamics of cultures were being scrutinized by Christian humanists. Well before the collisions of id and ego, libido and super-ego were discovered by psychologists working with clinical data, the struggle between the lower reason and the higher was described and defined, and with a greater awareness of the full consequences of the conflict, by rhetoricians and poets, philosophers and theologians.

These men established lasting procedures and with them fundamental truths. They added a tender Christian conscience to the sturdy pagan consciousness—the grace of intellect working on the nature of history—and found, wherever they turned, details of the relationship between God and man which to them was history. The details were many, the relationship many-faceted, and the rhetoric, as a result, one of many dimensions. The art of self-recollection they demonstrated is a complex one, a subtle one, one of many veils and a hundred obscurities. But the shadows can be lifted, the veils torn aside; the self can be collected again, consciousness restored, understanding established, and upon all of this love reconstructed or even constructed for the first time. This is the resourceful reality and the grandeur of Christian humanism.

Notes

Chapter I: Lions and Gardens

[1] St. Gregory the Great, *Morals on the Book of Job* (London, 1883), I, 272–273.

[2] St. Irenaeus, *Adversus haereses,* trans. in *Documents of the Christian Church,* ed. Henry Bettenson (New York, 1947), p. 43.

Chapter II: The Patristic Assimilation

[1] St. Augustine, *The City of God,* trans. D. B. Zema, S.J., G. G. Walsh, S.J., *et al.* (New York, 1950), I, 386–387.

[2] St. Leo the Great, Letter XXIV.

[3] St. Augustine, *De Doctrina Christiana,* trans. J. J. Gavigan, O.S.A. (New York, 1947), p. 113.

[4] St. Gregory Nazianzen, *Funeral Orations,* trans. L. P. McCauley, S.J. (New York, 1953), p. 9.

[5] Werner Jaeger, *Humanism and Theology* (Milwaukee, 1943), pp. 23–24.

[6] St. Augustine, *De Moribus,* trans. in Charles Journet, *The Church of the Word Incarnate* (New York, 1955), p. 212.

Chapter III: St. Augustine: "And So It Shall Be Opened"

[1] St. Augustine, *Letters,* trans. Sister Wilfrid Parsons, S.N.D. (New York: 1951), I, 76, 77, 84.

[2] *De Doctrina,* p. 129.

[3] St. Augustine, *De Magistro,* trans. G. G. Leckie (New York, 1938), p. 56.

[4] St. Augustine, *Soliloquies,* trans. T. F. Gilligan, O.S.A. (New York, 1948), p. 423.

[5] St. Augustine, *De Ordine,* trans. R. P. Russell, O.S.A. (New York, 1948), pp. 239, 262–263, 311–312, 327–328.

[6] St. Augustine, *De Quantitate Animae,* trans. in Dom Cuthbert Butler, *Western Mysticism* (New York, 1924), p. 69.

NOTES

Chapter IV: Boethius: Wisdom's Consolation

[1] The quotations in this chapter are from the Loeb Classical Library edition of the *Theological Tractates* and the *Consolation of Philosophy*, trans. H. F. Stewart and E. K. Rand (Cambridge, Mass., 1918), pp. 53, 71, 157, 265, 267, 303, 411.

Chapter V: Gregory the Great: "And No Man Wonders"

[1] St. Gregory the Great, *Morals on the Book of Job*, I, 5.

[2] *Morals*, I, 7, 9, 10.

[3] St. Gregory the Great, *The Book of Pastoral Care*, IV.

[4] *Morals*, I, 355–360.

[5] *Morals*, III, 128–129.

[6] Gustave Bardy, *The Christian Latin Literature of the First Six Centuries* (St. Louis, 1930), p. 201.

[7] M. L. W. Laistner, *Thought and Letters in Western Europe*, A.D. *500–900* (London, 1957), pp. 108–109.

[8] *Morals*, I, 10–11, 15, 25–26.

[9] St. Gregory the Great, *Homilies on Ezekiel*, trans. in Butler, *Western Mysticism*, pp. 102–103.

[10] *Morals*, III, 358–359.

[11] *The Dialogues of Saint Gregory*, ed. E. G. Gardner (London, n.d.), pp. 96–97, 98.

[12] *Morals*, I, 324–325.

Chapter VI: St. Bernard: The Rhetoric of Mysticism

[1] Hugh of St. Victor, *De Sacramentis*, trans. R. J. Deferrari (Cambridge, Mass., 1951), pp. 5–6.

[2] St. Bernard, *On the Love of God*, trans. T. L. Connolly, S.J. (Westminster, Md., 1951), pp. 12–13, 35–36.

[3] St. Bernard, *Sermons* (Westminster, Md., 1950), II, 200.

[4] St. Bernard, *The Steps of Humility*, trans. G. B. Burch (Cambridge, Mass., 1940), pp. 147, 163, 165, 181, 201, 203, 205.

[5] St. Bernard, *Letters*, trans. B. S. James (Chicago, 1953), pp. 230, 110, 112, 480–481.

[6] *On the Love of God*, p. 70.

[7] St. Bernard, *On the Song of Songs*, trans. A Religious of C.S.M.V. (New York, 1952), pp. 267, 259–260.

Chapter VII: Thomas Against Thomas

[1] Martin Grabmann, *The Interior Life of St. Thomas Aquinas*, trans. Nicholas Aschenbrener, O.P. (Milwaukee, 1951), p. 22.

[2] St. Thomas Aquinas, *The Catechetical Instruction*, trans. J. B. Collins, S.S. (New York, 1939), pp. 27–29.

[3] *The Interior Life*, pp. 76–77.

[4] Aristotle, *De Anima, in the Version of William of Moerbeke and the Commentary of St. Thomas Aquinas*, trans. Kenelm Foster, O.P. and Silvester Humphries, O.P. (New Haven, Conn., 1951), pp. 300, 302–303.

[5] St. Thomas Aquinas, *The Trinity*, trans. Sister Rose Emmanuella Brennan, S.H.N. (St. Louis, 1946), pp. 61–62, 65, 66, 135–136, 188, 197.

[6] Gerald Vann, O.P., *Saint Thomas Aquinas* (New York, 1940), p. 62.

Chapter VIII: Dante: The Sacred Poem

[1] St. Augustine, *De Musica*, trans. R. C. Taliaferro (New York, 1947), p. 375.

[2] St. Bonaventure, *The Mind's Road to God*, trans. George Boas (New York, 1953), p. 20.

[3] Dante, *Inferno*, XXXIII.

[4] Dante, *The Divine Comedy*, trans. J. D. Sinclair (New York, 1948), III, 363.

[5] Dante, *De Monarchia*, I, i.

[6] Sinclair, II, 157.

[7] *Purgatorio*, XI.

[8] Sinclair, II, 367–369, 371, 393–395; III, 147, 151–153, 203, 303, 451, 479, 483–485.

Chapter IX: The Renaissance Assimilation

[1] Marsilio Ficino, *De Christiana Religione*, XXII, trans. in Paul Shorey, *Platonism Ancient and Modern* (Berkeley, Cal., 1938), p. 124.

[2] Ficino, trans. in P. O. Kristeller, *The Philosophy of Marsilio Ficino* (New York, 1943), pp. 302–303.

[3] Pico della Mirandola, *Oration on the Dignity of Man,* trans. E. L. Forbes in *The Renaissance Philosophy of Man,* ed. E. Cassirer, P. O. Kristeller, J. H. Randall, Jr. (Chicago, 1948), pp. 222, 230, 225, 237–238, 252–253, 250.

[4] Lorenzo de' Medici, *Cerchi chi vuol le pompe e gli altri onori,* trans. L. R. Lind in *Lyric Poetry of the Italian Renaissance* (New Haven, Conn., 1954), p. 231.

Chapter X: Shakespeare and St. John of the Cross: De Contemptu Mundi

[1] St. John of the Cross, *Dark Night of the Soul,* in *Works,* trans. E. Allison Peers (Westminster, Md., 1953), I, 451–452.

[2] St. John of the Cross, *Living Flame of Love, Works,* III, 140.

[3] St. John of the Cross, *Ascent of Mount Carmel, Works,* I, 229–230.

[4] *Ascent, Works,* I, 135.

[5] *Dark Night, Works,* I, 443–444.

Chapter XI: Pascal: Fire and Fact

[1] Butler, *Western Mysticism,* pp. 15–16.

[2] Blaise Pascal, *Shorter Works,* trans. Emile Cailliet and John Blankenagel (Philadelphia, 1948), pp. 205, 211.

[3] Blaise Pascal, *Pensées,* trans. H. F. Stewart (New York, 1950), pp. 3, 13, 25, 29, 83, 99, 101, 115, 123, 217, 251, 299, 151, 135, 307, 309, 317, 319, 345.

Chapter XIII: Newman and Dostoevsky: The Politics of Salvation

[1] John Henry Newman, *Autobiographical Writings,* ed. Henry Tristram (New York, 1957), pp. 270–271.

[2] John Henry Newman, *A Grammar of Assent,* ed. C. F. Harrold (New York, 1947), pp. 296, 305–306, 317, 263, 264, 265.

[3] John Henry Newman, *Lectures on the Present Position of Catholics in England* (London, 1851), pp. 241, 243–245, 263–264.

[4] John Henry Newman, "The Infidelity of the Future," in *Faith and Prejudice, and Other Unpublished Sermons* (New York, 1956), pp. 117, 126.

[5] John Henry Newman, *The Idea of a University*, ed. C. F. Harrold (New York, 1947), pp. 292–293, 306.

[6] *Letters of John Henry Newman*, ed. Derek Stanford and Muriel Spark (Westminster, Md., 1957), p. 198.

[7] John Henry Newman, *Lectures on the Doctrine of Justification* (London, 1874), pp. 268–269, 337–338.

[8] John Henry Newman, *Meditations and Devotions* (London, 1893), pp. 208–209, 277.

[9] F. M. Dostoievsky, *The Diary of a Writer*, trans. Boris Brasol (New York, 1949), II, 1000.

Index

A NOTE ON THE TYPE IN WHICH THIS BOOK IS SET

This book is set in Janson, a Linotype face, created from the early punches of Anton Janson, who settled in Leipzig around 1670. This type is not an historic revival, but rather a letter of fine ancestry, remodelled and brought up to date to satisfy present day taste. It carries a feeling of being quite compact and sturdy. It has good color and displays a pleasing proportion of ascenders and descenders as compared to the height of the lower case letters. *The book was composed and printed by The York Composition Company, Inc., of York, Pa., and bound by Moore and Company of Baltimore, Maryland. The typography and design are by Howard N. King.*